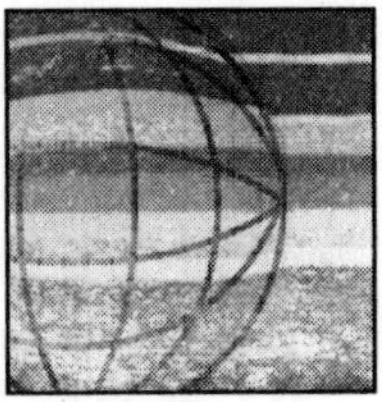

Vulnerability and Globalisation

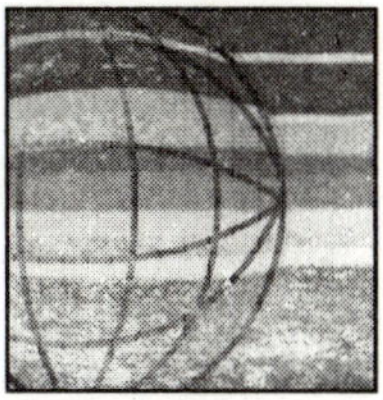

Vulnerability and Globalisation

Perspectives and Analyses from India

Edited by
N. Jayaram and D. Rajasekhar

RAWAT PUBLICATIONS
Jaipur • New Delhi • Bangalore • Hyderabad • Guwahati

ISBN 978-81-316-0489-2

Published by
Prem Rawat for **Rawat Publications**
Satyam Apts, Sector 3, Jawahar Nagar, Jaipur 302 004 (India)
Phone: 0141 265 1748 / 7006 Fax: 0141 265 1748
E-mail: info@rawatbooks.com
Website: www.rawatbooks.com

New Delhi Office
4858/24, Ansari Road, Daryaganj, New Delhi 110 002
Phone: 011 2326 3290

Also at *Bangalore, Hyderabad* and *Guwahati*

Typeset by Rawat Computers, Jaipur
Printed at Chaman Enterprises, New Delhi

for
S.L. Rao

Contents

List of Figures and Tables

Figures

Tables

Preface

Much has been written about globalisation, either eulogising it or vilifying it. Those who eulogised it have been forced to eat their words: instead of fulfilling its promises, globalisation has landed many an economy in crisis and caused unmitigated misery to large sections of the population, especially in the less developed countries. Those who vilified it, however, can hardly be complacent: globalisation cannot simply be wished away; it is there to stay. Globalisation, to be sure, has created new vulnerabilities for the vast masses, besides exacerbating their chronic vulnerabilities. What are these vulnerabilities in the context of India, and have they been or can they be managed? To discuss this and related questions, a two-day national seminar on 'Globalisation and the Management of Vulnerabilities' was organised at the Institute for Social and Economic Change, Bangalore on 26–27 March 2008. The seminar was jointly organised by the two co-editors: the first was then Director of the Institute and the second is a Professor at the Institute. The present volume is an outcome of the seminar.

In organising this seminar and in putting together this volume, we have incurred a debt of gratitude to many. Our thanks go to all the scholars who presented papers at the seminar (viz., R.S. Deshpande, Narendar Pani, P. Radhakrishnan, D. Rajasekhar, A. Ramaiah, V.M. Rao, Supriya Roy Chowdhury, and Manohar Yadav), who chaired the technical sessions (viz., Abdul Aziz, N. Jayaram, M.V. Nadkarni, S.L. Rao, and Michael Walton), and who participated in the panel discussion on 'Democracy, Dissent, and Agency in the Era of Globalisation' (viz., Abdul Aziz, M.V. Nadkarni, and V.M. Rao). We are doubly grateful to M.V. Nadkarni, Narendar Pani, D. Rajasekhar, V.M. Rao, Michael Walton, and

Manohar Yadav for taking the trouble of revising their presentations at the seminar as contributions to this volume. Our thanks are due to Indrajit Bairogya, Kaushik Basu, Pradeep Mehta, Architesh Panda, Tarodi Tunga, and S. Yogeshwari, the doctoral scholars at the Institute, for their contribution as rapporteurs. We are also thankful to other participants for their contribution during the discussion at the seminar.

While putting the volume together, we noticed thematic gaps. Hence, we decided to include two papers, two presentations at other fora, and a research report additionally. We are grateful to D.N. Dhanagare and P.K.B. Nayar for their kind permission to republish their articles, which had been originally carried by *Sociological Bulletin*. We are thankful to the Indian Sociological Society for its generosity in permitting us to reprint the articles by Dhanagare and Nayar. Manish Thakur and Gaurang R. Sahay kindly accepted our request to revise their presentations at other fora for inclusion in the volume. Similarly, D. Rajasekhar, Manjula R., and Suchira J.Y. consented to rewrite some part of their research report as an article for this volume. We are grateful to them all.

At the Institute Col. Ashutosh Dhar, L. Gopal, K.S. Narayana, A. Sathish Kamath, A.N. Ravishankar, Manjula R., Mohana Devi, and V. Sangeetha extended their wholehearted support and unstinted cooperation in their various capacities. We very much appreciate their support and cooperation, which went a long way in the successful organisation of the seminar. We are also thankful to the Indian Council of Social Science Research, New Delhi for the financial support it extended to the seminar.

Shri S.L. Rao, the then Chairman, Board of Governors, Institute for Social and Economic Change, Bangalore evinced keen interest in and was a pillar of support for all academic activities at the Institute. He took particular interest in the organisation of the seminar and also participated in it actively. In recognition of his contributions to the Institute and as a token of our affection to him, we dedicate this volume to Shri Rao.

We are beholden to our respective family members who have contributed to the seminar and the volume invisibly.

For the efficiency and speed with which the manuscript of our anthology has been turned into an attractive volume, we are thankful to the production team at Rawat Publications, Jaipur.

N. Jayaram and D. Rajasekhar

1

Introduction

Globalisation, Its Discontents and Beyond

N. JAYARAM

> I believe that globalization – the removal of barriers to free trade and the closer integration of national economies – can be a force for good and that it has the *potential* to enrich everyone in the world, particularly the poor. But I also believe that if this is to be the case, the way globalization has been managed, including the international trade agreements that have played such a large role in removing those barriers and the policies that have been imposed on developing countries in the process of globalization, need to be radically rethought.
>
> —Joseph Stiglitz (2003: ix–x)

> There are, of course, no magic solutions. But there are a multitude of changes to be made – in policies, in economic institutions, in the rules of the game, and in mindsets – that hold out the promise of helping make globalization work better …
>
> —Joseph Stiglitz (2007: ix–x)

Perhaps no other term has received as much scholarly and media attention in the last two decades as globalisation. The phenomenon encapsulated by this term appears to have become 'the most pressing issue of our time' (Stiglitz 2003: 4). Scholars across the social sciences have been engaged in research and analysis of the process, dimensions, and consequences of globalisation internationally or with reference to particular countries. For this, diverse analytical perspectives, some with explicit ideological positioning and others with tacit ideological underpinnings, have been used. Accordingly, the scholarship on globalisation is divided: at one extreme are its proponents who regard it as coterminous with progress and the most effective route to end poverty; at the other end are those vilifying it as the source of all contemporary social, political, economic, and cultural ills, not only in the developing world but also in the developed world. The debate, expectedly, has often tended to be polemical and rhetorical. In between these two extremes are scholars who view globalisation as a process, which, though historically inevitable, can be managed for alleviating the vulnerabilities resulting from it if not for reaping its promised benefits. As Samir Dasgupta puts it,

> ... globalization in itself, is neither a positive nor a negative trend. Rather, its ultimate effects on the well-being of people depend critically on several still unresolved factors. These include who is involved in the decisions that drive the process, which values are to dominate it, and whether the often vast inequalities that now exist between regions, socio-economic classes, and the like will endure, increase, or diminish. (2010: xiv)

To be sure, globalisation is not a new phenomenon. As early as in the mid-19th century Karl Marx (see Sweezy 1968) had observed that capitalism as an economic system is by definition and necessity an international economic system. In the 1960s, Andre Gunder Frank (1978, 1982) analysed the implications of the phenomenon when advancing his thesis on 'capitalist accumulation' and the 'development of underdevelopment'. And, before the term 'globalisation' acquired currency, Immanuel Wallerstein (1979) spoke of 'the capitalist world economy' and 'the world systems theory'. Of course, it is not just the term that is new; what is new is the pervasiveness of the phenomenon and the speed at which it has engulfed all parts of the world: it has intensified 'consciousness of the world as a whole' (Robertson 1992: 8) and 'local happenings are [now] shaped by events occurring miles away and vice versa' (Giddens 1990: 64). Globalisation has changed the face of the world irrevocably: time has been compressed, communication revolutionised, the concepts of self and community metamorphosed, and the idea of the state and its boundaries challenged. All this has, no doubt, significantly affected the life and livelihood of the people in different countries, but not always for the better.

Of the various facets that globalisation has affected profoundly, socio-economic inequality has been crucial. While there is some minimum consensus on the idea that globalisation has exacerbated inequalities both within and between nations, the exact nature of that relationship and its wider implications, however, remain unexplored, inadequately systematised, and inconclusively theorised. Both social scientists and policy makers have acknowledged that globalisation incorporates some in a rising tide of wealth and consumption while excluding the vast majority. The discussion around globalisation has consequently moved from 'trickle down' to 'globalisation with a human face', with a defined emphasis on social security, and so on. Both governments and multilateral institutions have acknowledged that policies which are more inclusive of wider sections of the population, than what a purely market-oriented model of growth would allow, must be put in place. In both national and international policy regimes, it is no longer contested that certain growth-oriented marketisation policies need to be moderated in order to cushion certain sections of the citizenry from the impact of globalisation.

Despite this emerging consensus, the exclusivist nature of the growth that globalisation has created continues to be a source of serious concern. In many developing countries, public spending on social sectors has continued to decline and large numbers of citizens remain outside the mainstream market economy. All of these magnify an enduringly negative dimension to the concept of globalisation. The current reality of political economy, however, is defined by two facts: (i) that globalisation is an irreversible process, and (ii) that the potential of economic growth opened up by globalisation creates a framework of opportunities, which no nation can afford to ignore. As Joseph Stiglitz remarks, 'governments need to – and can – adopt policies that help countries grow but that also ensure that growth is shared more equitably' (2003: xi).

Thus, it becomes important to substantively address the following questions: (a) In what ways can this process be negotiated or managed so as to create a degree of social balance between the imperatives of growth and justice? (b) How can the respective boundaries of the state and the market be redefined so that the impulse to growth does not exclude institutions that address both justice and equality? (c) In what ways can both a democratic polity and an active civil society contribute to this process? To discuss these and related questions, a two-day national seminar was organised at the Institute for Social and Economic Change, Bangalore on 26–27 March 2008.

Addressing the foregoing questions, the seminar discussed many thematic points about globalisation. First, while poverty and inequality certainly preceded globalisation, the current concern with rising inequalities rests on the observation that certain processes are set forth through the process of globalisation that displace certain sections of the population. Thus, for example, the process of public sector reform or privatisation may well displace a large number of workers from permanent employment. In a context where the market does not offer formal sector jobs, informalisation becomes the norm: contractualisation and casualisation of employment, the swelling of the unorganised/informal sector, self-employment in petty trade, increasing number of ill-paid citizenry lacking social security and who are unable to create for themselves, or for their next generation, access to education and skills that would enable them to enter a fast moving, high technology, outward-oriented economy, and so on are the classic manifestations of informalisation.

Second, with the onset of globalisation, there has also occurred a dramatic expansion of the so-called export-oriented zones, the competitiveness and profitability of which are governed by the comparatively cheap labour that is available in countries like India. Such sectors, while closely integrated with the international market, nevertheless have wage levels and working conditions far below internationally, or even nationally accepted labour standards. Thus, as new pockets of poverty and deprivation are created within urban spaces, there is an urgent need to consider institutional and legal mechanisms which can reverse these trends, and address issues of fair wages, while at the same time retaining the economic vibrancy that drives an export-oriented sector.

Third, we also need to look at vulnerabilities which are intensified in the process of marketisation, whether in the area of food securities, farmers' distress, or where traditional livelihoods may be threatened through acquisition of land for industrial expansion.

What would be the institutional mechanisms to address economic hardships created in the moment of transition between a system of protection and subsidies towards one of competitive profitability?

Fourth, the question of state responsibility for human development needs to be squarely confronted. Cases of late industrialisation, represented by East Asian national industrial corporations, are often cited as examples of private sector-led, export-oriented development. However, it is important to remember the central role of the state in human development in such economies during their period of export-led growth. Thus, it is now part of a shared political economy understanding of the success of national industrial corporations that huge state investment in primary, higher, and technical education and in health, created a foundation of skilled humanpower that was able to benefit from as well as to drive the high technology and export-led growth in many of these countries. In countries such as India, unfortunately, the period of rapid economic growth in the past decade of economic liberalisation, has also seen the decline of public spending on social sectors, both at the central and at state government levels. Thus, there has to be renewed attention not only on ways in which public expenditure on social sectors can be prioritised, but also, critically, on how education policy, for example, can be reformulated to meet the requirements of both efficiency and equity. How, for example, does one conceptualise, or re-conceptualise, reservation/affirmative action in the current scenario where private sector/multi-national capital will increasingly become the driving forces of economic activity?

Finally, local politics, particularly within democratic political systems, frequently challenge the logic of globalisation and the market when these threaten local livelihoods, property rights, and so on. This was most recently seen in the political turbulence in Nandigram in West Bengal over the acquisition of land – under the Special Economic Zone (SEZ) scheme – by the government for the setting up of a car manufacturing unit to be owned by the Tatas (see Mukherji and Ghosh 2010). As a consequence of the violent and highly charged politics on this issue, the state government announced a freeze on land acquisition under the SEZ scheme. It is in this context that one needs to re-examine the politics, broadly defined, of economic liberalisation. This politics refers not only to overtly political challenges to globalisation, such as the one mentioned above, but to a more diffused, broadly based sense in which marketisation policies are being resisted by local groups. This resistance may emerge from farmers' lobbies, which engage in a broad critique of WTO (World Trade Organisation) agreements, from NGOs/civil society organisations which resist the privatisation of water, or urban land policies, or from groups that resist the coming of multi-nationals. To what extent do these movements define the context within which marketisation policies are being pursued? Is it possible to devise institutionalised forms of dialogue between governing agencies and such movements?

The Bangalore seminar, which dealt with these themes as they relate to India, was attended by thirteen scholars drawn from different social science backgrounds, of whom eight presented papers, and four participated in a panel discussion. The trans-disciplinary discussion among anthropologists, economists, political scientists, and sociologists was insightful as well as interesting. The seminar was inaugurated by N. Jayaram, the then Director, Institute for Social and Economic Change and Michael Walton, the then V.K.R.V. Rao Chair Professor at the Institute delivered the valedictory address.

The discussion at the seminar offered pointers and guidelines to the participants to revise their presentations for publication; some of them, of course, decided not to publish them. Put together in the volume are the contributions of participants who turned in the final version of their presentations. In the process of compiling this volume, the editors discovered gaps in coverage, especially concerning perspectives. Hence, it was decided to include five papers that did not originally form presentations at the seminar: two of these happened to be the presidential addresses delivered by D.N. Dhanagare and P.K.B. Nayar at the 28th and 33rd editions of the All India Sociological Conference held at the Indian Institute of Technology, Kanpur in December 2002 and the Karnatak University, Dharwad in December 2007, respectively; the other three being unpublished seminar presentations – by Manish Thakur and Gaurang R. Sahay – and part of a research report – by D. Rajasekhar, Manjula R. and Suchitra J.Y.

The Present Volume

The present volume is organised under two parts: the four chapters in Part I discuss various perspectives on globalisation and the seven chapters in Part II present analyses of specific themes. Part I begins with D.N. Dhanagare's discussion on the genealogy of 'globalisation' as a concept, and explicates its nuances. Dhanagare reviews the analytical insights of scholars and subject experts – like Thomas L. Friedman, Anthony Giddens, Ronald Robertson, Alberto Martinelli, L. Sklair, and Immanuel Wallerstein – on the subject. He juxtaposes 'modernisation–modernity' and 'world systems theory' as the two key theoretical paradigms for understanding the nature of inter-relations and economic linkages leading to cultural influences across countries. Dhanagare's examination of the nature of international integration that has taken place through market leads him to conclude that globalisation is just another way of describing 'the fact that capitalist regime gets extended beyond political boundaries of nation-states'. He argues that such integration is 'neither necessary nor sufficient condition for developing a truly sustainable "world community"'. For him, 'globalisation vià the market is incapable of inculcating a sense of identity, history, and social purpose among people. Such a "we" feeling can alone generate moral strength and survival instinct among social aggregates in times of crises'.

Dhanagare highlights the negative impact of the market-driven global integration on the less industrialised developing countries in general and those belonging to the disadvantaged, weaker, and marginalised sections in particular. His analysis points to the reinforcement of existing vulnerabilities besides the creation of new ones. He writes, 'Champions of globalisation often gloss over the fact that "food security" is quintessentially a poverty problem.... Invariably, lack of food is not due to a shortfall in food production, but because the poor who need the security badly lack purchasing power...' He finds the conditions of the working class, in both organised and unorganised sectors, in these countries no better under a globalised economy. What is pathetic, the trade unions, which had earlier played a significant role in influencing and humanising capitalist system within the nation-state framework, find themselves helpless in the globalisation phase of capitalism.

Dhanagare draws attention to far-reaching consequences of 'cultural invasion' of global capitalism for the developing countries: 'aggressive marketing and consumerism are clearly precipitating a serious conflict of cultures'. The people of these countries 'have started seeing their identity, or even reinventing their tradition – whether religious, ethnic, or cultural – as a rallying point'. Not surprisingly, assertion of such identities has often led to enmity and conflict.

Dhanagare's disenchantment with the discontents of globalisation during the last quarter century leads him to look for 'an alternative vision of globalisation'. The elements of such a vision, according to Dhanagare, can be found in India's 'philosophical traditions, spiritual resources, and civilisational wisdom', and is

> best encapsulated in ancient sayings like: '*vasudhaiva kutumbakam*' (let the whole globe be our family), '*aa no bhadraha kratavah yantu vishwatah*' (let noble thoughts come to us from every side) and '*krunvanto vishwamaryam*' (let us make the whole world *Arya* [persons of noble disposition], that is, let us equip people's minds with noble thoughts, ideals, and actions all over the world).

This vision, Dhanagare emphasises, is humanistic vision: it 'predicates autonomy to individuals, groups, communities, and nation-states, freedom of choice of a development path, and is also founded on the principles of brotherhood, peace, and coexistence'. It is also close to the principles enshrined in the Constitution of India.

For India, that is yet to get over 'late-development effect', Dhanagare opines, shying away from globalisation is no response and 'mystifying it will provide no answers to the problems it precipitates'. Viewed thus, the task of social scientists in India appears to be two-fold: (i) critiquing and demystifying the present globalisation phenomenon, and (ii) working towards a vision based on existent realities and indigenous cultural traditions and values that have been enshrined in the Constitution.

Social justice is a vantage point for examining the consequences of globalisation. In his chapter, P.K.B. Nayar turns attention to the idea of social justice in the context of globalisation, especially, the processes of liberalisation and marketisation that it has promoted. He discusses the role of two related agencies vis-à-vis social justice, namely, the state (the empowering agency) and the civil society (an enabling agency).

Given that 'social justice' is essentially 'an ethico- philosophical concept', Nayar explains the difficulties in defining it. Clarifying the concept, he explores John Rawls' theory of justice and Howard Adelson's views on social justice. He also differentiates between 'social justice' and 'human rights': social justice applies to groups and human rights to individuals, though in many cases, 'the dividing line between the two is hazy'. In UN parlance, 'human rights' is preferred over 'social justice', as it is easier to operationalise the former than the latter.

Nayar argues that 'social justice has found only qualified application in modern times in spite of the wild cry for it from several quarters, including the UN system'. To explain this paradox, he takes us through the journey of the concept of social justice across the world, starting from the *Code of Hammurabi* (c. 1780 BCE) through the United Nations Universal Declaration of Human Rights (1948) to the International Covenant on Civil and Political Rights (1976) and the International Covenant on Economic, Social, and Cultural Rights (1976). Nayar provides a brief account of the Indian hermeneutics on the concept of social justice, especially the concept of *dharma* and the contributions of Mahatma Gandhi, Vinobha Bhave, and Babasaheb Ambedkar.

On the central thesis of his chapter, Nayar notes that while the state is not a precondition for social justice in pre-political societies, it is 'a precondition for, and guarantor of, social justice' in modern times. He discusses the constraints that modern state encounters and limitations it faces in enforcing social justice: 'The different boundary-overlaps and disputes and consequent trade-offs and conflicts between the state and the contending forces would necessitate a dilution of many of the well-meant elements of social justice'.

Given the limitations of the state in realising social justice, can civil society organisations (CSOs) play an effective role in enhancing social justice? Nayar addresses this question with reference to India, especially considering the popularity that CSOs have gained among 'international aid-giving circles' and 'most of the organisations in the UN system not only recognising their services and potential but also giving them consultancy status'. He observes that, in the case of India, on the whole, CSOs have performed a very useful role, especially in developmental activities, but only a few of them are engaged in the promotion of social justice. Their role in enhancing social justice is not appreciable.

Nayar is apprehensive that the three 'Ds' – denationalisation, deregulation, and disinvestment – associated with globalisation, will 'put an end to the regulatory and redistributive potential of the state and would be a big threat to social justice at both national and international levels'. 'Globalism', he feels, 'cannot act as a gospel for social justice because the law of the market has no provision for it'. This is also compounded by the fact that the capacity of the governments in the developing countries to initiate social justice measures is progressively becoming weaker and circumscribed.

More importantly, globalisation has ruined rural economy in many a developing country. 'Those who suffer from social injustice' in developing countries 'are so pre-occupied with eking out a bare means of livelihood that the very word social justice seldom occurs in their minds.' In some of these countries, international economic aid is seen to be counterproductive. Strings attached to foreign aid are often invisible and turn out to be a noose which a donor country can tighten to increase its grip over the recipient country.

Finally, Nayar finds the politics of coalition governments in India to be detrimental to social justice. Coalition governments are 'more concerned with their survival than the welfare of the governed and have no time to plan or execute programmes of social justice'. Whatever social justice programmes implemented by the government are suspect, as they are directed more 'towards vote banks than the real victims of social injustice'. Nevertheless, political parties and civil rights groups use 'social justice' as a catchy slogan in their manifestos and agenda.

The neglect of social justice seems to be closely related to the decline of the welfare state. Based on a review of the literature on the subject, in his chapter, Manish Thakur analyses the implications of the interface between globalisation and the new middle classes for the decline of the welfare state in India. Focusing on their diasporic aspirations, consumerist values, quest for a pan-Indian/global identity, notwithstanding their socio-cultural diversity, he charts out the changing location of middle classes in relation to the Indian nation-state, on the one hand, and the globalising market, on the other. He ties up 'issues concerning culture, identity, and the lifestyle of the middle classes with the larger issues of change in political processes and public policy'.

Thakur begins with an analysis of the distinctiveness of the Indian middle classes, highlighted by B.B. Misra in the early 1960s, and the distinction between the 'old' and the 'new' middle classes in the sociological understanding of social stratification in India. He identifies two distinct analytical trajectories in the literature on the Indian middle classes that approximate the respective roles of the state and the market: the political economy and the culturalist traditions. The 'differing analytical weight of the nation-state and the market (as the institutional site of consumption practices) in the making of Indian middle classes', Thakur argues, 'also connotes the distinction between the "old" and the "new" middle classes'.

According to Thakur, the liberalisation of the Indian economy has thrown open access to a variety of consumer goods and lifestyles for the middle classes. 'If large number of middle-class Indians has come to define life through acquisition of goods and have started deriving better part of their identity in terms of what they possess and can exhibit', Thakur argues, 'then their collective articulation of hopes and frustrations is bound to impact on the policy regime and the welfare character of the state'. He cites the dismantling of the policy of import substitution as an instance of meeting the appetite of the middle classes for various kinds of consumer goods.

Thakur examines two contrasting theses concerning the impact of globalisation on the state's role vis-à-vis welfare policy measures: one that argues that it has adversely affected social welfare programmes of the state, and the other holding that it has created economic conditions that require the state to play a more important role in social security in the long run. The latter thesis, Thakur notes, 'necessitates the reworking of the usual globalisation versus welfare state binary as state often promotes, rather than reluctantly accepts, globalisation'. He, therefore, feels 'it would be a trifle premature to write an obituary to the welfare state. True, it is being redefined but the reports of its death may appear to be a bit exaggerated. Yet there are loud proclamations on the withering away of the welfare state'.

How would Mahatma Gandhi have looked at globalisation? Based on his extensive reading on Gandhiana, M.V. Nadkarni addresses this interesting question. As a prelude to his analysis of the Gandhian perspective on globalisation, he examines the three views on the process: 'a narrow, purely economic view ..., a broader but still an anthropocentric view, and a still broader view comprising the whole global eco-system'. True to the Gandhian standpoint, the purpose of his chapter 'is not to oppose either globalisation or economic growth totally, but to emphasise the need to be sensitive to their downsides, since these downsides may have serious repercussions on the poor and the deprived in whose name these two processes may be tried to be defended'.

Nadkarni argues that 'globalisation by itself cannot yield miracles'; 'it may result in unanticipated adverse consequences too', He emphasises that the 'government knows what it should do, and is willing to exercise its intervention when needed, in national or public interest'. As regards globalisation of capital flows, he clarifies that it is an 'explicitly economic process', which may have political dimensions either as a cause or as an effect: 'Economic instability, induced by hot money movements, could very well, and very quickly, lead to political instability as well.'

On the human dimension, Nadkarni draws attention to 'the dominance of market culture in the globalisation era and a replacement of most of the traditional way of life and culture in favour of a homogeneous market culture, where culture itself becomes an instrument of global capitalism'. At the broadest level, globalisation is taking place in 'the global eco-system', in which human-market intervention has played a destructive role: fast shrinking drinking water resources, degradation of land, depletion of ozone layer, climate change, declining capacity of the oceans to absorb excess carbon from the air, depletion of bio-diversity, and increasing extinction of wildlife. 'Global eco-system knows no political boundaries of countries, since environmental impact of human intervention in one country spreads to other countries too in no time', observes Nadkarni.

To be sure, globalisation as we understand today was not an issue during Gandhiji's time; instead, it was colonialism, which was 'a globalising force'. As Nadkarni notes, there is much in the Gandhian thought that offers us useful criteria to analyse and assess globalisation in its present avatar. At the outset, he dismisses the naïve view that, since Gandhiji stood for *swadeshi*, *swaraj*, and self-reliance, he would have opposed globalisation *per se*; in fact, 'Gandhiji himself debunked this naïve view ...'

For Gandhiji, *swadeshi* meant, besides using the local produce, '"reliance on one's own strength"': 'so long as one relied on own strength, taking care that this strength is not eroded, one was free to use what was produced elsewhere'. He, in fact, warned his followers against making a 'fetish' of *swadeshi*. Gandhiji preferred '*swaraj*' (self-rule), a more inclusive and positive term ('which meant freedom of choice and freedom to act', over 'independence', a term with negative and narrow connotation.

According to Nadkarni, Gandhiji's main concern was with 'the freedom of the individual, since, for him, individual was the basic unit of the economy, polity, and society'. He, therefore, views Gandhiji's insistence on decentralisation as a precondition for individual freedom: 'Freedom of the individual certainly involved freedom to associate with others on equal terms and form groups, but the latter should not so dominate the individual as to be oppressive.' Under globalisation, when the state and the institutions of civil society facilitate the market forces, 'the individual becomes simply a non-entity, despite the formal elections'. A check on this danger, which is not imaginary but real, is what Gandhian approach would call for. In the Gandhian social schema, individual deprivation has no justification. Globalisation riding 'on the back exploitation or exploited individuals' would amount to violence, which also mean deprivation. All this has serious implications for development projects.

From a Gandhian perspective, poverty and deprivation are not the only consequences of globalisation to worry about. The adverse effects of globalisation on environment and the eco-system also need to be considered. The concern about environment has to do with the tendency of globalisation to promote limitless consumerism, particularly on the part of the elite and the middle classes, a point to which Thakur too has drawn attention in his chapter. In Gandhian view, according to Nadkarni, 'unbridled consumerism is morally and spiritually degrading'. Furthermore, via consumerism, as Thakur avers and Nadkarni endorses, globalisation also tends to homogenise culture and lifestyles. How are we to ensure that globalisation does not curb local initiatives, cultures, and freedom, and 'the Gandhian individual would be in control of the process, rather than be its helpless victim?' The debate on globalisation must address this important question.

The seven chapters in Part II present analyses of specific issues relating to socio-economic vulnerabilities under globalisation. Michael Walton provides a detailed analysis of the relationship between globalisation and vulnerabilities with special reference to India. Those opposing globalisation argue that it has heightened vulnerabilities, with the poorer sections of the population being the worst hit. 'Is this true? Does this mean globalisation is a bad thing? Or can it be managed?' – asks Walton. He explores two theses in this regard. Drawing from economics, the first thesis posits 'that globalisation *can* be a source of increased vulnerability, but whether it is so in practice depends on interactions with domestic conditions'. Going beyond economics, the second thesis argues 'that both the assessment of vulnerability and likely responses are linked to power and identity – at both the aggregate and local levels'.

Of the various dimensions of globalisation, Walton deals with the economic aspects of globalisation, and particularly the effect of increased integration of a country into international markets. According to Walton, 'It is hard to separate increased integration into international markets from the broader market-oriented liberalisation within the domestic market. In India, as in many countries, the processes were proceeding simultaneously.'

Walton's focus is on economic vulnerability: 'the probability of adverse short-run *changes* in well-being of an individual, household, or group – the downside of risk and uncertainty': 'changes in incomes and wealth, losses in health status, and adverse effects on dignity and identity' are its different dimensions. While insecurity resulting from uncertainty has costs, it proves to be more costly for poorer households and individuals, and larger the declines greater are the welfare costs. 'Adverse shocks can be a *source* of long-term welfare declines, when this leads to distress sales of land or cattle, pulling kids out of school and into work, or long-term effects of loss of work on the employability of workers.' Walton explains the kinds of shocks that matter in India.

Walton places the problem of vulnerability in the analytical context of market functioning and government responses. He views economic vulnerability as 'a symptom of market failures, but both its nature and the responses depend on interactions with social structure and politics'. This vulnerability differs across wealth and socio-cultural categories and groups with distinct social categories. The problem is compounded because governments also 'do a bad job of provisioning for security'. India is no exception in this regard.

How did the industrialised countries of the West address issues of vulnerability? Are there 'useful lessons for India from the post-Second World War political consensus that laid the basis for the broadening of welfare states in industrialised countries'? In these countries, Walton observes, 'the extension of the state into supporting risk management went hand in hand with the deep increase in international integration'. He discusses the provisioning for social welfare in the Scandinavia, Continental Europe, and the United Kingdom, and the distortions thereof.

In the light of his analysis, Walton finally discusses some 'design principles' and 'the current policy mix'. He emphasises 'that government-mediated action to support management of risks faced by households is desirable on efficiency and equity grounds' is more important with globalisation. He makes out a case for a sound policy *mix* involving action in all three areas: 'of risk reduction, *ex ante* risk management, and *ex post* coping'. On technical design of the insurance and coping-related instruments, 'the central issues concern the relationship between the structure of risks, the nature of market failures, and instrument design. Instrument design, in turn, concerns the mix, targeting (who uses the scheme) and effects on behaviour'. In the light of his discussion on 'design principles' and 'policy mix' in managing vulnerability, Walton reviews the National Rural Employment Guarantee Act (NREGA) and the programme implemented under it.

In conclusion, Walton argues that 'institutionalised risk-management structures are a *complement* to globalisation':

> Building a comprehensive, institutionalised system of social protection in India will involve confronting all these issues: of the relationship between design, efficiency, and equity; of the political economy of securing support for an institutionalised system; and of recognising the interactions with the structure of social identity in India society. This will involve transforming the functioning of the Indian state, which is significantly embedded in historically shaped structures of power and identity.

Narendar Pani looks at the relationship between globalisation and cities. As a prelude to his analysis, he discusses the multiplicity of definitions of globalisation and cities. The conceptual framework that he suggests for understanding the relationship between globalisation and cities captures as much of the wide variations in definition of both as possible. Apparently, his approach may misleadingly suggest 'an open-ended system where nothing can be said with certainty'. Hence, he hastens to clarify, 'If we were to look at flows of goods and services both within a city and between those in the city and those outside, some consistent patterns could well become discernible. *A particular flow of goods and/or services can then form a circuit that tends to reinforce itself*' (emphasis original).

It is true that 'among the processes thrown up by globalisation and each other, it is those that develop into effective circuits that tend to influence the dynamics of a city'. Potentially, each process – be it an industry or a marriage bureau – generates a specific circuit of its own, and the various processes and the circuits generated by them interact with each other in a city. 'The circuits may exist entirely within a city, may provide links between the local and the non-local within a country, or might provide links across nations'. According to Pani,

> *The process of globalisation can be unpacked into a number of different, economic, social, political, cultural, environmental, criminal and other circuits. These circuits of globalisation may be accompanied by the development of circuits within a region that cut across national boundaries as well as circuits within a nation that cut across the local and non-local. The circuits of globalisation, and the circuits that link the regional as well as the local and the non-local within a country, interact with conditions in the different arenas in which they operate, as well as with each other, in the process generating even newer conditions. And cities are among the most prominent of these arenas.* (emphasis original)

Pani extends this framework to understand the vulnerabilities of cities to globalisation. He argues that globalisation has a multitude of effects and hence 'we cannot make a blanket statement about globalisation being a positive or negative process'. Since these effects vary from place to place, the assessment of globalisation has to be made locally. Furthermore, 'the wide range of inter-connected effects also makes the process very difficult to resist. Those who strongly dislike one effect of globalisation may be tempted to adopt another.' Pani observes,

> Any suggestion that we could reduce the vulnerabilities of globalisation by simply stopping the entire process would be unrealistic. The variation from place to place and situation to situation implies that we cannot have a common approach to reduce the vulnerabilities of globalisation. What we could develop is a common method of looking for potential vulnerabilities before we can develop situation specific responses to the pressure.

Pani outlines a framework that will help us identify potential vulnerabilities in the arena of the city. He delineates and discusses three broad categories of vulnerability of cities due to globalisation: (i) those resulting 'from the circuits of globalisation competing with the circuits that already exist within a city', (ii) those existing 'within the circuit of globalisation itself', and (iii) those arising from 'the pressure the process of globalisation exerts on the economic, social, cultural, and political infrastructure that exists within the city'. Since the nature and extent of these vulnerabilities vary from situation to situation, the responses too would be different – to ease the pressure, to develop the ability to withstand the pressure, to develop alternatives to make the pressure irrelevant, or a combination of all these. What Pani has done is to provide us with a simple framework 'that tells us where to look when we try to understand the vulnerability of cities to globalisation'.

V.M. Rao turns attention to the rural communities in India which are passing through what he calls 'a churning process' resulting in breakdown of traditional structures and processes and exposing them to unpredictable changes. He identifies globalisation, along with its accompaniments of urbanisation, spread of markets, and accelerated growth, none of which is inclusive, as an essential element of this process. While a few people have risen from rags to riches, overall, Rao finds the impact of globalisation on the rural community to be adverse: from loss of traditional livelihoods to being forced to cope with vulnerabilities, the plight of the overwhelming majority is unenviable.

This predicament of the rural community, Rao holds, is not inevitable, and appropriate policies and strategies can transform the process of adjustment to globalisation into 'one of inclusive growth and more harmonious society'. He points to the fact that, in a democratic polity like India, 'the vulnerability and distress resulting from the adjustment process ... generates political pressures counteracting the negative fallout of the process'. In his chapter, Rao provides an analysis of the adjustment process in India.

After describing the features of the globalising world, Rao analyses the main factors underlying the socio-economic transformation that rural India has experienced in recent decades. For this, he constructs an analytical framework based on two contrasting rural types: 'Traditional Rural Community' and 'Urban Layout'. Rural communities in the country are at different stages between these two analytical types. Probing this transition, Rao feels, can bring out vividly the processes of change that the rural community is undergoing.

Obviously, different strata of the rural community experience the opportunities and vulnerabilities resulting from globalisation differently. Rao distinguishes three such analytical strata: (i) 'a gradually expanding creamy layer of elites living in the village but belonging to the wider urban world with active economic and social relations outside the village rather than within', (ii) 'an intermediate strata of upwardly mobile people – mostly farmers – struggling to get out of subsistence agriculture to join modern, commercialised agriculture producing for distant markets and using purchased inputs coming from outside', and (iii) 'a large and heterogeneous lower stratum (about 75 per cent of people in the village) consisting of the chronically poor, deprived, and suppressed sections at the bottom; an enterprising section striving to move up; and those downgraded from the intermediate strata having failed in their efforts to become upwardly mobile'.

According to Rao, though all these strata are affected by rural transformation triggered by globalisation, it is the last strata, mostly made up of the rural poor, which is affected most. He discusses the vulnerability of the rural poor and the security requirements to enable them to protect themselves and to benefit from development processes. To add 'a bit of flesh and animation' to the statistical data that he has used for his analysis, Rao concludes his chapter by providing the profiles of two rural poor households: one of 'a typical agricultural labourer still in the poverty trap' and the other that of 'a construction worker who is emerging out of the trap, but the improvement in his income is apparently too modest to enable him to kick it away fully'.

Findings of Census 2011 reveal that for the first time since 1921 India's urban population has gone up by more than its rural population. This is a pointer to the gravity of rural distress, as much of the growth of urban population is due to migration from the rural areas (see Sainath 2011). Rural distress is the theme of Gaurang R. Sahay's chapter. Contrary to expectations in the official circles, Sahay notes that in the agricultural sector the economic reforms based on the Structural Adjustment Programme (SAP) have not lived up to their promises. 'They, in fact, resulted in large-scale crisis in rural India by creating some new problems and exacerbating the existing ones, and by increasing vulnerability and insecure conditions of peasants and agricultural labourers.'

Sahay analyses data from government reports and academic research to show how the reform measures have adversely affected agriculture, which is the main source of livelihood of about 57 per cent of the country's population. Of the different dimensions of the vulnerabilities, which have either resulted from or exacerbated by globalisation and liberalisation are the increasing landlessness and inequality in landholdings, declining productivity in agriculture and increasing marginalisation of peasantry, changing cropping patterns and diminishing food security status, declining growth rates of agriculture, diminishing profitability of agriculture, wearing away of real incomes of farmers, slowdown of exports and increased uncertainty vis-à-vis cultivation, the reduction of input subsidies, declining gross capital formation in agriculture, decline in public investment in agricultural research and extension and in irrigation, decline of social and development banking and the return of the moneylenders, and uncertainty and risk in the output side of agriculture.

There are several manifestations of the post-reform crisis confronting the rural community, the gravest being the large number of cases of suicides by farmers and peasants. Sahay documents and reviews the literature on suicides by farmers to analyse the magnitude and trends in the phenomenon. Limitations of data notwithstanding, it appears that the number of farmers' suicides has remained more or less steady during 1998–2001 (between 16,000 and 16,500 suicides per year), saw a steep increase about in 2002 and fluctuated (at around 17,000 to 18,000 per year) during 2002–06. There has been a small decline in the number of farmers' suicides in 2007 and 2008.

Sahay draws attention to the high degree of variation in the number of farmers' suicides across the states. The problem appears to be most acute in Maharashtra, Karnataka, Andhra Pradesh, Madhya Pradesh (including Chhattisgarh), Kerala, Tamil Nadu, Pondicherry, and West Bengal. Assam, Gujarat, Haryana, Orissa, Bihar (including Jharkhand), Uttar Pradesh (including Uttarakhand), Himachal Pradesh, Punjab, Jammu & Kashmir, and Rajasthan account for a comparatively lower number of farmers' suicides. The number of farmers' suicides appears to be 'inconsequential' in most of the north-eastern states and union territories. To delineate the patterns in farmers' suicides, Sahay summarises K. Nagaraj's study on the subject in terms of the four-fold classification of states and union territories on the basis of number, rate, intensity, and trend of such suicides.

Considering that the process of globalisation is irreversible and the high rate of economic growth that India has experienced during the period of reforms, it is often suggested that the resolution of the agrarian crisis should be explored within the existing economic framework. Hence, expert committees and social scientists who have enquired into the crisis have suggested many policy measures to overcome the vulnerabilities of the rural communities. Summarising these recommendations, Sahay comments that they have been 'a part of the discourse on agriculture in India for the last few years', but the approach of successive governments towards these has been lacklustre. According to Sahay, therefore, it is not surprising that 'agrarian crisis has persisted and the incidence of farmers' suicides has remained unabated'. What he finds puzzling, however, 'is the near absence of farmer/peasant movements, which India was earlier famous for, against the state asking for the implementation of these measures'.

Workers in the unorganised sector, who constitute over 90 per cent of the workforce in India, are more vulnerable under the influence of globalisation. Obviously, the provision of social security ('protective measures to assist households and people facing severe shortages in income and basic survival needs due to different work, health, or family related risks') is of utmost importance for managing the vulnerability of the unorganised workers. While these workers significantly contribute to the nation's wealth, they lack sufficient and reliable access to social security. D. Rajasekhar dwells on this irony.

As a background to his analysis, Rajasekhar outlines the demographic, labour market, economic, and fiscal situation of the country. He notes that 'the high congruence between informal work status and poverty/vulnerability' is almost complete in the case of casual workers, as 90 per cent of them belonging to the poor and vulnerable group. More important, 'overwhelmingly, this group includes the Scheduled Castes, Scheduled Tribes, OBCs [Other Backward Classes], and Muslims'. Rajasekhar examines the government's policies and programmes relating to the provision of social security to the unorganised workers.

Rajasekhar observes, 'Unlike social security benefits for the organised sector workers that take the form of entitlements and which are budget-financed, those for the unorganised sector workers only take the form of schemes'. According to him, the social security policies and programmes for the unorganised workers suffer from many limitations. There is 'no consistent policy on social security in the country' and the government schemes and programmes are formulated randomly to meet some expedience. The multiplicity of governmental schemes lack overall cohesion in design and management, and the approach is fragmented. The expenditure on social security has been measly (less than 2 per cent of GDP), and the eligibility criteria are too tight as to exclude many a vulnerable person. To compound all this, the unorganised workers lack bargaining power and even awareness on social security schemes.

Given that an overwhelming majority of the unorganised sector workers lack access to sufficient and reliable social security, 'what risks do they face and what coping mechanisms do they adopt?' Based on the studies that he and his colleagues have undertaken, Rajasekhar addresses these questions. He views risks as 'emergencies', both predictable and unpredictable, as 'for households typically lacking risk-management tools, predictable events would also have negative welfare effects'. The evidence reveals that the incidence of crises or emergencies was the highest among the unorganised agricultural workers belonging to the scheduled castes and scheduled tribes. 'Health emergencies were the most significant crises faced across all categories of workers ...', imposing a heavy cost burden on the households concerned. To cope with these emergencies, these households borrowed from moneylenders, from relatives, but the employers played a limited role in this. In brief, 'there has been extreme dependence by the unorganised workers on informal sources of risk management...', and this perpetuates their vulnerability.

What do the unorganised workers perceive as their social security needs? Rajasekhar answers this question by summarising the findings of some studies that he and his colleagues have conducted in 2005–06 on agricultural labourers, construction workers, domestic servants, *agarbathi*-rollers, and garment workers. According to him, 'unemployment benefits, old age pensions and medical benefits (sickness) were the three key needs', though there were differences in felt needs across the different categories of workers and in terms of age, sex, education, regions, etc. Differences were also found as regards the willingness of the workers to participate in contributory social security schemes and the amount they were willing to contribute.

In conclusion, Rajasekhar argues that there is 'a need to provide adequate and reliable social security to the unorganised workers as an entitlement' and that 'the social security benefits need to be universal rather than scheme-based'. These, he regards, as the key instruments 'to reduce income gaps, to redistribute incomes, and to ensure the vast majority of the unorganised workforce do not face social harshness'.

Of the various categories of workers in the unorganised sector, as Rajasekhar had observed, those belonging to the scheduled castes and scheduled tribes were the most vulnerable. In his chapter, using 'social justice' as the anchoring point, Manohar Yadav discusses the vulnerabilities of the scheduled castes in the context of globalisation. According to him, globalisation has 'a trajectory, record, and consequences of its own in India. It has passed through different historical phases and each phase has produced unique contextual results.' In each phase of globalisation, most of the benefits were garnered by the high and the privileged castes and some religious groups. His impressions suggest that the chronically indigent sections did not benefit from the fruits of globalisation, and the dalits have been worst hit. A similar point was also made by P. Radhakrishnan at the seminar.

Yadav traces the vulnerability of dalits through history. Contrary to expectations, the British rule, he argues, excluded the dalits from the modernity that it introduced and reinforced their vulnerability. While positive beginnings were made soon after independence to change this situation for the better, the efforts lost both 'force and direction'. The dalits could not benefit much from the policy of protective discrimination, especially reservation in government jobs, as 'they were not equipped with literacy and education to qualify themselves to utilise the new opportunities ...'. According to Yadav, 'Not until the Fourth Five-Year Plan period could dalits receive any serious relief in crucial matters like poverty, hunger, and unemployment ...'.

In the present phase of globalisation, Yadav feels the bleak realities of the dalits have persisted. He quotes Duncan Forrester's observation that 'whatever index one may use – poverty, social status, health, life expectancy, literacy, education – [they] come under the bottom of the scale'. He finds the vulnerability of the scheduled castes is graver as compared to those of the tribal communities and other most backward castes. He discusses the condition of the scheduled castes as regards land and employment, education, and assets, and the related policy measures initiated by the government.

While governmental intervention through policies and programmes is, no doubt, indispensible for the amelioration of the condition of dalits, Yadav makes the important point that dalits must 'take stock of their own situation and see whether they have a role to play in their own betterment'. This is important considering the rise of the dalit entrepreneurial class in the wake of the opportunities provided by globalisation (see Aiyar 2011). At the seminar, A. Ramaiah argued that these opportunities open a window for the empowerment of dalits. Yadav bemoans that 'dalits have not made much headway in the development of institutional and cultural resources in the cause of their upliftment', and stresses that 'the dalit intellectuals and the elite of the community have a significant function in this respect'.

To address vulnerability and to manage risks, especially those confronted by the rural people and the scheduled caste households, micro-finance has widely been advocated. Micro-finance implies the provision of financial services – such as savings, credit, and insurance – for the poor 'to meet consumption credit needs, or to start new economic activities, or to strengthen the existing ones'. These programmes, it is believed, have the potential to reduce poverty and empower the poor, especially in the context of globalisation and privatisation. Does micro-finance reduce vulnerability of the dalit households? Based on a comparative study in Karnataka and Tamil Nadu, in the concluding chapter, D. Rajasekhar, Manjula R. and Suchitra J.Y. try to answer this question.

As a background to their study, Rajasekhar et al., outline the situation of dalit households in Karnataka and Tamil Nadu vis-à-vis the national level. They discuss in particular landownership, deprivation in capabilities, and quality of employment and earnings. They then profile the background of the sample households and the micro-finance benefits, especially savings and credit benefits, received by them. This is followed by an analysis of the relation between micro-finance and access to basic amenities, health, and education among the sample households.

Analysing the relationship between membership in micro-finance groups and vulnerability, Rajasekhar et al., reiterate that the sample households have benefited from both savings and credit facility, though the extent of benefits varied between the two states and the project areas within each state. They analyse the relationship between micro-finance through self-help groups and the levels of savings, frequency of availing loans, income generation, and meeting emergencies. The self-help groups have been a mechanism through which the households 'come together, discuss their problems, and solve them collectively'. Though it is too early to confirm, an analysis of the links between self-help group membership and levels of vulnerability in this chapter shows that 'micro-finance would have only limited impact on vulnerability of dalits household'.

As compared to Karnataka, Rajasekhar et al., found the self-help groups in Tamil Nadu 'to have been more successful in enabling member dalit households to attend group meetings, to contribute larger amounts of savings, and in providing loans to meet consumption and production credit needs. This has had some positive impact on the member households to cope with vulnerability'. The dalit households, however, faced vulnerability on many other counts and not all of them were addressed by micro-finance programme. Rajasekhar et al., opine that micro-finance programme can be more effective in reducing vulnerability among poor in general and dalit households in particular only 'if they provide access to appropriate insurance (social security) and savings products either on their own or in collaboration with other actors such as government or banks'.

Coda

There is euphoria that in the globalisation era, India has put behind 'the Hindu rate of growth' and her economy has achieved a high growth rate, almost touching double digits. It is also argued that such robust economic growth is indispensable for sustained reductions in mass poverty. But, growth does not necessarily benefit all: 'It is not true that "a rising tide lifts all boats". Sometimes, a quickly rising tide, especially when accompanied by a storm, dashes weaker boats against the shore, smashing them to smithereens' (Stiglitz 2003: 78).

Obviously, not all policies undertaken to promote growth have contributed to reducing poverty; some of these policies have, in fact, actually exacerbated poverty, constraining the poor to inhabit what Abhijit Banerjee and Esther Dufflo (2011) call 'a poverty zone', where their future incomes over a life are likely to be lower. For this globalisation cannot be blamed *per se*; mere condemnation of globalisation will not help much. As Stiglitz observes, 'globalization itself is neither good nor bad' (ibid.: 20). While for many, it has, no doubt, been 'an unmitigated disaster,' its 'power to do enormous good' (ibid.) cannot be dismissed as wishful thinking. What is called for are 'pro-poor growth strategies' (ibid.: 82), that is, policies that simultaneously promote growth and reduce poverty.

Articulating such policies and strategies require a sound understanding of the problem and an evaluation of the programmes that have been already implemented. The information and analyses provided in this volume, it is hoped, will result in better policies, which will lead to better outcomes.

References

Aiyar, Swaminathan S. Anklesaria. 2011. 'The Unexpected Rise of Dalit Millionaires', *Sunday Times of India* (Mumbai), 31 July 2011: 22.

Banerjee, Abhijit and Esther Dufflo. 2011. *Poor Economics: Rethinking Poverty and the Ways to End it.* New Delhi: Random House India.

Dasgupta, Samir. 2010. *Globalization and Humanity.* Jaipur: Rawat Publications.

Frank, Andre Gunder. 1978. *Dependent Accumulation and Underdevelopment.* New York: The Monthly Review Press.

——. 1982. *On Capitalist Underdevelopment.* Bombay: Oxford University Press.

Giddens, Anthony. 1990. *The Consequences of Modernity.* Stanford, CA: Stanford University Press.

Mukherji, Partha N. and Bhola Nath Ghosh. 2010. 'Democratic Centralism, Party Hegemony, and Decentralisation in West Bengal', *Sociological Bulletin,* 59 (2): 199-215.

Robertson, Ronald. 1992. *Globalisation: Social Theory and Global Culture.* London: Sage Publications.

Sainath, P. 2011. 'Census Findings Point to Decade of Rural Distress', *The Hindu* (Bangalore), 26 September 2011: 1 and 9.

Stiglitz, Joseph E. 2003. *Globalization and Its Discontents.* New Delhi: Penguin Books India.

——. 2007. *Making Globalization Work.* London: Penguin Books.

Sweezy, Paul M. 1968. *The Theory of Capitalist Development.* New York: The Monthly Review Press.

Wallerstein, Immanuel. 1979. *The Capitalist World Economy.* Cambridge: Cambridge University Press.

Part I
Perspectives

2

Globalisation

Towards an Alternative View[1]

D.N. DHANAGARE

During the past decade and a half, no other concept, with perhaps the solitary exception of 'gender', has stirred a major discourse in social sciences as the term 'globalisation' did. It is not just an accident that the term came speedily into academic parlance following almost on the heels of the Dunkel Agreement that finally led to the formation of the World Trade Organisation (hereafter WTO). This synchronisation of social science discourse on globalisation and the institutionalisation of WTO is a striking instance of how developments in the world economy keep impinging on societal processes and institutions, induce new patterns of change, and necessitate reassessment of the adequacy of concepts and approaches in social sciences for understanding complex social reality.

The term 'globalisation' refers to the growing economic integration at international level based significantly on the activities of multinational corporations (hereafter MNCs). These activities involve financial exchanges, evolving production strategies, marketing rights and responsibilities across boundaries of nation-states, and, of course, accelerating growth by deploying the new information technology. Although not an entirely new phenomenon, the globalisation process in the 1980s and 1990s led to surging of international trade and investments mostly centred around and dictated by the advanced industrial capitalist

---

This chapter originally appeared in *Sociological Bulletin*, 52 (1), March 2003, pp. 4–31. It is reproduced here with the kind permission from the author and the Indian Sociological Society.

economies. Because of the intensification of the economic integration process, more recently, many developing countries have chosen to get more closely integrated into the network of global economy. In their anxiety to rebuild their economies, most developing postcolonial countries perceive such integration as a short cut to realising their long-cherished developmental dreams. By the standards of the industrially developed countries of the West, however, the process of globalisation in several developing countries, including India, remains at an incipient stage.

The globalisation debate in general is focused largely on more recent developments, whose impact is not confined either to a single nation-state, continent, or to a subcontinent. Consequences of the global economic integration are seen spread over a wide range of non-economic spheres of life all over the world. It is commonly understood as a process that rapidly transforms an otherwise disparate and heterogeneous world into a compressed, but not necessarily homogeneous, entity and yet at the same time it 'intensifies consciousness of the world as a whole' (Robertson 1992: 8). It is generally claimed that globalisation accelerates and reinforces interdependence of markets, peoples, and their cultures and nation-states. Therefore, some sociologists approach the problematic of globalisation via considerations of modernity. In his model of the global system, Anthony Giddens, for example, defines globalisation as 'intensification of worldwide social relations which link distant localities in such a way that local happenings are shaped by events occurring miles away and vice versa' (1990: 64). He emphasises four dimensions of globalisation: the nation-state system, the world capitalist economy, the world military order, and the international division of labour. Each of these four, according to him, is an extension of societal modernity and an offshoot of its basic institutional features. He, therefore, postulates modernity as inherently globalising and, hence, today's globalisation is no more than the fundamental consequence of the modernity project of the West (ibid.: 52–63, 177). However, cultures are not and, in fact, cannot be, obliterated by modernity because 'features of globalisation and modernity relate specifically to the separation and recombination of space and time that are so crucial to the dynamism of modernity' (ibid.: 20–21, 59–71).

The claim by Giddens that globalisation does not involve any dismemberment or dissolution of non-western cultures (the 'other' of the West) practically borders on optimism with utopian-futuristic streaks. As we shall see later, this use of 'modernity prism' for understanding globalisation is really not very common among contributors to the contemporary debate. Today, the concept of 'globalisation' revolves mainly around social consequences of integration with world economy via the market and multinationals. The thrust of the current debate is as much on understanding the devastating effects of global economy on less developed countries as it is on revealing mechanisms that monopoly capitalism deploys to perpetuate its domination. These concerns are discussed emphatically by economists and by other social scientists alike. It, however, needs to be emphasised that although theoretical relevance of 'globalisation' is being taken seriously by all social scientists (including those of the Marxist and neo-Marxist persuasions), the debate as yet has not gained maturity and sophistication as a major social science discourse (Sengupta 2001: 3137).

The origin of the concept of 'globalisation' is usually traced to Marshal McLuhan (1960), who first introduced the idea of what is today called 'global village' – a notion that implied a sort of compression of the world and intensification of consciousness of the world as a single entity. This shrinking of the world, in the early 1960s, was then attributed to the growing impact of media revolution, more specifically to the television. The visual medium and its multichannels abetted market invasion on peoples and cultures. Their influence on human experience has been so deep and all-pervasive that it became a part of our being, our consciousness and our very existence.

It is necessary to explicate the notion of globalisation first. While oversimplifying its meaning, Thomas L. Friedman has defined globalisation as 'the integration of everything with everything else'. This nominal definition tends to hide more and reveal little about the meaning structure. Globalisation involves a process of change that is too simple and yet paradoxically too complicated to grapple with. 'It is a process of integration of markets, finance and technology, especially information technology [hereafter IT] in a way that shrinks the world to a miniature in size and enables people from different parts of the globe to reach around the world faster, deeper and cheaper' (Friedman and Kaplan 2002: 64). This characterisation of globalisation, however, projects it as if it is confined to the sphere of market and economic activities alone. E. Anitat has talked of globalisation as 'the process through which an increasingly free flow of ideas, people, goods and capital leads to the integration of economies and societies' (2002: 4). Exuding his confidence about what globalisation has fetched for humankind, Anitat argues that such global integration has boosted growth and incomes and has thereby helped to raise general standards of living in less developed and underprivileged parts of the world. With globalisation not only sophisticated technologies have become available to developing countries, but also marked improvements in average literacy, quality of health, and general life expectancy and, above all, greater integration have taken place and these have promoted human freedom. This has been possible because information sharing and market expansion now provide increasing choices to people (ibid.).

The growing interest in 'globalisation' has to be understood in the context of developments since the early 1960s that mark an important watershed in world history. After the World War II, the Berlin Wall had been erected signifying the bipolar world as well as the ideological divide between two superpowers that mothered their respective spheres of geopolitical influence. The world economy was clearly divided between two blocs represented by 'free market economy' and 'administered economy', between capitalism and socialism. Only modern communication system – the media – contributed to 'global consciousness'. Nonetheless, the term 'global community' was seldom used, since the media then fully acknowledged nationality and autonomy of a particular media system. In other words, despite the emergence of a new global awareness, increased communication had not overshadowed or obliterated the remnants of identities of nation-state, ethnicity, caste, religion, race, language, and region even within a nation-state, let alone across nation-states. Their insularity was consciously protected by the 'Berlin Wall', 'Iron Curtain', or a 'Warsaw Pact' and by protective tariffs. Behind these walls and fences, nation-states could preserve their own unique forms of cultures, traditions, lifestyles, and politics, not just their economies.

The nature of interrelations and economic linkages leading to cultural influences came to be understood within two dominant theoretical paradigms, namely, 'modernisation–modernity' and 'world systems theory' – the latter one as cogently articulated and propounded by Immanuel Wallerstein (1980). These two conceptual apparatuses practically kept the social science scholarship preoccupied from the 1960s till the 1990s. Contributions of neo-Marxists like Paul Baran (1957), Samir Amin (1982, 1997), Hamza Alavi (1982) and Andre Gunder Frank (1978, 1982) to theories of development and underdevelopment, are replete with concepts like 'core', 'centre–periphery', 'international division of labour', 'capitalist world economy', 'monopoly capitalism', and the like that are found in Wallerstein's writings abundantly. Without going into the details of these two paradigms, it should suffice to note that they are precursors of the present-day discourse on 'globalisation'. Quite surprisingly though, Wallerstein (2000) considers globalisation as no more than a buzzword that describes the current situation in which the end of the 'Cold War' has led to the emergence of a unipolar world with an unassailable supremacy of the USA both in global economy and geopolitics. To him, globalisation is meaningless as an analytical concept. It is being given legitimacy by spokespersons of the neo-liberal creed that ideologically sustains the pro-global regime. The concept only serves primarily as a political prescription (or exhortation) for the developing world to opt for all kinds of short cuts to integration with the capitalist global economy (ibid.).

Nature of Integration through Market

The current debate on globalisation focuses on the role of international trade and market as a cohesive force mainly assisted by modern media and IT. It would, therefore, be necessary to examine the nature of the global integration that is taking place today. John Kenneth Galbraith, an eminent economist, was once asked whether globalisation is truly metamorphosing economy in any fundamental way, and his reply was: 'such a reference to a *new* economy is just short of fraudulent' (Galbraith 2001: 10). He was only suggesting that forms of expression change more frequently than does substantive content to which they refer. What was once termed 'capitalism' is now being called a market economy or corporate system. Such euphemistic change, however, does not alter the quintessence of capitalism and its ultimate goal, that is, profit maximisation through monopolies at any cost, that was, and continues to be, the hallmark of capitalism. But then the new expression 'market system' is preferred because it is seen as a more bland, ideologically neutral, and yet a sophisticated way of describing the gory side of capitalism. Globalisation is, thus, yet another way of putting the fact that capitalist regime gets extended beyond political boundaries of nation-states. Systems of formal governance are relegated to the status of subordinate partners while the business, dominated by MNCs and their managerial class, controls decision-making process, and occupies a pre-eminent position in global economy.

The rapid changes in the transnational business world are usually attributed to the revolution in the new digital technology and IT. It is often said that information superhighways are *the* routes through which globalisation process takes deep and firm roots. The high-speed digital technology is its principal vehicle that enables globalisation to change economies and societies – their norms and rules of the game, especially those of the transnational business world. The unstoppable speed of the new IT has thus accelerated the process of integration of the world economies. It is seen in the ever increasing exports of goods and services, on the one hand, and the growing trend of cross-border investment flows, mergers, and acquisitions of manufacturing companies, on the other.

More specifically, far-reaching globalisation of the finance sector in recent times has been facilitated by electronic communications. All financial and market transactions (transfer of money, bank accounts, loans – lending and borrowing, securities, investments, sale and purchase of stocks of companies, etc.) can now be conducted from, and transferred to, any part of the world in practically no time. Thus, IT has enabled principal companies and actors in the international market to organise themselves as global enterprises. Banking, the backbone of finance sector, for instance, has also become a substantially global phenomenon. According to one estimate, 'the world's total bank deposits owned by non-residents of a country rose from $ 20 billion in 1964 to $ 7,900 billion in

1995. Electronic payments through the Society for Worldwide Inter-bank Financial Telecommunications (SWIFT) has itself arranged more than $ 5 trillion worth payments per day in 1999' (Scholte 2002: 22–23). The magnitude of these financial exchanges on a global scale is simply mind-boggling.

Global financial governance, however, seems to have a weak structure and an arbitrary system of decision-making. Apart from the fact that the global financial system is haunted constantly by anxiety over stability of currencies and security of investments, the system clearly favours the North as against the South, big corporate players than upcoming entrepreneurs, and developed industrial capitalist countries more than their developing counterparts. 'In the absence of strong civil society initiatives, this global financial system tends to function in a partisan manner while its governance is insufficiently participatory, consultative, transparent and publicly accountable' (ibid.: 3). A study conducted by the Organisation of Economic Cooperation and Development (OECD), consisting of some twenty-nine highly industrialised countries worldwide, has revealed that 'the value of cross-border mergers and acquisitions by US-based MNCs grew six-fold from 1991 to 1998. Similarly, between 1990 and 1999, the number of international business alliances (for sale, marketing, and development agreements) rose from just over 3,000 to almost 60,000' (Ferranti 2000: 1–2). Such an exponential growth in financial transactions in the developed capitalist world is not, however, seen in their exchanges with the less developed countries.

Such research findings on rapid integration of economies within a global space present only a partial picture of reality. They tend to create an impression as if a unified integrated one world – a global community – has arrived not only in economic terms but also in social and political terms. Truth claims of such assertions, often made more tacitly than explicitly, need to be scrutinised with great care and caution. Triumphalists of globalisation always paint a rosy picture of a transnational business class as a cohesive and unified entity. The fact that transnational corporations (hereafter TNCs) have truly become global institutions in structural and functional terms is often overstated. An impression is thus sought to be created that the corporate business world is fast shaking off the national anchorages, nostalgia, attributes, and obsessions of its constituents. L. Sklair's (2001) thesis on globalisation is a good example of such an overstatement. While suggesting the active constructors of the global system, following many a predecessor systems theorist, Sklair has highlighted three analytical divisions between the economy, polity, and culture-ideology. He has further argued that TNCs dominate the economic sphere, while their cultural ideology of consumerism – the chief driving force in the sphere of culture and ideology – plays the role of a surrogate of market force. The transnational capitalist class takes over the control of the political sphere (ibid.: 20–55). This theoretical position is founded on the assumption of transcendence of not only nation-state boundaries, class interests defined primarily in terms of ownership of means of production (in the classical Marxist sense), but also of cultural tastes, habits, choices, and practices. In the event of the latter happening, with the extension of the TNCs, the transcendence would entail a near complete homogenisation of culture and ideology.

The core of Sklair's argument is that a transnational class is rapidly emerging. It is comprised of (a) TNC executives, (b) globalising bureaucracy and politicians (whose services are lent by nation-states, who occupy decision-making positions in international organisations or structures of governance – such as the United Nations, UNESCO, UNDP, IMF, World Bank, European Union, Commonwealth and SAARC secretariats, and the like, (c) globalising professionals (such as IT specialists, and finance and management consultants), and (d) merchants and media. Some of these research findings and statistics do establish the fact that in recent decades this transnational class and the corporate groups they preside over are inclined to go for direct foreign investments in the form of collaborations, or financing subsidiaries to begin with, followed by gradual mergers and takeovers. Sometimes it is also seen that the TNCs, thanks to the ingenuity of their executives and management experts, are effectively dealing with two major crises facing the global society today, namely, the crisis resulting from extreme form of class polarisation and the environmental crisis. The crises are handled so adroitly that some TNCs are now actively advocating the notion of 'sustainable development', production of environmentally safe commodities and services, and are championing the cause of social justice by selectively appropriating the language as well as rhetoric of non-governmental organisations (hereafter NGOs), primarily to pre-empt or ward off any activist intervention.[2]

Sklair's thesis raises more fundamental questions: whether globalisation has really resulted in increasing free international competition; whether production processes and outputs are getting internationalised, leading to a quantum jump in international labour migration; whether new forms of global governance are really crystallising; and whether or not globalisation process would finally disintegrate nation-states and obliterate cultures and civilisations. In other words, does globalisation truly lead to the formation of a world community and foster at least a *quasi-gemeinschaft* solidarity across nation-state boundaries and corporate business class? To answer this question it would be instructive to examine whether the TNCs – the prime catalysts of globalisation – are really moving in the direction of internationalisation of capital ownership and development of a genuinely transnational business community. Recently, W.K. Carroll and Fennema (2002) have studied some 176 leading MNCs in the world economy over a period of two decades between 1976 and 1996. This important empirical study, using a longitudinal research design, found that most of the world's largest business corporations continued their operations within national boundaries. Although some financial flows, investments and production activities did go beyond national corporate networks, nearly three quarters of their business linkages were domiciled in the same country (ibid.: 413–14). Even a transnational network, developed around large financial institutions too, was found to be no more than a mere superstructure that rests on resilient national institutions. Thus, Wallerstein's argument that capitalism has essentially been a world system all through history (Wallerstein 1980) stands substantially undermined because MNCs and their so-called corporate forms of governance seem to operate predominantly within national networks. Thus, neither in corporate ownership nor in forms of governance a truly global framework seems to be emerging in structural and functional terms. This is not to suggest that barring its euphoria no transnational corporation or business class is emerging. Some interlinkages are developing, no doubt, but they are seen operating on a moderate scale only. Financial markets have become global and more integrated but the governance of MNCs, whether from the North America or from Europe, remains firmly embedded in national and regional structures and cultures (Carroll and Fennema 2002: 403–9).

The Future of Nation-States

The present globalisation discourse also touches upon the issue of the future of nation-states under the condition of global financial integration. The triumph of TNCs and their finance capitalism over microcosms of nation-states raises the question whether globalisation will strengthen or weaken nation-states? Two diametrically opposite views are advanced. A more optimistic vision is that globalisation actually strengthens the state by redefining its role in changed economic conditions resulting from global integration via market and finance capitalism. The other, more pessimistic, view is that the globalisation process will not only weaken but will also hasten the demise of the nation-state. On a more optimistic side it is argued that once a technology-driven globalisation sets in, it starts shrinking the world. As people get used to reaching around the world faster, deeper, and cheaper, they also start thinking globally. The logic is very simple. Technology builds capabilities, and capabilities create human intentions 'to act globally' regardless of whether or not a formal structure of global governance (like WTO) exists. When declining costs and increasing returns entice people, companies and institutions to tie up with foreign collaborators for maximising their profits, their increasing global interactions create a semblance of disorder. Nation-states then start using primordial and cultural identities as instruments to assert their choice of staying in or out of global trade and market competition as and when it suits them. The situation is also conducive for breeding a sense of insecurity and business instability. As the need for morality of order gets reinforced naturally then everyone is willing to give up a share of one's independence for the sake of 'world government' (Friedman and Kaplan 2002: 65). The scenario reminds us of famous arguments of 'contract theorists' about the origin of the state as a regulating institution.

Today, not even few social scientists think that a 'world government' is round the corner. In fact, some theorists go even to the extent of visualising or positing nation-state as no more than a bubble that would soon evaporate in the face of the emerging world community and a global system of governance. It is argued that historically nation-state developed only through the growth of civil bureaucracy, an army, and diplomacy that catapulted in the formation of a nation as an 'imagined community'.[3] The bubble of nation-state actually results from modernising initiatives of industrial capitalism. Usually nationalist elites, supported and bolstered up by the national bourgeoisie, often resort to evoking primordial, ethnic, and cultural-symbolic roots and identities of people (see Gellner 1983; Anderson 1991; Smith 1991).[4] Globalisation is that final phase of capitalism when it completes the entombment of sovereign nation-states. Kaplan (see Friedman and Kaplan 2002: 67) has cited the example of the European Union (hereafter EU) emerging out of the coal and steel consortium in the early 1950s with only a few nation-states, but later gradually developing into a superstructure. Kaplan, therefore, argues that the state is weakening in Europe with the formation of EU.

In the context of growing anxiety over the future of nation-states, it is significant to note that A. Martinelli (2002: 9–11) views the globalisation process as eroding the very foundation of sovereignty and autonomy of nation-states. This is largely because global finance capitalism compels nation-states to adopt neo-liberal economic policies to stay in the competitive world market. Sovereign states have, therefore, no option but to come to terms with gradual loss of sovereignty and erosion of their power. Martinelli also thinks that EU is a step towards global governance. He is, however, not arguing that nation-states disappear altogether under the bulldozing impact of global economic system. He is only saying that 'they undergo a deep transformation'. In other words, it amounts to saying that nation-states are not demised, but they get reconstituted or reconstructed. Projecting EU as a model of supranational system of governance, Martinelli is simply highlighting the experiment as a convincing demonstration of how the two concepts of autonomy and sovereignty have been rendered obsolete and redundant by the globalisation process (ibid.: 13–14).

Quite surprisingly, Martinelli takes no cognisance of Amin's position on the true nature of 'so-called' European integration under globalisation. While discussing changes that capitalism goes through during globalisation, Amin has stressed the need to separate the grain from chaff. He has almost drawn up a balance sheet of what the European Economic Community (hereafter EEC) has and has not been able to achieve by way of economic integration through the market. He draws our attention to the fact that what truly holds the European community together is the fear of revival of Germany as a major industrial and military power. This shared fear is the motive force underlying the other member nation-states voting for European unification. Beneath the facade of unity of EU there have been ideological pulls and counter-pulls on the 'right' (that is, pro-USA) and on the 'left' of the political spectrum. The latter position is obviously 'pro-Russia' as a checkmate for the united Germany. Certainly nationalism and national priorities have had an overwhelming influence on the member-states of EU since its formation (Amin 1997: 108–12). Economic gains of EEC in the form of visible growth have been attributed by Amin (ibid.: 113) to a kind of social compromise between capital and labour in post-War Europe. Quite paradoxically, the success of EU is largely because national policies, built around Fordism and welfare state, have been determining the extent of individual nation-state's participation in the EEC experiment. Notwithstanding the triumphalists' discourses around the united European community, the fact remains that 'Europe has not made itself an irreversible history', and that the future of its integration as yet remains an unsettled issue. To prove his point Amin (ibid.: 118–19) has cited four examples of how the member-states of EU have steadfastly kept four sensitive issues of national economic interest outside the purview of the European Union:

(i) Research and development policy, being closely linked to development of military capacities, is still guarded as an exclusively national responsibility of each of the EU members.

(ii) Transparency in economic policy and practice, on which rests a truly competitive market, is readily discarded. Basic principles of a free market are often bypassed owing to pressure of national interests and policy preferences.

(iii) Though active partners in the European economy, MNCs still have to operate only within the bounds of national commercial laws of respective member-states of EU.

(iv) Media (movies, TV, etc.), that is, 'culture' has been completely excluded from the sphere of fierce commercial competition within EU.

Therefore, EU has really not achieved even truly integrated economic governance, except in areas marked out and approved by its sovereign member-nation-states.

What is often glossed over in the discourse on globalisation is the fact that the concept presupposes construction of an effective global production system. Advocates of global integration share a faith that the globalisation process is indeed leading to disintegration of national productive systems that they consider as both necessary and desirable. Often the domineering presence of MNCs in a national economic space is taken as an unassailable proof that global productive system has come to stay. Economic, mainly financial, integration through the market may have accelerated the pace of exchanges between nation-states and their principal corporate actors. However, to assume that such frequent exchanges necessarily lead to shaping of a new global society – civil, economic and political – appears to be a far-fetched idea. It is as much an unattainable dream as it is an ahistorical viewpoint simply because a community or society needs a shared vision, values and sentiments. Just shared economic interests, pursued with the calculus of balance of payments, trade deficits and profits, do not suffice. That shared vision is possible only when commonality of interests transcends pure economic interests or financial integration. As things stand today centrifugal tendencies do operate quite visibly even within EU and other formations like the Group of 7/16/20, Commonwealth, ASEAN, SAARC, and similar other regional formations. 'Fear of the other' seems to be a common running undercurrent of all centrifugal activities and initiatives within such formations.

It is necessary to emphasise that globalisation is the ideology of capitalist superpowers that harbour 'a utopian vision of running the world like a market'.[5] On a more political and pragmatic side, it involves an exhortation for the less developed economies on the one hand and a project to effect disintegration of nation-state entities on the other hand, to fragment power and achieve social disaggregation, even ruthlessly if necessary. The final aim of this project is to render nation-states as economically parasites, politically powerless and socio-culturally faceless before bulldozing power of the market with MNCs driving from the backseat. Protagonists of the globalisation thesis, who assume that the process is inevitable, often miss the fact that global hierarchy or ascendancy remains perpetually unstable or shaky due to vicissitudes of a world market occasioned by a combination of devaluation of currencies, costs of production, and collapse in commodity prices. Today, a developing country with fragile economy may lack the capacity and resources to compete in the world market, but a decade or two later the same country may realise its development potential fully. It needs to be stressed that a hierarchical structure founded on the pedestal of market, commodities, and financial power is not irrevocable. Japan and Germany at the end of the Cold War are not the same as they were at the end of the World War II. Hence, though a market-centred vision of globalisation legitimises hierarchy, it is not very conducive for sharing of community sentiments. The market is only an institutional mechanism for one-sided accumulation. Furthermore, it has no history of being poor-friendly. In the economic history no economic theorist has ever claimed markets to be a pro-poor institution. Although competitors in the market might have contributed to infrastructure development and to some social welfare measures here and there through aid, credit (soft loan), or through foreign direct investments, generally the market tends to polarise societies not only in the relative but also in absolute terms. Therefore, financial integration of world economy through market mechanisms is neither necessary nor sufficient condition for developing a truly sustainable 'world community'. This dictum is true as much for national, regional, and local levels as it is for the global scale. Hence, globalisation via the market is incapable of inculcating a sense of identity, history, and social purpose among people. Such a 'we' feeling can alone generate moral strength and survival instinct among social aggregates in times of crises.

Developing Countries, the Poor and Globalisation

What impact the market-driven global integration is having on the less industrialised developing countries and their vast population, especially those belonging to the disadvantaged, weaker and marginalised sections – such as the small and marginal farmers – that is, primary producers, agricultural labourers and more so the women in India? Considerable attention is now being paid to this question in the debate on globalisation. Policy makers, development administrators, and international funding agencies, besides of course NGOs, are presently preoccupied with searching for a viable and more sustainable alternative for the developing countries. More recent debates have tended to zero down on minimum food security for the poor in less industrialised countries in the face of globalisation. The need to launch some kind of 'stop global and shop local' campaign is underscored by such debates. Because, the most important manifestation of globalisation process is that it inevitably leads to increased international trade, including trade in food, across the world that is really avoidable. Besides, economic globalisation tends to turn agricultural farms more capital-intensive. This change is conducive to corporate controlled agriculture that is spreading to countries where the great bulk of farmers is poor with small and marginal holdings. Once global agribusiness and biotechnology corporations are allowed to penetrate and destroy local economies (in the hope that the free market economy will make food cheaply available to the needy), incomes of small-farm owners in the developing countries start declining (Shiva 2000). The globalisation of non-sustainable industrial agriculture (often promoted in the form of monoculture) gets established, it creates perpetual dependence among small farmers from developing countries making it impossible for them to survive. This has risked their minimum livelihood.[6]

Generally, increased international trade is justified by WTO on the grounds that it can promote economic development, that it is *the* solution to world poverty, and that it has a built-in guarantee of minimum food security to the poor in developing countries. In reality, however, WTO has promoted an unnecessary trading and export-import activity involving foods and cereals. Moreover, WTO is unable to control unfair trade practices of some developed nations against developing countries effectively. The idea that farmers, whether small or big, can make more profits by growing food (cereals, fruits, poultry, etc.) for market, especially for export, is theoretically sound. However, things just do not work out that way. The ground realities have shown time and again that once small farmers get drawn into the vortex of export–import activities under the WTO regime, they are forced to drop prices of their produce if they wish to compete with capitalist farm producers from the developed world. In a sense small producers from developing countries have to compete with rich farm producers from the developed countries as unequals, because the level of farm subsidies given by the latter can never be matched by the former, that is, countries like India.[7] China, for instance, presently supplies about 80 per cent of the demand for green tea in the international market. Anticipating an upsurge in demand from the western developed countries for green and organic tea (that is reported to have health promoting properties), China is now getting ready to meet the increased demand by flooding the world market with tea at rock bottom prices to push out potential competitors like tea producers from India and Sri Lanka (Hines et al. 2002: 40). The latest victim of this global competition is the edible oil industry in India. It appears to be nearing the threshold of extinction because of low import duties that have led to highly subsidised soya and palm oil imports from Malaysia that are flooding the Indian domestic market today.[8]

Any attempt by developing countries to protect their small-farm producers by putting trade barriers and tariffs are stoutly opposed by the corporate business lobby using the WTO sanctions effectively. In conformity with the WTO norms, India had to remove some of the trade barriers on foods by the year 2000 following a complaint by the USA. Consequently,the prices of export items like coconuts, coffee, and paper have plummeted by 80, 60, and 45 per cent respectively (see Hines et al., 2002: 38). Even the gap between the industrial urban economy and the rural farm setting is getting widened. For example, corn as an ordinary cereal is sold for ₹ 15 per kg, but the processed corn flakes produced by the cereal company Kellogg's are sold for ₹ 200 per kg.

Integration with the global economy, thus, accentuates disparities, and polarises sections of a society and also nation-states. It produces a strange paradox that increased economic growth through global commerce entails absolute deprivation and denial of minimum food security to the poor and vulnerable sections, and threatens sustainability of the local economy (see Shiva 2000: 17–19; see also Bagchi 1999).

Champions of globalisation often gloss over the fact that 'food security' is quintessentially a poverty problem. It simply means that lack of food is due to the lack of means to acquire or buy it. Invariably, lack of food is not due to a shortfall in food production, but because the poor who need the security badly lack purchasing power – a fact highlighted by the familiar findings of Nobel laureate Amartya Sen from his studies in China and India. Therefore, despite economic globalisation and growth in international trade, in general, 'protectionism' continues to be a serious problem that subverts the sustainable agriculture sector in developing countries (Schuh 2002: 15–16). This explains why the globalisation process has failed to capitalise on international trade as a means to ensure food security to the poor from developing countries. Experience of the past decade suggests that the WTO modalities are rapidly pushing small-farm producers into the ranks of the poor in developing countries.

Conditions of working class, in both organised and unorganised sectors, in developing countries seem to be no better under a globalising economy. Throughout the history working class movements and trade unions have always sought to influence and humanise capitalist system within the nation-states framework. In the globalisation phase of capitalism, however, MNCs and TNCs have rendered economic borders more permeable. They have thereby undercut the capacities of national governments to regulate them, particularly in developing countries (Ross 2000: 1–2). India is no exception to this trend. Consequently, the labour is facing a new problem under globalisation, as markets keep expanding in their reach as well as in their power beyond labour organisations' will and capacity to affect MNCs. Secondly, in a developing economy like India, organised non-agricultural industrial labour is only a fraction of total workforce and a great bulk is found in the unorganised sector. Here, the transition to a free and organised labour market has been exceptionally slow. Furthermore, different parts of India are unevenly developed – a fact that tends to weaken labour and especially the bargaining power of their unions because of intra-labour competition.

Indian experience with MNCs is that they are willing to pay handsome wages – more attractive than wages offered by their Indian counterparts, let alone the wages paid in the nationalised/public sector. While enticing the labour with better wages, greater job security and further prospects, MNCs successfully seek cooperation of workers and their unions winning them away from the national government. Almost compelled to move rapidly in the direction of economic reforms – that is, deregulation, privatisation, liberalisation, and patronisation to foreign direct investments, etc. – the national economy is already finding itself in the tentacular global capitalist system. Therefore, the most important challenge Indian labour is facing as a result of globalisation is that the traditional industrial working class is practically pushed into the background and is likely to become invisible soon because of four processes, namely, tertiarisation, feminisation, casualisation, and precarisation.[9] These processes unleashed by globalisation are adversely affecting labour and their unions that hitherto depended on the traditional support base of organised 'blue-collar workers'.

As regards the effects of globalisation on female labour in India, studies have come out with diverse, at times even conflicting, findings. According to some researchers, liberalisation and opening of avenues for international trade can offer opportunities and provide employment to women workers. If India's share in world trade is expanded, then increased export–import activities can provide income-generating opportunities to women who are currently found mostly in the unorganised sector. A.K. Mehta (1999: 70–71), for instance, has pointed out that exports in handicrafts and hand-made carpets (its share in export being 20.41%), textile fabrics and manufactures (its share being 23.28%), and agricultural and allied products (such as tea, spices, and fish processing, their total share being 17.61%) are some potential areas of more opportunities for women's employment that globalisation is opening up. But then, effects of increased international trade on women as producers and consumers can be both positive and negative. If sectors having employment potential for women are identified and if, side-by-side, sectors where women's employment is getting drastically curtailed are also spotted, then alternatives can be found through planned development. In the event of that happening women workforce too can readjust itself with forces of globalisation. Theoretically, it sounds both valid and convincing. However, the ground realities of unorganised labour market and weakening bargaining position of workers, especially female labour in a developing country like India, do not bear out this optimism. To cite only one example, the textile industry in Mumbai was a strong forte of women workers until the 1920s. As unions managed to get security for labour under various industrial Acts and labour laws, their numbers started declining. In 1985, there were 2,50,000 textile workers in Mumbai. Their strength has come down to just 40,000 in 2000–01. In 1950, 40 per cent of textile workers were women. It is less than one per cent today. Similarly, the Mumbai-based industrial plant of Hindustan Liver – an MNC – had as many as 1,600 workers during the 1960s decade, of which 600 were women employees. The total number of workers came down to just 800 in 1993, with only three female workers among them (Dewan 2002: 1–3). Some studies have even reported that sex-based division of labour persists in India to the disadvantage of women workers in various fields: that women remain underrepresented in government services and great bulk – 92 per cent of total working women in India continue working in informal and unorganised sectors (Jain 1996: 405–08). Therefore, the general feeling shared in the developing world is that gains from globalisation are going to be negligible and the only visible impact is likely to be negative for female workers. Some also fear that globalisation can further accelerate the pace of feminisation of poverty that, in turn, will deepen miseries of women, particularly from the underprivileged sections of Indian society.[10]

Cultural Impact of Globalisation in a Unipolar World

An unintended but important consequence of modernity and aggressive modernisation projects, assisted and funded by developed western countries, is that people in the developing world have started seeing their identity, or even reinventing their tradition – whether religious, ethnic, or cultural – as a rallying point. Assertions of such identities often lead inevitably to enmity and conflict. During the Cold War years, the world was polarised with friends on one side and enemies on the other. In contrast, 'under globalisation world tends to turn friends and enemies into competitors', claims Friedman (2000: 12). Nonetheless, fierce conflicts and warfare seem to be tormenting our contemporary history. Conflict becomes unavoidable, according to Samuel P. Huntington (1996: 20), because cultural identities are basically civilisational identities and the most dangerous enmities are occurring today among cultures lined up on two sides of the great divide between the western and non-western civilisations. The conflict is getting further accentuated by the way market-centred globalisation is making deep inroads into local and regional cultures that feel their very survival is threatened.

The western worldview has been 'universalistic, positivistic, generalising and even totalising' (Singh 2002: 40–41) especially during the colonial era. It tended to treat local, regional, and parochial cultures and their traditions in the non-western world condescendingly, at best, and disdainfully, at worst. With the emergence of the unipolar world under the domination of western capitalism, cultural impact of market and trade relations is further intensified. Culturally, globalisation involves some kind of homogenisation that basically means Americanisation (Friedman 2000: 9). From the 1980s, particularly from the early 1990s, since India joined WTO, its economy is being rapidly drawn into the global economic network. As consumerism spreads, changes are visible in people's lifestyles, cultural tastes, food habits, dress codes and choices, and in modes of entertainment; changes even in norms and values are quite striking. Market mechanisms and media is the armoury with which global capitalism successfully demolishes all walls of resistance to its expansion. Revolution in electronic communication (such as radio, TV, cinema, telephone, fax, email, Internet, etc.) has produced an indelible impact on local, regional, and national cultures because these media can now reach swiftly even the remotest corner of any country. It should not be an exaggeration to say that in every Indian village beer bars and McDonald's fast foods will become available earlier than potable drinking water does. For more authentic news on casualties in accidents, cyclonic storms or communal riots, India's elite switches on to channels like BBC or CNN. This situation is often characterised as a 'cultural invasion' that global capitalism plans as an offensive without the inconvenience of resorting to traditional warfare. Aggressive marketing and consumerism are thus clearly precipitating a serious conflict of cultures.

As stated earlier, the conflict emanating from globalisation is essentially a civilisational conflict. As Huntington has argued that 'after the end of the Cold War, as influence of the West is waning, the balance of power is shifting clearly in favour of Asian civilisations. The new world order is emerging in which societies sharing cultural and civilisational attributes, affinities and history have started reaffirming their own cultural identities and values' (1996: 20–21).

Such assertions perhaps constitute a defence mechanism against the onslaught of globalisation. In this scenario, the United States has to keep blowing hot and cold. On the one hand, it has to advocate globalisation ideology less by choice and more by compulsion of the market. On the other, it has bluntly to resort to brutal warfare against those non-conformist nation-states or 'super-empowered individuals' (like President Saddam Hussain of Iraq, Col. Gaddafi of Libya, or Osama bin Laden),[11] because they not only challenge the very notion of a unipolar world, but also question the legitimacy of the United States to preside over it.

Since the end of the World War II, the USA has been consolidating its control over the resources and assets of the developed capitalist industrialised world and over the oil-rich Middle East. After the collapse of Soviet Union in the early 1990s, capitalism has practically trounced its principal ideological and political rivals – such as fascism followed by communism and socialism. The USA's top priority then shifted to bringing all the former colonies shared by different empires (British, Dutch, French, Portuguese, Spanish, etc.) under one roof and to remove politico-administrative barriers to her financial empire. The USA thought that it alone had the will, capacity and ability to keep all the former colonies tied to the global economy. For this integration, some visible growth and economic development were promoted in the developing world through aid, soft loans, and foreign direct investments, and by deploying modern technology on a large scale. Furthermore, to meet any exigency or challenge to its domination, the USA had to be prepared militarily with latest technology, including nuclear armaments, of mass destruction. To complete the 'end of history' project, the media and Cyberspace networks are now being used for legitimising the globalisation ideology and a network of new NGOs has also been created.[12] Francis Fukayama (1992) calls it as 'the triumph of liberalism and market capitalism'.

To understand the cultural impact of the globalisation process better, the distinction between 'internationalisation' and 'globalisation' would be quite pertinent here. Before the World War II, the imperial powers, to a certain extent, promoted international understanding and tried to encourage transnational and cross-cultural solidarity with a broad liberal humanistic vision. In doing so, however, cultural autonomy of colonies was seldom harmed. Today, globalisation has only one-point agenda, namely, to make markets truly global by fostering commodification of everything including all forms of cultural creativity. Very attractive products of local cultures (ethnic, tribal, indigenous, etc.) are now wrapped up in beautiful packages and sold globally. Whether it is a Madhubani painting, an ethno-medicine, a folk dance, embroidery of a bridal dress, a dalit's autobiography, or even a food recipe, everything is produced locally but marketed globally. Therefore, whether globalisation constitutes a threat to local and regional cultures becomes a moot question that Indian discourse on the issue must address itself to. In his two recent essays, Yogendra Singh has admitted that local cultures are coming under tremendous pressure of globalisation, market economy, and the media power reinforced by IT. Yet a robust faith in cultural resilience of Indian local communities makes him optimistic about the ability of local cultures, tribes and castes to engage themselves with globalisation creatively and then try 'refractory and pragmatic adaptations'. Being optimistic about India's positive cultural response, Singh holds that adaptive reconciliation with the forces of globalisation would eventually strengthen, instead of weaken or threaten, local or regional cultures and identities (2002: 62–65). However, to say that for traditional local artisans, craftsmen and artists, globalisation is a friendly process because it creates spaces for their economic empowerment and social mobility (ibid.: 103–4), and to argue that globalisation would enhance cultural consciousness of local, regional and ethnic communities, amounts to either overstating the case or glossing over the ground realities, if not to expressing a pious hope.

Such hopes are betrayed by everyday experiences in recent decades. The overstated virtuosity of globalisation notwithstanding, its record so far has been far from unblemished. While globalisation means greater interdependence, it seems simultaneously to cause increasing fragmentation of the world. The Human Development Report too has stated that 'economically and politically, frustration in developing countries about the skewed distribution of global power has seldom been greater' (UNDP 2002: 101). The bulldozing on-march of globalisation has provoked strong reactions especially among the youth from countries that have been at the receiving end of the global capitalist and market-dominated network (Bhagwati 2002: 2). Despite the triumph of global capitalist system, both as economy and as an ideology of governance for domination via the market, the fact remains that it could not realise goals of social justice in appreciable measure. This limitation of global capitalist system, even under its corporate incarnation, is being realised increasingly both by its core insiders and by peripheral outsiders. Hence, in the globalisation phase, capitalism produces anti-capitalist critics who tend to respond to the global integration more with passion than with reason. One of more recent additions to enemies of globalisation has two faces: religious fundamentalism and international terrorism that are acting in unison as if they are two sides of the same coin.

Most of us remain dimly aware of the fact that fanaticism, fundamentalism, and ethnic strife have been on the rise for many decades all over the world, not in the Islamic part alone. Secondly, it is not historically correct to trace the origin of these fundamentalist and terrorist tendencies to the happenings of 11 September 2001, when terrorists exploded the twin towers of the World Trade Centre in New York and to the series of events that followed. According to the Initiative on Conflict Resolution and Ethnicity

(ENCORE) Organisation, a variety of ethnic strife has affected as many as 43 countries around the world (Norberg-Hodge 2002: 36). Therefore, the growing trend of ethnic conflicts and religious fundamentalism has to be understood primarily as a repulsive response to the pernicious impact of the global consumer culture on diverse, even unique, local cultures. Local communities feel both unstable and unsafe in the face of global market forces – bolstered up by media that too are controlled by MNCs. The media impact on local communities and cultures is so shattering that the consumer culture has pushed them to the threshold of extinction. Local economies are being swallowed gradually by the global capitalism and traditional cultures are being displaced by the ever-expanding global market and consumer culture. Local communities in the developing world are silently, and somewhat helplessly, watching that their plentiful raw material and natural resources are getting depleted and these are replaced by scarce imported materials produced by TNCs. At the same time, 'local communities are experiencing a steady and systematic undermining of their self-esteem' (Norberg-Hodge 2002: 37–38). While introducing new brands and products of MNCs/TNCs, their professional advisers and marketing consultants inflict a sense of shame on the people about their local products, customs and food habits, etc., quite subtly and suggestively through commercial advertisements.

This kind of erosion of local cultures by the process of homogenisation, and particularly by the promotion of global monoculture, has disastrous consequences. To achieve development at any cost, many developing economies are pressurised to make structural adjustments, introduce neo-liberal measures, reduce social sector spending, and undertake massive programmes of infrastructural development that are unsustainable in the long run (Dev and Moosi 2002). Much of the development initiatives in developing countries is geared to serve the needs of global capitalism to exploit their cheap labour, material resources, and vast markets. Development under globalisation gets heavily concentrated in urban industrial, metropolitan cities and tends to leave out rural hinterlands to fend for themselves, to face acute problems of poverty, unemployment and even drinking water. It is this kind of impact of globalisation that prepares a breeding ground for religious fundamentalism and for terrorist activities. In fact, decentralised development is a precondition for nurturing local cultural diversities because that development is not only adapted to local cultures but it is also sustainable.[13]

There is some room for optimism, as Friedman has suggested, that globalisation system can still be sustained without letting any major cultural conflicts, without competitors being perceived as enemies. Having its own power structure, globalisation has to build itself around three sets of balances that overlap and affect each other. First is the traditional balance between the nation-states. With the emergence of the United States as the superpower without any rival, this balance has, however, been upset considerably. In the second place is the balance between the nation-states and global market, which implies that investors from all over the world must have a sense of security of their investments if the global economy is to maintain its efficiency and profitability. The third balance has to be between individuals and nation-states, particularly because in certain historical situations 'superempowered individuals' become larger than life size for their nation-states (Friedman 2000: 13–14). However, these balances are often beset by powerful nations, like the USA, and their political leadership that keep subserving the interests of their own MNCs and aim at perpetuating asymmetrical relationships between nation-states and the global market. That defies all principles of equity, social justice, autonomy and sovereignty. Erosion of local cultures and national sensitivities – a logical corollary of the global market – then results in conflict inevitably.

Towards an Alternative Vision

The foregoing, somewhat extensive, review should suffice to show that effects of globalisation are taking away from people in local communities even their basic rights to life and livelihood. For India, it took it nearly half a century since the adoption of the Republican Constitution to turn people's entitlements into rights. These very basic human rights now appear to be threatened by a totally market- and commodity-centred globalisation. The situation, therefore, calls for a debate on the possibility of an alternative vision of globalisation. In our view, such an alternative can be traced and rediscovered in the Indian tradition. It would be worthwhile to explore how best we can draw selectively upon the history of India's past collective experiences and achievements. Indian philosophical traditions, spiritual resources, and civilisational wisdom contain a global vision – a vision that is neither commodity- nor market-centred, nor is it focused on material calculus of gains and losses, profits or deficits purely in material–monetary terms. Such an alternative vision is best encapsulated in ancient sayings like: '*vasudhaiva kutumbakam*' (let the whole globe be our family), '*aa no bhadraha kratavah yantu vishwatah*' (let noble thoughts come to us from every side) and '*krunvanto vishwamaryam*'(let us make the whole world *Arya*, that is, let us equip people's minds with noble thoughts, ideals, and actions all over the world).[14] To realise this vision, neither any commercial or military war has to be fought, nor conquests of other's territories are necessary, nor external markets need to be captured through media aggression and offending advertisements. It is a humanistic vision that predicates autonomy to individuals, groups, communities, and nation-states, freedom of choice of a development path, and is also founded on the principles of brotherhood, peace, and coexistence.

Such an alternative vision comes very close to the principles enshrined in the Indian Constitution. Nonetheless, while searching for a globalising vision in the ancient Indian tradition and civilisational history, a caution is necessary. Often it is suspected, and rightly so, that such a search will entail revival of traditional Brahmanical ideas, ritual practices, and cultural domination. It must be remembered that *varna*/caste distinctions, associated with a spectrum ranging from ennobling to debasing actions, discrimination and injustices based on purity and pollution were justified using the theory of *karma* and *punarjanma* as an ideological tool of the Brahmanical order and its hegemony. However, a careful glance at some Indian philosophical traditions, such as *Vedanta* (mostly contained in rich *upanishadic* literature), would reveal that the concept of *advaita* (non-dualism or monism), suggests that *atman* and *paramatman* (self and the supreme consciousness) are not two separate entities; rather the 'other' is very much an integral part of the 'self', while the self is inseparable from the *Brahman*.

Such traditions contain elements of a truly secular, humanistic, non-hierarchical, and non-discriminatory worldview.[15] *Yoga* is yet another tradition – involving theory and practice – that is now accepted as a scientific way of establishing, or bringing back, harmony with one's true self – a precondition for lasting happiness and peace of mind, and for achieving 'liberation' in existential sense, if not for attaining spiritual purpose or bliss in life.

It is not being suggested here that facts like elitist character of the sacred knowledge and learning in the Brahmanical order, resulting in alienation of the toiling and illiterate masses, should be ignored. On the contrary, it needs to be emphasised that knowledge subsequently became the chief source of temporal power superior to the power of the sword. The knowledge of *Vedanta* (mostly written in Sanskrit – a language unintelligible to the masses) became the main instrument for stabilising the cultural power of the few. However, it is also noteworthy that this domination of ritualised knowledge power did not go unchallenged. India's long history is replete with a series of pan-Indian and grassroots level people's struggles and protest movements against the Brahmanical orthodoxy. From Lord Buddha down to Mahatma Phule and Dr Ambedkar, and from Lord Mahavira to Narayana Guru, and to Mahatma Gandhi – everyone contributed richly to these protests and sought to build a non-discriminatory egalitarian society.

Considering the whole world as a manifestation of the supreme consciousness requires some kind of spiritual realisation that has some streaks of mysticism. However, Swami Vivekananda gave that pursuit an existential meaning and a social purpose. In his worldview, real salvation comes only through a selfless service to the needy and all religions are similar. Indian religion, chiefly Hinduism, has always treated all religions to be true. 'It has taught the world both tolerance and universal acceptance'.[16] In an obvious reference to the famous 'Columbia' – Liberty statue (that stands at the Hudson Bay, New York) – Swami Vivekananda, in his Chicago speech back in 1893, offered the following advice for the American people:

> Hail, Columbia, motherland of liberty! It has been given to thee, who never dipped her hand in her neighbour's blood, who never found out that the shortest way of becoming rich

> was by robbing one's neighbours, it has been given to thee to march at the vanguard of civilisation with the flag of harmony. (1989, Vol. 1: 20)

These words of wisdom have been either forgotten or their meaning misread by the American superpower. To dominate the unipolar world, today, the United States, assisted by its MNCs, is doing exactly the opposite. Likewise, the record of protagonists of *Hindutva* in contemporary India is no different because they have either banished the ethos of tolerance and universal acceptance or have consigned it back to history. Religious fanaticism and market fanaticism are not only flourishing simultaneously, but are also competing with each other in the current phase of globalisation. Swami Vivekananda's message in the closing part of his famous speech at Chicago has still some relevance to the globalisation debate today. To him 'each of the world religions must assimilate the spirit of the others and yet preserve its individuality and grow according to its own law of growth': 'Help and not Fight', 'Assimilation and not Destruction', 'Harmony and Peace and not Dissension' (ibid.: 24). If this message is carried beyond religion in the domain of economic integration, it has the potential to provide an alternative global vision.

Globalisation via the market has brought humanity at the crossroads of history today as 'social systems and secular order are simply crumbling down under the weight of ideologies'. Therefore, social scientists need to 'traverse beyond the realm of concepts and clouds of despair'. As Romano Prodi has put it: 'The proper response to globalisation is not to build protective barriers or walls to insulate economies and societies from each other, but to harness the forces of globalisation and make them work for the good of all the countries – rich and poor' (2002: 8).

In this essentially normative statement, Prodi only suggests that globalisation rests on an effective system of global governance that is possible only when as partners nation-states adhere to the agreed rules and operate within a transparent, participatory, and an accountable set of institutions. Global order is, or has to be, a moral-ethical order. Powerful nation-states will have a tendency to pressurise the weak and less developed ones and thereby to perpetuate their domination. Growing polarisation between affluence and poverty, between over-consumption and malnutrition, and the iniquitous distribution of power in global system is then glossed over. Whether science and technology or systems of production and market, they must be founded on ethical values of human dignity, freedom, and equity, and must honour minimum rights of life and livelihood. Otherwise, globalisation would be no more than a shibboleth for reinforcing unipolar domination through global market and finance capitalism. For Indian society, that is still trying to get over late-development effect, shying away from the globalisation could be no response; similarly, mystifying it will provide no answers to the problems it precipitates. This should be a sufficient pointer to the task of critiquing the present globalisation phenomenon and its demystification that should preoccupy sociologists everywhere in years to come.

Notes

1. Presidential address delivered at the XXVIII All India Sociological Conference, Indian Institute of Technology, Kanpur, 18–20 December 2002.
2. Some professional NGOs in developing countries are financially supported by leading international funding agencies and organisations from the developed world. It is estimated that between 1,00,000 and 5,00,000 NGOs were actively doing development work at the grassroots level in India in 1999–2000. During the 1990s, foreign funding to some of these NGOs increased by 13.5 per cent per annum, and every year on an average ₹ 2,200 crores worth of foreign exchange came in to support some of these NGO (see HIVOS 2002: 53–54; see also Dhanagare 1993).
3. The phrase 'imagined communities' was introduced in social science discourse by Benedict Anderson (1991).
4. Wallerstein (1986: 56) has argued that nationalism in general, including in India, in historical terms is a relatively new concept and it is clearly a product, indeed a late product of world capitalist system. Any nation-state serves the purpose assigned to it within that system and hence its existence is contingent upon that purpose. When that function is over, the existence of that nation-state cannot be guaranteed or taken for granted indefinitely.
5. This expression has been taken from Amin (1997: 128).

6. A graphic description of the disastrous effects of monoculture on the ecosystem with rich biodiversity in Latin America is available in Baran (1982: 195–204).
7. For disparities in levels of agricultural subsidies received by farm producers in the developed and developing countries, see Dhanagare (1999: 250–54).
8. Nearly 70 per cent of India's demand for domestic consumption of edible oil is met by such imports (see Hines et al., 2002: 38–40).
9. Some of these terms have been taken from Ross (2000).
10. Similar views and findings have been reported in more than one study (see Sethi 1999, particularly the essays by Mahanto and Sonowal (pp. 160–61) and by Gawari and Singh (pp. 187–88) in that volume, and Sangari and Chakravarty 1999).
11. The phrase 'super-empowered individuals' is taken from Friedman (2000: 14–15).
12. For a more elaborate statement of this argument or reasoning, see Ahmad (2001: 25–27).
13. For a detailed exposition of this point of view on sustainable decentralised development of local cultures and economies, see Norberg-Hodge 2001.
14. The term '*Arya*' came to acquire a rather devious connotation of an ethnic/racial identity, particularly during the British period, to mean 'people of superior social origin with specific phenotypical features'. Originally, in the epic literature, '*Arya*' was used as an honorific while addressing a person of noble disposition, enlightened thoughts, and actions. In *Ramayana*, for instance, Sita repeatedly addresses Rama as '*Arya*'.
15. See, for instance, Aurobindo's 'Introduction' to his celebrated commentary on the *Upanishads* (1996: 1–13).
16. This is taken from Swami Vivekananda's address to the World Parliament of Religions at Chicago, on 11 September 1893 (see Vivekananda 1989, Vol. 1: 3).

References

Ahmad, A. 2001. 'Globalisation: A Society of Aliens?' An article originally published in *Frontline*, and its translation in Marathi by Nalini Pandit appeared in *Thinkers' Academy Journal*, 10 (2): 24–31.

Alavi, H. 1982. 'The Structure of Peripheral Capitalism', in H. Alavi and T. Shanin (eds.): *Introduction to the Sociology of Developing Societies*. London: The Macmillan Press, pp. 172–92.

Amin, S. 1982. 'The Disarticulation of Economy within Developing Societies', in H. Alavi and T. Shanin (eds.): *Introduction to the Sociology of Developing Societies*. London: The Macmillan Press, pp. 204–9.

——. 1997. *Capitalism in the Age of Globalisation*. Delhi: Madhyam Books.

Anderson, B. 1991. *Imagined Communities*. London: Verso.

Anitat, E. 2002. 'Surmounting the Challenge of Globalisation', *Finance and Development*, March: 4–7.

Aurobindo, S. 1996. *The Upanishads: Texts, Translation and Commentary*. Pondicherry: Sri Aurobindo Ashram.

Bagchi, A. 1999. 'Globalisation, Liberalisation and Vulnerability: India and Third World', *Economic and Political Weekly*, 34 (45): 3219–30.

Baran, P. 1957. *The Political Economy of Growth*. New York: Monthly Review Press.

——. 1982. 'A Morphology of Backwardness', in H. Alavi and T. Shanin (eds.): *Introduction to the Sociology of Developing Societies*. London: The Macmillan Press, pp. 195–204.

Bhagwati, J. 2002. 'Coping with Anti-Globalisation: A Trilogy of Discontents', *Foreign Affairs*, January–February: 2–7.

Carroll, W.K. and Fennema. 2002. 'Is There a Transnational Business Community?', *International Sociology*, 17 (3): 393–420.

Dev, S. Mahendra and J. Moosi. 2002. 'Social Sector Spending in Nineteen Nineties', *The Hindu*, 1 February: 8.

Dewan, R. 2002. 'Gender and the Dominant Development Paradigm: A Conceptual Note' (a paper presented at a seminar on 'Globalisation and the Academia: Challenges and Prospects' at K.C. College, Mumbai, 22 January 2002).

Dhanagare, D.N. 1993. 'NGOs and Foreign Funding', *Man and Development*, 20 (2): 133–46.

——. 1999. 'The New Farmers' Movement in Maharashtra and its Response to New Economic Reforms', in F. Oshikawa (ed.): *South Asia under the Economic Reforms* (JCAS symposium series 6). Osaka: Japan Centre for Area Studies, National Museum of Ethnology, pp. 247–61.

Ferranti, M. 2000. 'Globalisation Tidal Wave', *Infoworld*, 23 (48): Item No. 3819925: 1–2.

Frank, A.G. 1978. *Dependent Accumulation and Underdevelopment.* New York: Monthly Review Press.

——. 1982. *On Capitalist Underdevelopment.* Bombay: Oxford University Press.

Friedman, T. 2000. *The Lexus and the Olive Tree.* London: Harper Collins.

Friedman, T. and R. Kaplan. 2002. 'States of Discord' (a debate), *Foreign Policy*, March–April: 64–70.

Fukayama, F. 1992. *The End of History and the Last Man.* New York: Free Press.

Galbraith, J.K. 2001. 'What Happened to the Good Society?' (an interview recorded and transcribed), *Current*, July–August: 5–13.

Gellner, E. 1983. *Nations and Nationalism.* Ithaca, NY: Cornell University Press.

Giddens, A. 1990. *The Consequences of Modernity.* Stanford, CA: Stanford University Press.

Hines, C.; Lucas, C. MEP and V. Shiva. 2002. 'Local Food, Global Solution', *The Ecologist*, 32 (5): 38–40.

HIVOS. 2002. *HIVOS Annual Report: 2001.* Bangalore: India Regional Office.

Huntington, S.P. 1996. *The Clash of Civilisations and the Making of World Order.* New York: Simon and Schuster.

Jain, L.C. 1996. 'Cooperatives: An Appropriate Vehicle for Women's Empowerment', in N. Rao et al. (eds.): *Sites of Change: The Structural Context for Empowering Women in India.* New Delhi: FES and UNDP, pp. 400–20.

Martinelli, A. 2002. 'Markets, Government, Communities and Global Governance' (Presidential address delivered at the XV World Congress of Sociology, Brisbane, 7–13 July 2002: 1–26).

McLuhan, M. 1960. *Explorations in Communication* (ed. E.S. Carpenter). Boston: Beacon Press.

Mehta, A.K. 1999. 'Globalisation and Women', in R.M. Sethi (ed.): *Globalisation Culture and Women's Development.* Jaipur: Rawat Publications, pp. 55–76.

Norberg-Hodge, H. 2001. *Ancient Futures.* Saginaw, Texas: The Rider Publications.

——. 2002. 'Globalisation and Terror', *The Ecologist*, 31 (10): 36–39.

Prodi, R. 2002. 'Heal the World: EU and India Have a Moral Duty', *The Times of India* (Pune), 23 November): 8.

Robertson, R. 1992. *Globalisation: Social Theory and Global Culture.* London: Sage Publications.

Ross, G. 2000. 'Labour versus Globalisation', *Annals of the American Academy of Political and Social Sciences*, Vol. 570 (July), pp. 14 and 78 as abstracted by the American Information Resource Centre, New Delhi.

Sangari K. and U. Chakravarty (eds.). 1999. *From Myths to Market: Essays in Gender.* Shimla: Indian Institute of Advanced Study/Delhi: Manohar.

Scholte, J.A. 2002. 'Civil Society and Global Finance: Contributions and Challenges', *Work in Progress* (a review of research activities of the United Nations University), 16 (3 Pacific affairs section): 22–24.

Schuh, G.E. 2002. 'Global Food Security', *Economic Perspectives* (an electronic journal of the US Department of States), 7 (2): 15–17.

Sengupta, C. 2001. 'Conceptualising Globalisation: Issues and Implications', *Economic and Political Weekly,* 36 (13): 3137–43.

Sethi, R.M. (ed.). 1999. *Globalisation, Culture and Women's Development.* Jaipur: Rawat Publications.

Shiva, V. 2000. 'Globalisation and Poverty', Ruth Lecture, *Resurgence*, 202 (September–October): 15–19.

Singh, Y. 2002. *Culture Change in India: Identity and Globalisation.* Jaipur: Rawat Publications.

Sklair, L. 2001. *The Transnational Capitalist Class.* Oxford: Basil Blackwell.

Smith, A. 1991. *National Identity.* London: Penguin Books.

UNDP. 2002. *Human Development Report: 2002.* New Delhi: Oxford University Press.

Vivekananda, S. 1989. *The Complete Works of Swami Vivekananda* (Vol. 1). Calcutta: Advaita Ashram.

Wallerstein, I. 1980. *The Capitalist World Economy.* Cambridge: Cambridge University Press (Paris: Editions de la M.S.H. Reprint).

——. 1986. 'Does India Exist?' (paper presented at session: Historical Sociology in India, XI World Congress of Sociology, New Delhi, 18–23 August: 1–6).

——. 2000. 'From Sociology to Historical Social Science: Prospects and Obstacles', *British Journal of Sociology*, 51 (1): 19–35.

3

Social Justice in a Globalised World

Encounters with State and Civil Society[1]

P.K.B. NAYAR

Social justice has fared badly in the last twenty-five years, especially after the surge of globalisation with its chief handmaids, namely, liberalisation and marketisation. History has not been on the side of social justice and, in spite of tall promises solemnised through country constitutions and legitimised by the United Nations through the Universal Declaration of Human Rights (UDHR), social justice has not progressed an inch further in today's world; on the contrary, social injustice has increased and is threatening to assume alarming proportions everywhere.

An examination of the present state of this phenomenon and the factors contributing to it should be of interest to all concerned, and more so to sociologists, who do not seem to be so enthusiastic in putting it as a priority item in their study or research. In the present exercise, I have taken two related social agencies for analysis of social justice: (i) the state, which is the empowering agency, and (ii) the civil society, which is an enabling agency. It is hoped that an analysis of the dynamic relationship between social justice, on the one hand, and state and civil society, on the other, would bring to light many elements that would have been overlooked or underemphasised by those concerned and situating these agencies in juxtaposition with social justice would help

This chapter originally appeared in *Sociological Bulletin*, 57 (1), January–April 2008, pp. 3–29. It is reproduced here with the kind permission from the author and the Indian Sociological Society.

appreciate the potential role the state and civil society organisations could play in advancing the cause of social justice.

In this chapter, I am envisaging but not arguing that social justice is a condition prevailing in a political system and that civil society is an aid for the enforcement and enhancement of social justice. This is not affirming that the state is a precondition for the existence of social justice or that civil society is always an aid to it. In fact, while civil society in the modern sense of the term came into existence only recently, the state as a political entity and as an agency for establishing and enforcing order in society has had a long and historic past. At the same time, the concept and practice of social justice predate both these and go back to the origin of civilised human kind, if one concedes that social justice has an ethico-philosophical and moral basis and is at the back of all human values. Viewed thus, social justice is an abstraction that emerges from an innate urge embedded in human nature that in any interaction among humans (what we call social interaction) a person should get what he or she deserves as a fellow member in the interaction process. In this sense, social justice has in it two elements: intrinsic and comparative. Intrinsic justice relates to micro-level analysis and says that one should not get any undeserved benefits, nor should he/she be made to bear undeserved burdens (Principle of Equity). Comparative justice deals with macro-level analysis (Principle of Equality). This aspect is better developed and better known because it assumes basic equality of all human beings. Indeed, comparative justice has received more attention today, especially from civil society organisations (CSOs) than intrinsic justice and it has several ramifications.

Social justice, being more an ethico-philosophical concept, is difficult to define and even more difficult to achieve than the other two concepts in our schema. Social justice is seen by some as an attribute emanating from a 'just society', which is generally thought of as a society which affords individuals and groups 'fair treatment' and a 'just share' of the benefits of society. However, different proponents of social justice have developed different interpretations of what constitutes fair treatment and a just share. Hence, a postulation of social justice with just society does not make our work easy because we have added more terms to our repertory and now have to grapple with additional concepts like fair treatment and just share.

The problem is further obfuscated by the emergence of several forms of justice, many of which overlap with social justice. There are, for example, concepts like natural justice, retributive justice, distributive justice, civil justice, economic justice, and so on, all of which have some interface with social justice at some point. There is a lot of disagreement among political, juridical, and moral leaders on the meaning and scope of these terms as well.

Most political parties today advocate social justice and this is more so in a democratic regime because of its capacity to pull up popular votes. In fact, it finds a place in the manifesto of most of political parties, but on what constitutes social justice and how this could be achieved parties are poles apart (ranging from left-wing radicals to right-wing conservatives). From the juridical point of view, social justice is enacted through the legal framework and operationalised through fundamental rights. But, here also, what is legally right and how one enforces one's fundamental rights are disputed points. In different guises, social justice finds a place in all religions – righteous, upright, humane, moral, natural, divine, and so on. It is considered to be ethically and morally unjustifiable to keep a segment of the people poor and downtrodden in society and all religions are eloquent against this malady.

Like civil society, social justice as a concept and as an ideology assumed prominence only in recent times, may be in the last two centuries – more exactly after the Industrial Revolution in the West. Most writers on social justice are of the opinion that it was Tapperelli who first used the term in 1845 (see Adelson 1995: 36), that is, when Western Europe began to consciously introduce some sort of distributive justice in their societies, which were disturbed by gross inequalities caused by the fast-changing production system. The Industrial Revolution widened the cleavage between the rich and the poor. In fact, the poor were pushed into the tornado of misery, with their little means of subsistence wiped out and their labour made redundant. Some countries in Europe brought about legislation (for example, the Poor Law in England) to ameliorate the misery of the poor and to give them some relief from it. To be sure, such steps were not taken as part of a package to establish social justice but as ad hoc measures to relieve the sufferings of a new class of destitute. No ideology was involved and no commitment to provide justice to the downtrodden or to the underprivileged was on the accepted agenda.

But, even before the emergence of a new class of destitute, as a goal to be achieved, the concept of social justice and its application at the state level had a long legacy, going back to even pre-historic times. This was not because of the precipitation of a social emergency like the one contributed by the Industrial Revolution, but as part of a religious and moral code for the guidance of all, especially the rulers.

Social justice postulates that society is responsible for the undeserved suffering of its members and, as such, society as a whole should repair the deprivation and should construct social means to ensure that such harm is avoided. The logic of why society should come to the rescue of the unfortunate individual is this. If, a wrong is done by an individual on another, the erring individual can be asked to restitute the aggrieved appropriately. If, on the other hand, a person has to suffer an undeserved burden for no apparent fault of his/her, there is no individual offender who could be identified and society has to come to his/her rescue. As a matter of fact, this problem has been faced by all societies – ancient and modern – at all times. In societies where religion had a strong hold, justice was done as the will of god. Norms and values were accordingly evolved and social justice was advocated on ethico-moral and philosophical grounds. In this sense, social justice had no political overtones even though rulers were expected to administer even-handed justice to all subjects. Another constituent of social justice was the notion of natural law. Nature was viewed as being just to everybody and natural law was thought of as guiding everything in nature and as such was viewed as a normative force. In both cases (religious and natural), social justice has a metaphysical base and cannot be equated with dispensation through ordinary laws.

Any analysis of social justice will have to first grapple with the word 'justice'. Justice can be conceived as a virtue from two angles: as a property of persons, and only derivatively of their actions and the institutions they create; or as a property of actions or institutions, and only derivatively of the persons who bring them about. The source of justice may be thought to be harmony, divine command, natural law, or human creation; or it may be envisaged as subordinate to a more central ethical standard. The demands of justice are pressing in two areas: equity and equality. Equity, sometimes called distributive justice, requires fair treatment, giving people what they deserve, maximising benefit to the worst off, protecting whatever comes about in the right way, or maximising total welfare. Equality means that all are treated equally – in terms of holding and enjoying the socially desirable goods and services. Actually, the second subsumes the first and could be envisaged as a sublimated version of the first, even though for analytical purposes they have to be kept separately.

The most comprehensive and systematic approach to the theory of justice in recent times is that of John Rawls (2000). Rawls' primary objective is to explain how it is and under what circumstances that citizens are obliged to obey the laws which the state creates. According to him, justice is the first virtue of all social institutions. Each person possesses an inviolability founded on justice, which even the welfare of society as a whole cannot override. For this reason, justice means that the loss of freedom for some is made right by a greater good shared by others. It does not allow that the sacrifices imposed on a few are outweighed by the larger sum of advantages enjoyed by many. In a just society the liberties of equal citizenship are taken as settled. The rights secured by justice are not subject to political bargaining or to the calculus of social interests.

On these grounds, Rawls envisages a society in which people cooperate to achieve common ends and, when these ends are distributed, each of them would prefer to have a larger share. Under such circumstances, a set of principles is required for choosing among various social arrangements which determine this division of advantages and for underwriting an agreement on the proper distributive shares of each. These principles are the principles of social justice. They provide a way of assigning rights and duties in the basic institutions of society and they define the appropriate distribution of the benefits and burdens of social cooperation. This arrangement presupposes three things: (i) coordination, (ii) efficiency, and (iii) stability. First, the plans of individuals need to be fitted together so that their activities are compatible with one another and they can all be carried through without anybody's legitimate expectation being severely disappointed. Second, the execution of these plans should lead to the achievement of social ends in ways that are efficient and consistent with justice. Finally, the scheme of social cooperation should be stable over time for the endurance of justice.

Rawls continues: the primary subject of justice is the basic structure of society, more exactly the way in which the major social institutions distribute fundamental rights and duties and determine the division of advantages from social cooperation. The major institutions are the political constitution and the principal economic and social arrangements. The legal protection of freedom of thought and liberty of conscience, competitive markets, private property in the means of production, and the basic family structure are examples of major social institutions. Taken together as one scheme, the major institutions define men's rights and duties and influence their life prospects, what they can expect to be and how well they can hope to do. The basic structure is the primary subject of justice because its effects are so profound and present from the start. The intuitive notion here is that this structure contains various social positions and that men born into different positions have different expectations of life determined in part by the political system as well as by economic and social circumstances. It is these inequalities, presumably inevitable in the basic structure of any society, to which the principles of social justice must in the first instance apply. The justice of a social scheme depends essentially on how fundamental rights and duties are assigned and on the economic opportunities and social conditions in the various sectors of society.

Rawls does this through the device of a hypothetical agreement, made under conditions of equality so that there are no disparities in the bargaining power of constituent members. This hypothetical agreement justifies the coercive use of state power, because, guided by it, a state would take a form to which all would, under conditions of freedom, consent. Rawls called this theory *Justice as Fairness*.

It is not necessary to present the whole gamut of arguments put forward by Rawls to explain our problem. However, Rawls' argument about the origin of the concept of justice and why the state has paramountcy in establishing and enforcing justice are very important. He says that the source of justice is the belief by all the concerned persons that there was originally a condition where everybody had equal access to justice, interpreted as fairness in interpersonal relations, and in order to preserve this, some conditions are necessary. These take the form of laws.

At this juncture, it is pertinent to introduce the point of view of Howard L. Adelson regarding social justice. According to Adelson (1995), social justice is neither charity nor correct enforcement of law. It is not legal justice. Nor should there be any confusion between secular law and divine or canon law. Nor should it be any confused with social democracy, nor does the entry into a social contract involve social justice. In the classical world of Greece and Rome, there was no social justice; actions were based on charity and dues for each man/woman were judged by the class to which he/she belonged. This is eloquently brought out by Aristotle when he said that justice lies in equals being treated as equals and unequals being treated as unequals (see Irani 1981: 37). So also, while ideas of representative government were developed during the course of the Middle Ages, those ideas did not lead to a concept of social justice since the deprived classes were not treated on par with the holding classes. Social justice, according to Adelson, was as foreign to the Middle Ages as it was to the classical world.

While the term 'social justice' is obviously of very recent origin (Adelson 1995: 31), probably from the early 19th century, the concept of a society based upon the equality of man and requiring humane treatment of the lower, poorer classes, as a right of those classes and as a duty of the more fortunate, appears to be a product of particular circumstances prevailing in some societies in the ancient world. These circumstances did not appear concurrently or uniformly in all societies. Even when they appeared in some societies, they were erratic in the sense that they were short-lived and the idea of social justice generated by these circumstances was not continued either in thinking or in actions in the later periods. The conception of social justice as distinct from the mere call to individual or even national righteousness, or as an overwhelming belief in the harmony of the various classes, which was celebrated as an ideal in the classical world of the Greeks and the Romans, is also misplaced. In earlier times, even when those in charge of taking up the cause of the poor claimed that they were trying to establish social justice, it was distinct from the use of the term 'social justice' in the modern world. The concept that the more fortunate should assist the less fortunate because it is an obligation on the part of the former and a right to ask or even demand for such assistance on the part of the latter, had a metaphysical content in earlier times but it has a human rights content in modern times. An ordered class structure (in the sense of harmony between classes) does not qualify for social justice under this reasoning. The proposition of social justice is built on the premise that all men are equal in some basic respects and, as such, deserve equal treatment or equality in the sharing of social wealth. The necessity of treating all equally, however, arises only if one believes that all human beings, or at least the segment of humankind to which the principle of social justice is to be applied, are, in fact, equal in some sense with those dispensing assistance. It is not moderation and balance in human relationship. It is a belief that blatant inequality is not acceptable in social relationships

Since Adelson's objective in his paper was not to give an update on social justice, he does not go into an examination of the modern application of the concept nor engage in making a comparative study of ancient and modern exercises in social justice. But Adelson has a point which has not been adequately appreciated by other previous writers, and since the whole concept is modern, it is necessary to establish a bridge between Adelson's approach to social justice and the approaches of modern governments and CSOs to the issue of social justice.

According to Adelson, a hierarchically-oriented class society does not go with social justice, however just it may be in the dispensation of justice to the different strata. For this reason, both Greek and Roman societies were class-based – master and slave in Greece and Patrician and Plebeian in the Roman empire. In the

Middle Ages, the prevalence of status groups ingrained in the feudal system went against it. Even as late as the 18th century, the American Revolution, which stood for the rights of all men to life, liberty and property, and the French Revolution, which stood for liberty, equality and fraternity denied such privileges to some categories of citizens. Adelson points out that American independence was built on slave labour and the chief architect of the Constitution of America, Thomas Jefferson, and his associates were slave owners. The French Revolution did not recognise women on par with men in the matter of liberty and equality. In fact, in this respect, they were status quoists.

Again, according to Adelson, the social contract theorists who held sway over the political thought in Europe and America for quite some time in the recent past did not mention anything about distributive justice. Adelson's views on social justice, it has to be pointed out, represent the extreme puristic view of social justice which hardly existed anywhere in the world but could be used as an ideal type for analytical and comparative purposes.

In fact, the argument in the instant chapter is that social justice has found only qualified application in modern times in spite of the wild cry for it from several quarters, including the UN system. If social justice is justice shown by a privileged group of people in society to an unprivileged group, whatever may be the motivating factor behind it, attempts of modern governments to introduce benefits to the poorer segments of the community should be considered as social justice measures. Distributive justice is the crux of the issue here. Since governments cannot leave this to be done by the haves out of their goodwill they have enacted legislations and formulated welfare measures to implement it. We are here concerned as much with the content and concern in social justice as with the outcome of its implementation.

At this point, we have to differentiate between the concepts 'social justice' and 'human rights'. In general, it may be said that social justice is applied to groups and human rights to individuals. In many cases, the dividing line between the two is hazy. The UN parlance prefers the usage of the term 'human rights' over 'social justice' because it is easy to operationalise.

Concept of Social Justice Across the World

One of the earliest surviving codes which bear any symbolic relationship with social justice is the *Code of Hammurabi* (c. 1780 BCE) which prescribes punishment for violation of laws protecting, *inter alia*, the rights of women, children, and slaves. The famous *Cylinder* of Emperor Cyrus the Great of Persia (539 BCE), so called because the edicts appear on a cylindrical material, is recognised by many as the first human rights document. It declared that citizens of the empire would be allowed to practise their religious beliefs freely. It also abolished slavery. In an era where slaves typically did all strenuous and dirty work, all the palaces of the kings of Persia were built by paid workers. These two reforms are endorsed in the Biblical literature which state that Cyrus released the followers of Judaism from slavery and allowed them to migrate back to their land. In the Persian empire, citizens of all creeds and ethnic groups were also given the same rights, while women had the same rights as men. The Cyrus Cylinder also documents the protection of the rights to liberty and security, freedom of movement, the right of property, and economic and social rights to all citizens in the kingdom.

Christianity gave great importance to justice, and many of the tenets of the Bible contain exhortations for kindness to the downtrodden and the less fortunate, especially women and children. According to the apostles, justice is to be enforced not so much by the state, but by the code of conduct through the guidance and supervision of the church. In Christianity, the principle of social justice lies in the teachings of God which emphasise love towards fellowmen and the practice of righteousness. Virtuous conduct towards all is the basis of social justice.

Islam also gave great importance to social justice, as is shown by its treatment of women, ethnic minorities, and the poor. John Esposito (1998: 79, 98) sees Muhammad as a reformer who condemned the practices of pagan Arabs such as female infanticide, exploitation of the poor, usury, murder, false contracts, and theft. According to Bernard Lewis, Islam 'from the first denounced aristocratic privilege, rejected hierarchy, and adopted a formula of the career open to the talents' (1994: 7). Lewis believes that the egalitarian nature of Islam 'represented a very considerable advance on the practice of both the Greco-Roman and the ancient Iranian world' (ibid.: 9).

Several 17th and 18th century European philosophers, most notably John Locke, developed the concept of natural rights – the notion that people possess certain rights by virtue of being human. His ideas were important in the development of the modern notion of rights. Lockean natural rights did not rely on citizenship or any law of the state, nor were they necessarily limited to one particular ethnic, cultural, or religious group. But these rights belonged to the world of scholasticism and were not reflected in the world of reality, his theory being more conceptual than operational.

Two major revolutions occurred in the 18th century: in the United States of America, in 1776, and in France, in 1789. The United States Declaration of Independence includes the concept of natural rights and proudly states that all men are created equal, that they are endowed by their creator with certain inalienable rights and among these are life, liberty, and the pursuit of happiness. Similarly, the French Declaration of the Rights of Man and of the Citizen defines a set of individual and collective rights of the people: liberty, equality, and fraternity. These are held to be universal – not only to French citizens, but to all men without exception. Notwithstanding Adelson's criticism mentioned earlier, these two examples have gone a long way in highlighting the significance of human rights as the *sine qua non* of dignified human existence.

The 1948 United Nations' Universal Declaration of Human Rights (UDHR) may be considered the first attempt to give these rights the imprimatur of international legitimation. The Preamble to UDHR recognises the inherent dignity and the equal and inalienable rights of all members of the human family as the foundation of freedom, justice, and peace in the world and urged member-nations to honour and implement them. While not legally binding, the declaration was the first international legal effort to limit the behaviour of states and press upon them duties to their citizens.[2]

In 1976, the UN adopted the International Covenant on Civil and Political Rights and the International Covenant on Economic,

Social and Cultural Rights. They commit the 155 signatory countries to work toward the granting of civil, political, economic, social, and cultural rights to individuals.[3]

However, with the exception of the non-deformable human rights (the four most important of them are the right to life, the right to be free from slavery, the right to be free from torture, and the right to be free from retroactive application of penal laws), the UN recognises that human rights can be limited or even pushed aside during times of national emergency. The result is that in several member-nations these rights are not enforced and in several others only partially enforced. Cases have not been wanting where countries openly flouted the UN advice to halt the inhuman and unjustifiable human rights violations. The human rights enunciated by the UN are not legally binding on the signatory countries.

The Indian Concept of Social Justice

From the Rig Vedic times, Indian society has shown deep concern for social justice. The Vedic concept of *dharma*, which is the kingpin of the whole social edifice, permeates every thinking and action of the individual from Vedic time onwards. In its pure form, *dharma* means 'that which helps the upliftment of living being'. Gokulesh Sharma, quoting Madhavacharya's commentary of *Parashara Smriti*, explains *dharma* as 'that which sustains and ensures progress and welfare of all in this world and eternal bliss in the other world' (1997: 412). Welfare of all is enshrined in the concept *'Lokaa samastha sukhino bhavantu'*, meaning 'let all people on earth be happy'. Actually, the Indian concept of social justice was the crystallisation and operationalisation of another basic concept *'Thath twam asi'* (that thou art). This thesis presupposes the ultimate interconnectedness of human beings, rooted in the view that each individual is a manifestation of the Universal Self and the Universal Self is identical with the Essence of Reality. We are thus embedded in a vast web of mutual responsibility in which empathy and compassion call for the minimisation of human suffering, and especially to see that we avoid human suffering by living in accordance with the detailed injunctions of *dharma* sometimes called *sanathana* (eternal) *dharma*. In both

Ramayana and *Mahabharata,* there are descriptions of *rajadharma* – the duty of a ruler based on the scriptures. As we all know, Mahatma Gandhi considered Rama, the towering figure in the *Ramayana* epic, as the best example of an ideal ruler and the concept of *Ramarajya* as the cherished goal of any state. Social justice was paramount in Gandhiji's ideal of *Ramarajya,* later elaborated by his worthy disciple Vinoba Bhave through the concepts of *sarvodaya* (prosperity for all) and *antyodaya* (prosperity for the downtrodden).

The recorded history of India does not provide any instance of a king who followed in the footsteps of Rama or took Rama as role model. The only approximation to the ideal of *rajadharma* was that of Emperor Ashoka (see below) whose edicts proclaim that the subjects are as sons and daughters to him. He must have derived inspiration in part at least from the *Arthasastra* of Kautilya (alias Chanakya or Vishnugupta) who was the minister of Ashoka's grandfather Chandra Gupta Maurya. Although written as a primer for the king's use, some chapters of this treatise, especially the third one on 'Judges', breathe the quintessence of social justice. While Kautilya prefers monarchy, he enjoins on the monarch a number of responsibilities as ruler towards the subjects

A few excerpts from the book are relevant here in order to understand the sweep of the concept of social justice (even in its crude form) in the mind of the author, especially since it was written as a guide for his master – the king. It exhorts that the king should always have an eye on the people's welfare as the primary goal of governance. 'In the happiness of his subjects lies the happiness of the king, in their welfare, his welfare; whatever pleases himself the king shall not consider as good. Whatever pleases his subjects, the king shall consider as good' (Radhakrishnan and Moore 1973: 243). In another place, he says that punishment should be even-handed to the king's son as to the enemy, according to the nature of the offence. A large part of the responsibility for social justice is entrusted to the judges who are exhorted to be above corruption and nepotism. 'The judges themselves shall look into the affairs of gods, Brahmans, ascetics, women, minors, old persons, sick persons and those who are helpless' (ibid.; see also Gokhale 1956: 4, 38; Kangle 1992: Vol. 2: 1–5).

According to the author of *Arthasastra,* the concept of justice extends to many issues: the weaker sections (women, minors, old persons, sick persons, as specified above), checking unfair practices in trade and commerce, measures to be taken in natural calamities like famine, earthquake, flood and fire, prevention of corruption and nepotism in the administration of laws and ensurance of good governance, prevention of cruelty to animals, and even protection of the environment. 'They shall be fined who hurt animals and cut the shoots of trees in city parks that bear fruits or yield shade' (Kangle 1992: Vol. 2: 249). The author is very conscious of public health policy and promotion of public health. This involved a ban on unwholesome food and drink, a strict control over physicians in the interest of patients as well as state provision for medical treatment of victims of diseases and epidemics. The need to protect the public against unfair practices that may be resorted to by artisans and traders is also highlighted. One cannot find such minute elaboration of items which we now include under social justice in any other single book written in ancient times. In fact, some of the social justice elements in *Arthasastra* come very close to the Universal Declaration of Human Rights by the United Nations.

Ashoka (3rd century BCE), established unprecedented principles of civil rights. During his rule, he pursued an official policy of non-violence (*ahimsa*) and the protection of human rights, as his chief concern was the happiness of his subjects. Ashoka also showed mercy to those imprisoned, allowing them outside one day each year, and offered common citizens free education at universities. He treated his subjects as equals regardless of their religion, politics, or caste. In the Mauryan empire, citizens of all religions and ethnic groups also had rights to freedom, tolerance, and equality. The need for tolerance on an egalitarian basis can be found in the edicts of Ashoka which emphasise the importance of tolerance in public policy by the government.

We have no instance of other kings like Ashoka (except perhaps Cyrus the Great of Persia) who publicly proclaimed the rights of their subjects and caused them to be written and positioned in public places for their information. Even in India, we do not have any other ruler after Ashoka in subsequent centuries, including the British, who espoused the cause of disadvantaged groups for special treatment. It was only with the dawn of freedom that thought was bestowed on the need to bring the socially and economically backward castes of India to the mainstream of life through affirmative action.

The State and Social Justice

Earlier, we have argued that the state is not a precondition for social justice. This is true only of pre-political societies. In modern times, however, the state is indeed a precondition for, and guarantor of, social justice.

The modern state is quite different from the state portrayed in classical political studies. To be sure, it has sovereignty or hegemonic power vis-à-vis other states, and also paramountcy or overriding authority over all individuals and institutions within the state. These two exclusive attributes would ideally place the state in the position of absolute monopolist of power and the last word in the dispensation of that power. Also, it purports to have a well-defined territory and a set of identifiable people ideologically bound by nationalistic ties. But how many states in the world can claim to have all these attributes? Take, for example, sovereignty. Let us examine the Indian situation. We have proclaimed ourselves to be a sovereign republic, but the sovereignty of the Republic of India is only notional and when it attempts to deal with things at the international level, it will find that its sovereignty, at least in diplomatic terms and to an extent in practical terms, is circumscribed.

Upendra Baxi observes, 'The modern state is increasingly interdependent in a globalising world, which attenuates the classical notions of state sovereignty' (2002: 136). According to him, most independent states, especially of the South, emerge as the managing committees of the bourgeoisie comprising of multinational foreign investors and international finance and capital monopolists (ibid.: 137). Baxi's is, of course, a bit exaggerated view, but not far from truth. In several cases, such situations should not be taken as a weakness of a country vis-à-vis other countries; they arise out of the basic need to adjust and cooperate with similar other nations in a live-and-let-live international climate in the family of nations. In realpolitik, the amount of freedom of a state vis-à-vis other states and in the totality of nations is decided by its capacity to influence other nations, whether through military might or economic or technological weight or through diplomacy or a combination of all these. The so-called superpowers have risen to that stature through these attributes.

At this point, a statement made in one of the recent UN publications is quite pertinent. Speaking about the sweep of UDHR, it says that 'the Nation States are no longer the sole powers determining the realisation of such rights for their residents, so the rights discourse is no longer limited to the context of states' (UN NGLS 2006: 3). The nature of and scope for adjustment and the freedom available within the accepted domain to act independently are based upon several factors which are not relevant here. I am only interested in pointing out that the classical attribute of sovereignty of the state needs reconsideration when studying the modern state.

Again, take the attribute of paramountcy – the overriding power over all individuals and organisations within a state's territory. On the one hand, the Constitution of India says that the state's power over the citizens is limited in identified areas and the state is obliged to honour it. The Indian Constitution has a chapter (Chapter III, Articles 36 to 51) on Fundamental Rights where the rights of the citizen are enumerated and the judiciary acts as a vigil on these rights/powers. (One may argue that the judiciary is an integral part of the state and cannot be considered as independent and in that case, fundamental rights do not limit the state's absolute power. However, for all intents and purposes, the judiciary imposes the upper limit on the state's arbitrary exercise of its paramountcy). Besides, the CSOs, which are legally subject to the state's laws and jurisdiction, in many cases, act as spokes on the wheel of the state's power. With the coming of global CSOs, the situation of a state's absolute independence has received another setback. Some of the global CSOs wield enormous power in terms of money, technology, cyber strength, scientific knowledge, and other subtle weapons of direct and indirect control and many of them are capable of domination over the weaker nations. In many cases, they receive direct and indirect support from their own governments or from inter-governmental funding agencies (sometimes called inter-governmental organisations or IGOs), and even from some of the agencies in the UN system. Perhaps, this subtle mechanism of control is more powerful than international diplomacy and many times more effective in reintroducing, through the backdoor and without any apparent resistance, imperialism and colonialism from which these nations have struggled hard to deliver themselves. In any case, they are a challenge to the sovereignty of a nation and the use of paramount power by it.

In this context, it is pertinent to view the state as a political system (in behavioural terms) or as a political society (in contradistinction from civil society) and bring within the system not only the state but para-political organisations which sometimes move with, sometimes against, and sometimes parallel to the state.[4] The use of this concept for analysis of the state would obviate some of the technical hurdles which delimit the paramountcy of a state.

Many states are also struggling hard against terrorist and fundamentalist groups which question their very claim for sovereignty and hegemony and they (states) have found that this is a hard nut for them to crack. The global trend is for such movements to cut across state boundaries which were so far considered inviolate. Cases are not few where the solemnity of territorial boundaries is being disputed by neighbouring states which put forward claims for part of the neighbour's territory or which have grabbed part of it and created an ongoing boundary dispute. Within a state, fissiparous tendencies are rife and in some countries claims for independent statehood are also rampant.

Finally, we come to the concept of identifiable set of people, homogenous in their goals and integrated by nationalistic ideologies. We have the phenomena of multiple organisations, associations, and institutions flourishing within a state's domain and claiming their own identities – ethnic, linguistic, cultural, and what not – some of which are at loggerheads with one another and with the state over rights and over territorial and goal-achievement matters. Multiculturalism is another factor which sows the seeds of disharmony within the ideology of nationhood. Political pluralism is an obsolete term now, especially with the rise of CSOs and

NGOs, some of which have manifestoes and action programmes which are at times in opposition with the state's policies and programmes. Some countries are now having problems with immigrants who may in course of time pose a threat to their own nationals. Many Gulf countries have immigrants who outnumber the domestic population and are compelled to compromise with many elements in their sovereignty in the process of adjusting to the demands of the immigrant population.

I have presented these constraints of the modern state rather elaborately to highlight the multifarious limitations of a state which would attempt at introducing social justice. In the context of the prevailing threats to a state's sovereignty and paramountcy, its capacity to enforce social justice will be severely circumscribed. The different boundary overlaps and disputes and consequent trade-offs and conflicts between the state and the contending forces would necessitate a dilution of many of the well-meant elements of social justice.

Since it will be a laborious process to examine the social justice programmes at individual country level across the world and since many countries do not have clear policies and programmes on social justice, we shall confine our exercise to the social justice programmes of the state in India. Thanks to the long legacy of the concept of *lokaa samastha sukhino bhavantu*, which is a part and parcel of the Indian mind, the overriding spiritual influence of Mahatma Gandhi with his concept of *Ramarajya*, and the domineering personality of Babasaheb Ambedkar in the drafting of the Indian Constitution, social justice has been a top priority item of the government in independent India. The architects of the Indian Constitution have taken great pains to incorporate social justice prominently in this document.

The Preamble to the Indian Constitution declares that in the Sovereign Democratic Republic of India, justice – social, economic, and political – shall prevail. In the Constitution of India, Part III, Articles 12 to 35, on the Fundamental Rights of the Indian Citizen, the rights ensuring social justice are elaborated in fuller detail. The emphasis on social justice is continued in several sections of the Directive Principles of State Policy (Part IV, Articles 36–51).[5] Though not justiciable, they are moral imperatives for the rulers in formulating policies and programmes of the nation. Statutory Commissions (on human rights, women, the minorities, the Scheduled Castes, the Scheduled Tribes, etc.) have been established from time to time to act vigil and to take up cases of violations of these constitutional rights. In the case of the weaker and marginalised sections, affirmative actions (protective discrimination) in the form of reservation and special programmes in the Five-Year Plans of the country also have been provided for. Many legislations have been enacted by parliament and the state legislative assemblies to guarantee the rights provided in the Constitution (for example, Dowry Prohibition Act, Untouchability Abolition Act, etc.). The country has a very active judiciary that promptly takes up cases of violation of constitutional law. Hence, from the point of view of social justice, India has cut a clear path.

However, on the side of implementation, one cannot say with enthusiasm that everything is in order or moving on smooth or correct lines or in the desired direction. Take, for example, the policy of reservation of seats for the Scheduled Castes (SCs) and Scheduled Tribes (STs) in the public sector and educational institutions. The architects of the Constitution thought that the target could be achieved in ten years. But this did not happen and the period has been extended after every ten years. Even so, one is not sure if the objective of reservation would be achieved. There are other items on which target achievement has been tardy, indefinite, or even nil: Uniform Civil Code and Reservation of Seats for Women in Legislative Bodies, to mention only two. Reservation in some areas, while intended to achieve social justice, has a built-in social injustice element also in it, because, if continued indefinitely, the communities adversely affected by it will have a feeling of deprivation of their rights and opportunities for ever, which will go counter to the principle of social justice.

The Government of India has very well recognised the fact that guaranteeing the rights of the citizen will not *ipso facto* enable the deprived communities to enjoy them. There should be also commensurate opportunities for skill development and capacity building for which other enabling facilities are also provided through social legislation and political and economic empowerment programmes. India's Five-Year Plans have special components for the SC and ST populations. The affirmative action (positive discrimination) package contains a number of educational, job, and other concessions for the socially and economically weaker sections to enable them to assert their rights and help raise their positions. But the benefits have not percolated to the intended beneficiaries and the impact of these programmes on the targeted groups has not been encouraging as is indicated by the underachievement of the final goals. The Government of India has, therefore, permitted CSOs to enter this field in a big way to help accelerate the goal achievement process (see Nayar 2005).

Civil Society and Social Justice

We shall now examine the role played by the civil society in India in enhancing social justice. Our concept of civil society is that it refers to the space between the family, the market, and the state, and comprises a plethora of organisations of all sorts ranging from charities to advocacy groups. It is the arena of voluntary collective action around shared interests, purposes, and values. In theory, its institutional forms are distinct from those of the state, family, and market, though in practice, the boundaries between state, civil society, family, and market are often blurred, contested, and negotiated. Civil society commonly embraces a diversity of spaces, actors, and institutional forms, varying in their degree of formality, autonomy, and power. Civil societies are often populated by organisations such as registered charities, non-governmental organisations, community groups, women's organisations, faith-based organisations, professional associations, including business associations, trade unions, self-help groups, social movements, coalitions, and advocacy groups. CSOs vary widely in membership and geographical coverage; some are local, some regional, some national, and some global. They espouse all shades of causes and concerns and promote interests that are occasionally at loggerheads with the interests and prerogatives of the state. Our concern with civil society revolves around its role in promoting social justice. Since our definition of social justice would cover both social justice *per se* and factors which enable and promote the achievement of social justice, we may extend the coverage of the capacity of civil society to reach out to these aspects also. In this sense, many CSOs can be said to be engaged in the promotion of a variety of activities which are in the realm of social justice.

Of late, CSOs have become highly popular in international aid-giving circles with most of the organisations in the UN system not only recognising their services and potential but also giving them consultancy status (Baxi 2002: 48).[6] The World Bank and WHO have many CSOs on their consultative status list. Other UN organisations like UNDP, ADB, etc. also engage CSOs to work for them. In fact, UN has openly admitted that CSOs do better jobs in areas requiring people's cooperation and participation than government agencies. Indeed, the contributions of many CSOs can be said to be welcome or helpful, especially to the development-oriented countries of the South today.

In the case of India, one may say that, on the whole, CSOs perform a very useful role, especially in developmental activities where the state lacks in at least the following: (a) finance, (b) knowledge of and expertise on local problems and needs, and (c) a flexible bureaucracy with a set of empathetic officials. The contribution of the NGOs[7] in the social service sector (health promotion, family welfare, HIV/AIDS control programmes, child development programmes, rural empowerment) has been widely appreciated by all (Tandon and Mohanty 2003: 342). However, out of the multitude of CSOs functioning in India, only a few are engaged in the promotion of social justice. We should eliminate others from our discussion as also the peripheral organisations that do social justice work of a composite nature. For example, self-help groups (SHGs) throughout India work for the empowerment of women and empowerment is basic to the enjoyment and enforcement of many of the rights provided in the Constitution of India. Organisations which run educational institutions also may be considered in this category, though, of late, some of the old and most of the new institutions in this field have turned out to be commercial and market-oriented agencies. There are also agencies which advocate environment protection which is considered as a part of the promotion of social justice.[8] Even so, the number of organisations engaged purely or mainly in social justice itself runs into hundreds and they do a lot of good work for promoting social justice. These also include organisations that operate from countries in the global North.

However, not all CSOs are performing supportive roles in their service-providing activities. There are some at least whose work is confined to receiving funds and utilising them for promotion of the interests of their members or promoters. There are also organisations which collect foreign funds and use them for anti-national activities. Fundamentalist and terrorist groups collect funds, domestic and foreign, and use them for anti-state activities. Several global CSOs not only have branches in India, but also fund Indian NGOs for not-so-national causes or social justice-oriented activities, even though they are apparently recognised as philanthropic, humanitarian, and human-rights-oriented organisations.

Some of the defects of the CSOs arise out of their structural peculiarities. To begin with, they do not have democratic structure and are not answerable even to their members. They are not transparent in their dealings and many of them are alleged to work on hidden agendas. They are supported by foreign funds or are branches of foreign NGOs which are receiving funds from shady agencies abroad and they are distributing these funds to their local units for equally shady activities. This is helped by the absence of any public audit of the funds received by them or scrutiny of the activities engaged in by them. Some of them, because of the huge resources they command and the critical nature of the work they do (for example, HIV/AIDS prevention, Tsunami relief) wield enormous power over the local administration. There is also criticism that some NGOs are engaged in anti-national activities and some even pose threat to the security of the nation. According to Baxi (2002: 130), destabilisation of governance regimes of the South is seen to be, and often is, the privileged function and role of some foreign funding auspices, and this is as true of the Cold War as of the post-Cold War practices of pursuits of human rights as an aspect of foreign, and global economic policies pursued by nations of the North. Some engage in social uplift services and at the same time carry out conversion activities using social service as a masquerade for the latter. Some are respectable names for good causes – for example, literacy promotion missions – but what they promote is alleged to be anti-national activities because their promotional work involves mostly sensitising people and distributing literature which either cultivate disharmony between communities and groups within the country or nurture anti-state feelings among the citizens. Also, there has been widespread criticism that some environmentalists are engaged in retarding economic development by canvassing against highly prioritised dams and highways rather than protecting the environment, which cause they apparently espouse. There are agencies which exist mainly to siphon off government funds/public money.[9]

At present, there is no agency to monitor or regulate their activities. There is no accountability on the side of the NGOs. Their patrons do not undertake any performance appraisal. Certainly, they are not accountable to those whose cause they espouse. Hence, with the respectable names they carry and the blessings and financial support they receive from reputed agencies, some indeed work for causes sometimes banned, sometimes disfavoured, and sometimes considered of low priority by the state. Hence, not all CSOs can be considered to be of service to the promotion of social justice or, for that matter, any just cause at all. As stated earlier, this should not be taken as a blanket criticism of all CSOs.

Global Civil Society Organisations

In this context, the case of global CSOs[10] and their contribution to national development and social justice need special mention. A number of the leading international NGOs, like Amnesty International, Greenpeace, and Action Aid, are directly working in the field of human rights. Many others also have human rights as their field of activity, but in an extended sense of the term. One welcome trend in the NGO sphere is that some of them are feeling the need for a human-rights-based approach in their objectives and programmes. NGOs working on international development are turning towards a rights-based approach to conceiving of and implementing development projects and advocacy, while their counterparts in human rights work pay closer attention to economic, social, and cultural rights rather than just civil and political rights. So, the discourse of human rights is becoming a common conceptual basis for these groups (Nelson and Dorsey 2003; see also Nyamu-Musembi 2002). Though few in number, as compared to country-based NGOs, the global NGOs have enormous potential in terms of resources, expert humanpower, and prestige and, for these reasons, wield substantial power and influence – both nationally and internationally. Many of them are promoted and, at least in part, funded by their national governments either directly or through their own developmental agencies such as USAID, CIDA, DANIDA, etc. In any case, they have primary loyalty to their sponsors and there is allegation that the humanitarian activities of several of the global NGOs are suspect and their services are not always in terms of national priorities, and certainly they are not accountable to the local population whom they are purported to serve.

A very recent UN Report (2006) has this to say:

> In a few years previous to the Tsunami, the media reported an increasing number of scandals involving charitable organisations in the US and around the world. To illustrate, in just a few months, major US newspapers such as the *New York Times, Washington Post,* and *Wall Street Journal* published over 30 articles about the ethical failures of such organisations. They flagged the sky-high salaries of top executives and expenses for offices, travel and other perks. They highlighted conflicts of interest, failures to adhere to organisation's missions, questionable fund-raising practices and a lack of transparency. They challenged the accountability of those who we thought we could trust. Opinion polls show that around the world the level of trust in non-profit non-governmental organisations is still higher than in business and government, *but is on the decline*). (Bendell 2006: x; emphasis added)

The author of this UN-sponsored publication even warns of '*the potential (of these NGOs) to undermine the sovereignty of constitutional democracies*' (ibid.: x; emphasis added).

The publication continues,

> Corrupt or self-interested use of non-governmental not-for-profit forms of organisations does exist around the world and threatens to undermine support to voluntary activity. In countries newly independent of the Soviet Union, and in Russia, the NGOs are often perceived as covers for organised crimes, in Bangladesh and Pakistan NGOs are sometimes seen as fronts for fundamentalist causes and in Central Asia they can serve as platforms for failed politicians. Consequently, the growth in NGOs should not be assumed to mean a growth in support for or positive contributions by NGOs. (ibid.: xii)

Very recently, writing in the *Economic and Political Weekly* (21 July 2007), Neera Chandhoke cast doubts on the global justice contribution of global CSOs. According to her, the global development agencies do not show any concern for the feelings or desires of the people they have come to serve. Not only do they not function on democratic lines but also they do not take into account the needs and aspirations of their clients.

> Democracy is about engaging with the state, it is about the right to protest, and above all, it is about the right to participate in the political domain. It is this aspect that might have gone missing in all the elegant and passionate prose on global justice. (Chandhoke 2007: 3021; see also Chandhoke 1995)

While civil society is a healthy and necessary compliment to democracy, some CSOs think that they should have primacy in dealing with their clients and that democracy should be their handmaid. This is supportive of the doubts expressed by D. Chandler that some NGOs are 'arguing against formal democracy, that democracy should come second to the ethical or moral concern that they champion' (2003: 341).

Of late, the need for transparency in dealings, democratic accountability in transactions, and sensitivity to the concerns and aspirations of the people they serve has been felt among the major global NGOs and, as a result of this concern, the UN–Non-Government Liaison Service (NGLS) has issued a Development Dossier titled *Debating NGO Accountability* (Bendell 2006). In the light of globalisation and increase in the number, magnitude, and sphere of activity of NGOs, it says that there should be democratic accountability for them and this should apply also to those organisations – religious, educational, and professional, including trade unions – which have considered themselves above this. It concludes by saying that 'no longer would people accept describing themselves as what they are not (non-governmental) but what they are for, by articulating the universal values that inspire their work' (ibid.: 78–79). This is especially necessary because they are now increasingly moving towards human rights approach.

Social Justice in a Globalised World

According to Baxi,

> human rights NGOs have moved from the position of 'movements' to that of 'markets'... NGOs of various kinds and at various levels emerge as economic actors insofar as these seek to mobilize resources for their work and as such many of them compete *inter se*. Some NGOs also seek to generate resources additionally through private individual citizen contributions. Human rights markets thus share the salient features of global service industries. (2002: 121)

Nor is this all. Baxi continues,

> ... human rights agencies are trying to market human sufferings under the title of human rights violation and they sometimes carry 'horror stories' to get sympathy and visibility without any compassion or sensitivity for the sufferings of the victims whose cause they espouse. This sort of rights organisations is not going to promote human rights'. (ibid.)

Baxi's point is that human rights NGOs cannot always be trusted in the matter of promoting social justice or human rights, as they have become highly market-oriented.

Globalisation with its three 'Ds' – denationalisation, deregulation, and disinvestment – is going to put an end to the regulatory and redistributive potential of the state and would be a big threat to social justice at both national and international levels. Globalism cannot act as a gospel for social justice because the law of the market has no provision for it. Competition knows no equity on which social justice is built. Governments in the South are also increasingly becoming weak due to a variety of globalisation factors and their efforts at introducing social justice measures are getting more and more diluted and circumscribed. Their capacity to initiate social justice measures is declining progressively. The rise of fundamentalism and terrorism has resulted in many of the social justice measures taken by the states in many parts of the world being contested and even neutralised.

The appalling poverty of many nations of the South, and the inability of their national governments to provide adequate food and shelter to their people, not to speak of other basic needs, have made social justice a right which people in these countries cannot even visualise, let alone covet or clamour for. For them, it is a luxury. Criticism has been levelled against the economic aid to Third World countries. Sometimes foreign aid becomes counter-productive. Foreign aid always has strings attached to it. Most of the time the strings will be invisible, but they could turn out to be a noose which a donor country can always tighten to increase its grip on the victim. Even the free trade doctrine of GATT and WTO can play havoc with the poor countries. According to Bryan Barry,

> Currently, the USA dumps corn, soya beans and rice on the world market at half the cost of producing it. Farmers in poor countries are ruined and are driven out into the already overburdened cities while whole countries that were formerly self-sufficient for food stuffs become importers. (2005: 34)

Undoubtedly, globalisation has ruined rural economy in many countries of the Third World. In these countries, those who suffer from social injustice are so preoccupied with eking out a bare means of livelihood that the very word 'social justice' seldom occurs in their minds.

In India, coalition governments have not been found to be committed to the promotion of social justice. They are more concerned with their survival than the welfare of the governed and have no time to plan or execute programmes of social justice. Parties in the coalition are more eager to use their position to bargain for their best advantage and benefits from their membership in the coalition and these bargains do not include social justice. Many of their programmes labelled as social justice are suspect. They are more directed towards vote banks than the real victims of social injustice. The presence of caste- and region-based vested interest groups makes whatever achievements in this field peripheral. Because social justice is a magical concept with magnetic powers and emotional overtones, political parties and civil rights groups wax eloquent on it and use it as a catchy slogan in their objectives and action programmes without any intention of seriously implementing it, or when implemented, make it at best perfunctory and at worst ritualistic and even farcical. In a multi-ethnic, multi-cultural and multi-religious state like India, social justice has different meanings to different groups of people and these groups are many times at loggerheads with one another. Governments, knowing that, by going quick with social justice programmes, they will be opening a Pandora's Box, are playing safe with them, while still paying lip service to the cause of social justice. This also keeps social justice a will o' the wisp.

Across nations, social justice suffers from a variety of evils, partly emerging from ideological differences and partly due to divides of all sorts – economic, geopolitical, and technological. The North-South divide and political instability and turmoil prevailing in many countries of the world have contributed their dominant share in blackening the face of social justice. Technology is inimical to the countries of the South. Cyber-poor countries are under severe handicap compared to the cyber-rich countries. According to Baxi, 'poverty is no longer to be identified in terms of material deprivations but in terms of access to information to cyberspace. Thus, one hears of "dead" or "wild" zones of the urban impoverished in terms of cyber-poverty rather than in terms of the right to food, housing and health' (2002: 160).

In the globalised world, social justice has a changed meaning and the groups of people who are deprived are: (a) *across nations*, those from the global South, and (b) *within nations*, those who are cyber poor. To be sure, cyber poverty is a bane mainly of the South, but it divides people within a nation as well. Globalisation is creating a new class of have-nots at both international and national levels who require affirmative action of a different sort. The Universal Declaration of Human Rights (UDHR) adopted by the UN in 1948 has not helped the cause of human rights any further, and with its limiting clauses, and with world politics running its present course, it will not make any dent on the cause of social justice and even on human rights either at international or at national level. We have countries galore which are openly flouting UDHR with impunity and they include countries big and small and from both North and South. In many cases, UN does not dare call a spade a spade and, even when the halt order is given, the defaulting countries pay deaf ear to it. Given these limitations, it will be too much to rely on UDHR for correcting the maladies at the global level. When we turn to the situation at the national level, one gets a feeling that the issue is being tossed from the frying pan to the fire. Where then can one turn for justice for the cause of social justice. Social justice everywhere is in grave peril. Will the state and civil society be able to take up the challenge of salvaging it, is a billion dollar question that is begging an answer.

Notes

1. Presidential address delivered at the XXXIII All India Sociological Conference, Karnatak University, Dharwad, 29–31 December 2007.
2. The human rights commonly include: (a) security rights that prohibit crimes such as murder, enforced involuntary suicide, massacre, torture and rape; (b) liberty rights that protect freedoms in areas such as belief and religion, association, assembling and movement; (c) political rights that protect the liberty to participate in politics by expressing themselves, protesting, participating in a protest movement; (d) due process rights that protect against abuses of the legal system such as arrest and imprisonment without trial, secret trials and excessive punishments; (e) equality rights that guarantee equal citizenship, equality before the law and non-discrimination; and (f) welfare rights (also known as economic rights) that require the provision of, for example, education, paid holidays, and protections against severe poverty and starvation group rights.
3. In 1993, the World Conference on Human Rights adopted the Vienna Declaration and Programme of Action. But many nations kept out of its acceptance and those who did accept it have records of non-implementation. The United Nations has set up a number of bodies to monitor and study human rights, and have appointed a (UN) High Commissioner for Human Rights (UNHCHR).
4. Political society includes political parties, interest groups, political movements and those institutions that provide the medium to channel political demands to the state. The argument is that the state cannot be viewed as a single institution but as a group of mutually interacting institutions (see Arora 1970: 1112).
5. The most relevant Article in this connection is Article 38 (1 & 2). Article 38 (1) says that 'the state shall strive to promote the welfare of the people by securing and protecting as effectively as it may a social order in which justice, social, economic and political shall inform all the institutions of the national life'. Article 38 (2) says that 'the state shall in particular strive to

minimise the inequalities in income and Endeavour to eliminate inequalities in status, facilities and opportunities not only amongst individuals but also amongst groups of people residing in different areas or engaged in different vocations.' Article 37, however, says that the provisions contained in the Directive Principles of State Policy shall not be enforceable by any court but the principles therein laid down are nevertheless fundamental in the governance of the country and it shall be the duty of the state to apply these principles in making laws.

6. According to Baxi, 'The UN conferences and summits have provided an unparallel opportunity to bring the world's burgeoning NGO communities together around issues such as bio diversity, population planning, development, women's rights, and habitat human rights. [....] Accredited human rights groups enjoy observer status in diplomatic conferences, where they seek to lobby governments to incorporate what they think to be more progressive texts or formulations' (2002: 62).
7. The terms 'Civil Society Organisations' (CSOs) and 'Non-Government Organisations' (NGOs) are often used indiscriminately and interchangeably. These terms, however, have different connotations: NGOs work in the space of civil society, but there are CSOs which cannot be strictly considered as NGOs. Looked at from another angle, all NGOs are CSOs, but not all CSOs are NGOs – for example, a terrorist group is a CSO, but not an NGO.
8. If we transform social justice into social rights or human rights as UN seems to have done, then a host of activities which apparently have no relation with human rights would come under social justice. For example, the editors of the *International Encyclopedia of Peace, Security, Social Justice and Human Rights* devote a whole volume (Volume III) to 'Social Justice' and the content of this volume is mainly UN Agenda 21: An Agenda for Development 1994. This agenda highlights eleven items, most of which relate to poverty alleviation, health promotion, environment protection, management of land resources and biodiversity (see Sinha and Cherry 1998).
9. Some global NGOs have active access to IGOs from where they collect handsome amounts of money, which they distribute to their subsidiaries and affiliates in the countries of the South for activities that are of greater interest to their sponsors and patrons than the receiving countries.
10. Some of the prestigious international NGOs are: Action Aid International, Amnesty International, CIVICUS World Alliance for

Citizen Participation, Consumers International, Greenpeace International, Oxfam International, International Save the Children Alliance, Survival International, International Federation Terre des Homes, Transparency International, Human Rights Watch, Human Rights First, Global Rights, International Justice Mission, International League for Human Rights, Physicians for Human Rights, and World YM/WCA.

References

Adelson, Howard L. 1995. 'The Origins of a Concept of Social Justice', in K.D. Irani and Morris Silver (eds.): *Social Justice in the Ancient World*. London: Greenwood Press, pp. 25–38.

Arora, Satish K. 1970. 'Economic Growth, Social Justice and Political Stability', *Economic and Political Weekly*, 5: 1110–12.

Barry, Bryan. 2005. *Why Social Justice Matters*. Cambridge: Polity Press.

Baxi, Upendra. 2002. *The Future of Human Rights*. New Delhi: Oxford University Press.

Bendell, Jem. 2006. *Debating NGO Accountability: NGLS Development Dossier*. New York: United Nations.

Chandhoke, Neera. 1995. *State and Civil Society: Explorations in Political Theory*. New Delhi: Sage Publications.

——. 2007. 'Global Civil Society and Global Justice', *Economic and Political Weekly*, 42 (29): 3016–22.

Chandler, D. 2003. 'New Rights for Old? Cosmopolitan Citizenship and Critique of State Sovereignty', *Political Studies*, 51 (3): 332–49.

Esposito, John. 1998. *Islam: The Straight Path*. London: Oxford University Press.

Gokhale, B.G. 1956. *Ancient India: History and Culture*. Bombay: Asia Publishing House.

Irani, K.D. 1981. 'Values and Rights Underlying Social Justice', in Randolph Braham (ed.): *Social Justice*. Boston: Martinus Nijhof, pp. 31–46.

Kangle, R.P. (trans.) 1992. *The Kautailya Arthasastra* (3 Vols). New Delhi: Motilal Banarsidass.

Lewis, Bernard. 1994. *Race and Slavery in the Middle East*. London: Oxford University Press.

Nayar, P.K.B. 2005. 'Civil Society, State and Democracy: Lessons for India', in N. Jayaram (ed.): *On Civil Society: Issues and Perspectives*. New Delhi: Sage Publications, pp. 124–36.

Nelson P.J. and E. Dorsey. 2003. 'At the Nexus of Human Rights and Development: New Methods and Strategies of Global NGOs', *World Development*, 31 (12): 2013–26.

Nyamu-Musembi, C. 2002. 'Towards an Actor-oriented Perspective on Human Rights' *(IDS Working Paper 169)*. Falmer, Brighton: Institute of Development Studies.

Radhakrishnan, S. and C.A. Moore. 1973. *A Source Book in Indian Philosophy*. Princeton: Princeton University Press.

Rawls, John. 2000. *A Theory of Justice*. Delhi: Universal Law Publishing.

Sharma, Gokulesh. 1997. *Human Rights and Social Justice*. New Delhi: Deep and Deep Publications.

Sinha, P.C. and K. Cherry (eds.). 1998. *International Encyclopedia of Peace, Security, Social Justice and Human Rights – Vol. III: Social Justice*. New Delhi: Anmol Publications.

Tandon, Rajesh and Ranjita Mohanty (eds.). 2003. *Does Civil Society Matter? Governance in Contemporary India*. New Delhi: Sage Publications.

UN NGLS. 1999. *Successful Approaches to UN-NGO Co-operation*. New York: United Nations.

——. 2006. *Development Dossier: Debating NGO Accountability*. New York: United Nations.

4

Globalisation, Middle Class Consumerism, and the Declining Welfare State

Some Sociological Reflections

MANISH THAKUR

There is a general consensus among social scientists about the simultaneous ascendance of globalisation and middle class consumerism onto the Indian scene. The burgeoning sociological literature on the Indian middle classes testifies to the growing significance of consumerism as a model of social participation (see Brosius 2010; Lukose 2009; Mathur 2010). This literature has focused on such issues as the re-imagining of citizenship as consumption and the resultant normative changes in the nature and character of the welfare state in India. However, in its enthusiasm to highlight the analytical novelty of consumerism as an embodiment of new visions of social life, it has somehow neglected, or rather failed to integrate its research agenda with, the older discussions on class and state emanating from the political economy tradition. Its firm anchoring in the cultural studies framework has predisposed these studies towards taking a positive view of the collective aspirational imagery, proliferating consumerist seductions based on the inalienable and insatiable

An earlier version of this paper was presented at the session on 'New Middle Class, New Welfare State?' of the Research Committee (RC 19) on 'Poverty, Social Welfare, and Social Policy' at the XVII International Sociological Association's World Congress of Sociology, Gothenburg, Sweden, 11–17 July 2010. I thank Professor N. Jayaram for his valuable editorial inputs.

right to desire, and the continuing mobilisation of populist consumerist aspirations. Not only has the planned economy been taken to be the main villain, but also 'from the very beginning consumerism was touted as a kind of sensuous antidote to the castrating agency of state planning, with its peculiarly bureaucratised rhetoric of austerity...the tactile quality of commodity images could, apparently, reanimate the self-realising energies that years of political exhortation had shrivelled' (Mazzarella 2003b: 62).

Amidst such celebrations, there has also been much scholarly angst pertaining to the *arriviste* classes (see Varma 1998). The rapid expansion of the *new* middle classes remains the mainstay of the consumerist apologia, and much of the blame for the deepening socio-economic divide between the consuming classes and the toiling and the excluded poor gets shifted to the vernacular rich who are swelling the ranks of India's middle classes without having any sense of its historic mission of *nation-building* and *Garibi Hatao*. In a way, this conceptual binary between the *old* and the *new* fits well with the differential reading of the state in the wake of globalisation. Whereas the state (both the colonial and the post-colonial) is credited with the creation of structural opportunities giving rise to the ever-expanding middle classes, the latter's coming of age is generally associated with the onset of a set of new socio-economic policies wrought under the aegis of globalisation. Ironically, the class, which once claimed to represent the nation and thus acquired legitimacy to capture the levers of bureaucratic control and power in a newly independent state, has turned itself into the greatest votaries of free market and a minimal state. Not surprisingly, the new middle classes are the social carriers of the discourses that advocate the substantially reduced role of the state vis-à-vis interventionist public policies and welfarism.

Against this backdrop, this chapter presents a critical appreciation of the available literature in terms of the implications of the interface between globalisation and the new middle classes for the declining welfare state in India. While much has been written about the cultural values of the 'old' and the 'new' middle classes, scholars have somehow not unravelled the ramifications of these changes for the continued sustenance of the Indian welfare state. The chapter attempts to bring out these silences and gaps in the existing studies, and outlines possible themes for further scholarly engagement. While briefly charting out the changing location of middle classes in relation to the Indian nation-state, and the equally important entity of the globalising market, it also discusses their diasporic aspirations, consumerist values, and the quest for a pan-Indian, or even global, identity notwithstanding their diversity and differentiation in terms of caste, religion, language, ethnicity, and region. Viewed thus, the chapter attempts to tie up issues concerning culture, identity, and the lifestyle of the middle classes with the larger issues of change in political processes and public policy. This is a modest attempt to integrate the literature emanating from the political economy and culturalist traditions so far as the understanding of the middle classes in India is concerned.

Middle Classes: Old and New

For long, students of social stratification have resorted to the variants of the Marxist class perspective to make sense of the social structure and change in contemporary capitalist societies. These theories of class have drawn their inspiration from Max Weber as well. There is a rich literature on the differing conceptualisations of class: the respective privileging of the economic basis of classes and the attendant polarisation of the bourgeoisie and the proletariat, and the equal, if not more, significance of occupational prestige, consumption, and style of life has been at the centre of animated controversies in sociology (see, for instance, Abercrombie and Urry 1983). In regard to the middle classes, much of this literature has focused on the problem of drawing categorical analytical (if not empirical) boundaries of the class given its heterogeneity, increasing differentiation, and growing fragmentation. The debate around proletarianisation and embourgeoisement has further complicated the host of theoretical problems about its relationship to the means of production and the form of its (contradictory?) relationship (antagonistic/non-antagonistic) with other classes in a concrete historical setting. Indeed, the 'political missions of the middle strata have been frequently seen as a function of the nature of its relationship with capital and labour' (Johnson 1982).

Surprisingly, the Indian middle classes have started getting scholarly attention fairly recently, though B.B. Misra (1961) had underlined the need for sustained empirical and theoretical investigation of these classes in his pioneering work way back in 1961. Misra was convinced of the distinctiveness of the Indian middle classes and was emphatic in his assertion that they were fundamentally different from their western counterparts: the middle classes in the West emerged basically as a result of economic and technological change and, for the most part, were engaged in trade and industry, whereas, in India, they emerged more as consequences of changes in the system of law and public administration than in economic development, and they mainly belonged to the learned professions. The fact that intelligentsia has been the dominant strand in the composition of the Indian middle classes has subsequently been stressed by a number of social scientists (see Bardhan 1989; Rudra 1989; Deshpande 1998; for a critique, see Béteille 1989).

Noticeably, in the discussions surrounding middle classes in India, the usual references are to the exercise of power and dominance either in relation to the regulatory apparatus of the state or to the congruence with other dominant classes in the ruling coalition in terms of control over the productive processes and the generation and appropriation of surplus. These preoccupations are not unusual, for the bulk of these discussions are primarily located within the political economy tradition (Bardhan 1998; Kohli 2009). Interestingly, it is the economists and political scientists who have taken the lead in scholarly considerations of the middle classes, unexpectedly leaving the sociologists and social anthropologists to arrive late on the scene.

Yet, the steadily growing contributions of sociologists and social anthropologists have brought to the fore a range of issues which were either neglected earlier or were understudied. The place of consumption in the self-definition of the middle classes has opened up an interesting line of enquiry for many promising researchers (Warde 1994; van Wessel 2004). At the heart of the consumerist lifestyle have been new forms of labour which enable this consumption and through which the image of the global consumer gets superimposed on the Indian middle classes (Mazzarella 2003a, 2003b, 2003c; Fernandes 2000, 2006). Membership in the salaried class of the growing private sector has opened up a vista of consumption through credit cards and easily accessible loans which were un-thought of before (Nisbett 2007). Moreover, these scholars have demonstrated key continuities between the middle classes in terms of educational strategies and reproduction of hierarchy through transmission of cultural capital and the manufacturing of hegemonic ideologies (Deshpande 1998). To the extent that a class has a shared moral universe, researchers have started according attention to family values, gender relations, and levels of consumption (see Osella and Osella 1999; Ahmad and Reifeld 2003; Béteille 2003; Voyce 2007; Jaffrelot and van der Veer 2008; Radhakrishnan 2008). Thus, the sociological literature on the Indian middle classes reveals two distinct analytical trajectories approximating to the respective roles of the state and the market. In fact, the differing analytical weight of the nation-state and the market (as the institutional site of consumption practices) in the making of Indian middle classes also connotes the distinction between the 'old' and the 'new' middle classes.

The Political Economy Tradition

Contemporary India has witnessed a broad consensus on economic liberalisation. Observers have underlined the centrality of the urban middle classes in supporting these reforms. In fact, 'private enterprise and business has attained a degree of social legitimacy which is remarkable considering the traditional social ambivalence towards the traders and moneylenders in India' (Panini 1995: 59). This fundamental change in the orientation and outlook of the middle classes where 'property and enterprise rather than office or regulation' (Béteille 1989: 154) has become the new mantra necessitates deeper analytical probe.

According to Pranab Bardhan (1989), there has been increasing social and economic interpenetration among the classes constituting the dominant coalition owing to the expansion of the social base of the professional classes. Rich farmers, industrialists, and traders have invested part of their economic capital to convert it into cultural capital for their progeny. So much so, that 'Marwaris with MBAs' is no longer a rarity. It is debatable if it has also led to the blurring of the rural-urban divide in terms of recruitment to the middle classes, for entry into the metropolitan segments of middle classes remain the preserve of the urban-English educated youth. Sure enough, the grip of the traditional literati over the state apparatus having little organic relationship with trade or industry and with social origins that did not have much stake in the fortunes of private capital has loosened a bit. For Bardhan, this has already started impacting on the flow of state services and other related public policy initiatives.

The contrast could not have been starker as middle classes not only had a stranglehold on the state apparatus after independence but also played a key role in building ideological hegemony around the pivot of the developmental state. Expectedly, the middle classes saw themselves as continuing the nationalist project by managing the developmental process on behalf of the nation. No wonder, the creation and moral privileging of this large, state-linked new middle classes has been posited as part of the process of development ideology of the post-colonial nation-building. For Satish Deshpande (1998), the creation of this class rather than promotion of indigenous industrial or agrarian bourgeoisie has been the most important impact of processes of development on the class structure. As he puts it,

> the concrete state initiatives that were part of development created both the demand for, and the mechanisms for the production of, a new managerial-technical elite that was granted a moral *carte blanche* by development. Unlike the industrialists or landlords, this class acquired the numbers, the legitimacy, and therefore the ideological confidence and social assertiveness that have made it a key political actor on the contemporary stage. (ibid.: 151–52)

The transformation of this state-centric middle classes that have made continuous claims on the state for access to benefits such as white-collar jobs by virtue of their supposed qualities of merit, hard work, talent, discipline, drive, and enterprise into consumer-based middle classes having transnational aspirations is one of the most interesting sagas of post-independence India. The relegation of the state-managed models of economic planning and development and the embracing of the market-based reforms are deeply implicated in this narrative. The waning of mutual dependencies between the state and the middle classes cannot be simply attributed to the general disenchantment with the 'licence-permit raj' that the growing significance of public enterprises in the Nehruvian model of development and the rapid growth in public sector employment had spawned.

No doubt, as long as the Nehruvian model lasted, the middle classes made hay by virtue of their control of networks of patronage through the distribution of economic resources and benefits, and also through economic claims on the state through white-collar union activity (periodic pay commissions, inflation-linked dearness allowance, housing, and medical facilities, subsidised education for children, subsidised travel, etc.). Arguably, it was the charm of the middle classes and the perceived entry barriers on the part of the groups and communities that have fuelled growing dissatisfaction and increasing pressures on the state for quotas of all sorts for middle class jobs as well as 'sons of the soil' movements in many parts of the country (Weiner et al., 1981).

Does it then mean that the increasing distance between the state and the middle classes is a function of the failure of the state to cater to the all-pervasive aspirations of middle-classisation on the part of the public at large? Or is it a function of the receding hold of nationalism in the public imagination? Or has globalisation become such an irreversible process and an enchanting discourse that reliance on the state has come to be seen as myopic for upward social mobility and consumerist needs by diverse publics?

Deshpande (1998, 2003) offers one particular response to these questions wherein the story of the Indian middle classes is told as their metamorphosis from being *proxy* to *portrait* of the nation. In his words,

> accompanying this transition is a change in its social stance vis-à-vis other groups within the nation. From its position as a 'proxy' for the nation, this class has now graduated to thinking of itself as a 'portrait' of the nation. That is to say, the middle class no longer claims merely to represent the people (who alone were thought to constitute the nation in the era of development), but rather that it is itself the nation. (1998: 162)

In Deshpande's reading, for the managerial/professional segments of the middle classes the benefits of globalisation seem clearly to outweigh the costs. Undoubtedly, it is they who constitute the privileged diasporics newly exposed to, and seduced by, the charms of a multicultural existence in a globalised world:

> this class segment is today interpellated by globalization in the same (or perhaps more intense) way that, a generation or two ago, it identified itself with development. Indeed, much of the celebratory rhetoric about globalization emanates from and is aimed at this group. *Having consolidated its social, economic and political standing on the basis of the developmental state, this group is now ready to kick it away as the ladder it no longer needs.* (ibid.; emphasis added)

What is remarkable is that this class segment has experienced no discontinuity between the state-led development of the Nehruvian era and the globalisation of our times. This smooth transition, a point well-articulated by Deshpande, certainly calls for further corroboration and investigation.

Whereas Deshpande (1998, 2003) underlines the active complicity of the middle classes in the production of economic ideologies, E. Sridharan (2004) adds nuance to the relationship of the middle class to economic ideology by looking at the sectoral composition of India's middle class. For Sridharan, the crucial variable is the share of public employees and public-subsidy-dependent farmers in the broadest middle class so far as support for economic reforms is concerned. He also takes note of the entry of the non-'twice-born' landowning dominant castes such as Marathas, Patidars, Reddys, and Kammas along with the Other Backward Classes (OBCs), religious minorities, the Scheduled Castes (SCs), and the Scheduled Tribes (STs). Moreover, he displays sensitivity towards the intermeshing of political and economic ideologies. In this regard, he mentions the common political preferences among the traditional upper castes and the rising dominant peasant castes, particularly in west and south India.

Sridharan further argues that the upper and dominant castes, the social bloc supporting the Bharatiya Janata Party (BJP), and largely middle classes, may also be supporting economic liberalisation for reasons other than the purely economic. In an interesting twist of the argument, he posits that these groups may have supported liberalisation because they support BJP and its coalition for essentially social reasons. In other words, the support 'for economic reforms among the middle class is not the result of any ideological shift in favour of liberalisation' (ibid.: 423). Rather, the support extended to economic reforms through BJP and its electoral allies by these social groups mainly reflects their class identification and aspirations. According to him, there is a large 'aspirational' middle class, beyond the economically defined middle class, particularly among the youths of all castes and classes. And, it is this 'aspirational' middle class which is the driving force behind economic reforms.

Evidently, to explain such a fundamental change in the domain of political economy and culture merely in terms of 'aspirations' of groups and communities to identify with the well-established middle classes displays too much of deference to social psychology. The assertion itself is questionable as it betrays flawed and partial understanding of the processes of interest articulation. The latter is not merely aspirational or ideological, but is also an outcome of structural distribution of opportunities and rewards in a given society.

The sociological and political convergence between the top and the middle that Sridharan puts forward is not a law of social evolution even in most capitalist democracies. Both Deshpande and Sridharan agree that the middle class would appear to have a wider socio-political and economic policy impact than its actual numbers might otherwise suggest. If it is neither numbers nor ideology, then we must look elsewhere for an explanation. Sure enough, Sridharan has advanced our understanding by questioning any unproblematic relationship between the growth of the middle class and the spread and the deepening of liberalisation policies. In its place, he sees contradictory signals emanating from the middle classes: they constitute a support base for liberalisation, while at the same time, the sheer weight of public employees and publicly subsidised agriculturists among their ranks have served to constrain the progress of certain types of economic reforms.

Relatively speaking, deregulation can be expected to command widespread support among the middle classes, as regulation is identified with corruption and inefficiency. Also, regional capital and medium-scale businesses are likely to warm up to deregulation as it helps them escape the vestiges of the 'licence-permit raj'. However, there is likely to be a contrary pull from the rising backward caste component of the middle classes who fear the loss of statist regulation for patronage, especially at the state level (Sheth 1999). Likewise, deregulation-induced shrinking of the state has the potential to take the sheen away from the caste-based quota in public employment and the state-funded higher education institutions. Yet, Sridharan does not foresee a situation where these economic reforms are either abandoned altogether or get retarded, they are to grow only gradually given the largely public employee and publicly subsidised farmer character of the broadest middle class.

Quite differently, Atul Kohli (2009) looks beyond the usual two supporting constituencies of the new discourse of liberalisation – business groups and the middle classes. He dismisses the first as having reactive rather than leadership roles in relation to economic policy, more of veto than agenda-setting power. He privileges structural mass base of capitalism as an explanatory variable. The middle classes supported liberalisation, he argues, because it offered concrete benefits to them from the outset, such as direct tax reduction and greater access to consumer goods. He factors in an emerging structural link between the growing middle class and the big business via the booming capital market: business increasingly finances itself by raising capital from the public. Big business thus acquires a mass social base, while the middle class acquires a stake in corporate profitability. This expanded mass base of capitalism cannot but have an impact on the development ideology woven around discourses of liberalisation and globalisation. Instead, it may contribute to making these discourses commonsense of the day the way the middle-classes' stakes in the statist development had made it look up to the state as the sole arbiter of nation's destiny.

The Cultural Studies Tradition

From a culturalist perspective, Leela Fernandes (2006) relates the formation of the new middle class to two of the central national trends that have shaped India since the 1990s – the rise of Hindu nationalism and the politics of economic liberalisation. Since the new middle class serves as an idealised standard for a range of social strata that make up the rural and urban middle classes, she examines a range of ethnographic data concerning newly available commodities, consumption practices, and urban lifestyles to shed light on its politics. She goes beyond the static, though fashionable, conception of the new middle class as a consumer group. What is interesting is her thesis that India's *new* middle class is not defined by new entrants to its ranks. The newness refers to a process of production of a distinctive social and political identity that represents and lays claims to the benefits of liberalisation rather than any fixed structural or social basis. In other words, the new middle class does not simply act on behalf of its predefined interests, but these very interests are created through specific sets of political, cultural and discursive processes: 'this middle class is not simply a new socioeconomic group; it embodies a changing set of socio-cultural norms for the Indian nation' (ibid.: 141). The general decline of the public normative interest in questions of poverty and workers' rights is a case in point.

At a structural level, this group largely encompasses English-speaking urban white-collar segments of the middle class who are benefiting from new employment opportunities, particularly in the private sector. Even as the entry to this social group is potentially open to other segments of the middle class and upwardly mobile working class, its reproduction draws upon historically produced inequalities. At the same time, its boundaries remain fluid and open to contestation as its claims of representative citizenship are challenged by social groups it distinguishes itself from – both the upper class and subaltern groups. It is this structural ambiguity and the attendant tension produced by its claims of natural or universal representativeness that imparts vitality to the middle-class politics.

Fernandes is not sure if the benefits from liberalisation are accruing uniformly to across the middle class. For instance, lower-caste groups are still dependent on state politics and state employment in gaining access to middle-class membership. Despite the fact that affirmative action policies have facilitated the entry of lower-caste groups into the middle class, one witnesses increasing reliance on privatised strategies rather than on organised political opposition on the part of middle classes while responding to processes of economic restructuring and accessing new careers and jobs.

In the urban/metropolitan context, the production of the identity of the new middle class is linked to a politics of 'spatial purification' (ibid.: 139) which centres on its claims over public spaces and corresponding movement to cleanse such spaces of the urban poor and working classes, and also the 'loose' women, to articulate its conceptions of civic life. What is quintessentially Indian in this new mode of politics is the ways in which both gender and class get coded by caste-based discourses and inequalities. Moreover, the new-middle-class politics is equally shaped by its relationship with a range of state practices and strategies. This complicity of the state demonstrates continuities across the facile binary between the state dependence of the Nehruvian middle class and the market orientation of the new middle class. What have indeed changed are the mechanisms and practices within civil society through which this class has come to shape the symbolic register of democratic politics. By virtue of its informal points of access to state power, and its representational claims through a plethora of civic associations, India's new middle class is engaged in an attempt to 'reclaim and redefine the substantive terms of democracy in exclusionary ways' (ibid.: 219).

There is no denying that consumption is not only central to the experience of modern life on the part of the middle classes, but is also shaping the relationship of the middle class to the nation and national culture and identity. Whereas the initial decades after independence saw the centrality of national identity to the experience of modernity among the Indian middle classes, liberalisation appears to have heralded their self-seclusion from the nation. Yet, consumption eludes moral legitimacy for the constitution of individual selves. Consumer culture is assessed more in terms of morality, that is, in terms of ideals of society set against the everyday experience of urban middle-class life than in relation to the nationalist discourses. At once, self-gratification and self-realisation through goods are condemned as moral deprivation and also seen as the necessary accompaniments of upward socio-economic mobility. According to van Wessel (2004), there is no unambiguous link between middle-classness, globalised consumption practices, and national identity. On the contrary, she finds a marked absence of nation or any variant of nationalism in moral discourses on consumption among the middle classes. There is an amoral sociality which is more sectional and reflective of intra-class concerns. National-global plays second fiddle to individuals and their locally rooted social world. Thus, even though middle classes may be well-above the mean, one does not come across attendant responsibility or obligation to work for the public good, nation, or inclusive development.

Nonetheless, media images produce a vision of the Indian nation based on an idealised depiction of the urban middle classes and commodity consumption. Globalised consumption becomes part of the national political culture and an indicator of Indian nation's arrival on the global stage as seen through the consumption practices of the urban middle class. The availability of commodities as a consequence of 'abroad is now in India' further reinforces the middle-class image of a new liberalising India pegged to global consumption benchmarks. One sees a curious conflation of the narratives of nationhood and development with the production of middle-class identity. They acquire the role of key protagonists in the collapse of nationalist imagery and the aesthetic of the commodity form. No wonder, a hegemonic urban middle-class lifestyle based on commodity consumption has come to articulate a new national cultural standard. On the one hand, this middle class-induced cosmopolitanism embodies a new compact between the nation-state, the private/corporate sector, and civil society; on the other, it reworks internal societal fault lines, such as caste, class, gender, and ethnicity. In any case, the current configuration of corporate-society-state relationship and the attendant re-conceptualisation of public interest in India would not have been possible without consumption being a powerful organising trope and permeating the imagination and practices of the middle class (Fernandes 2000). The symmetry of interests between them and non-resident Indians at a given historical conjuncture has but consolidated this new compact.

State, Classes, and the New Economic Ideology

As the foregoing discussion makes it clear, the socio-cultural practices of the Indian middle classes have to be considered in the context of liberalisation processes since the early 1990s and the rise of the Hindu nationalist and fundamentalist movements which are politically intertwined with this new economic ideology. For the middle classes, the increasing liberalisation of the Indian economy has meant an unprecedented access to foreign consumer goods and lifestyle. Expectedly, the popular discourses disproportionately highlight the economic aspects of this identity in terms of recently acquired purchasing power and the corresponding access to valued consumer goods. This characterisation *ipso facto* leads to the privileging of the market as a dispenser of identities and overlooks other aspects that are of greater sociological import.

For example, local or regional caste groups of low hierarchical position generally derive their social and economic position from an advantageous relationship with the state: they have benefited from governmental positive discrimination policies, which have helped them gain educational qualifications and permanent jobs in the public sector. The situation of the middle class of higher caste origin is quite different in relation to the state, which they commonly mistrust in present-day India despite their historically binding relationship (Saavala 2003: 231–32). This bond between caste and state, which crucially affects the new-middle-class status strategies, is a promising line of enquiry that has the potential to enhance our understanding of the much-talked-about disconnect between the state and the middle classes in India.

Quite symptomatically, one also notices the absence of a creative dialogue between the growing literatures on theories of consumer society and the empirical data obtaining in the Indian context. Like other fields, this may be just another instance of the uncritical application of the globally fashionable consumer culture theories to the Indian context. What Zygmunt Bauman calls 'the consumerist syndrome' (cited in Rojek 2004) may not be an apt description of a society where the majority of the population remains trapped in poverty. For the upwardly mobile, lacking any form of inherited material, social, or symbolic capital by virtue of their origins in low-caste groups, consumption could just be another strategy of social classification, seeking to draw a clear line between themselves and 'the poor' and identify themselves as middle-class people without being able to follow the established cultural code of the middle class to the full. The acquisition of the new-middle-class identities supposedly based on merit (formal education) and patterns of consumption could be a privatised escape route to get rid of the ignominy of low caste identities derived from alleged hereditary qualities. As Minna Saavala notes, 'new middle-class people acknowledge the basic principles of the encompassing hierarchy through their actions; without hierarchy as the fundamental context, their actions would not make sense' (2003: 245).

Given the centrality of 'classification struggle' (Bourdieu 1984), a struggle over definitions of middle-class respectability and attempts to identify one's social being as such, one could argue for the subordinate role of consumption in what remains essentially a society of producers, something that Thorstein Veblen studied and described. According to Bauman, Veblen's ostentatious consumption was a weapon in positional struggle, conducted mostly, perhaps solely, by the 'middle class' people as *individuals*. Viewed thus,

> conspicuous consumption was instrumental: a visiting card, or the way of notifying the 'significant others' selectively admitted to 'private views' just how high the *nouveau riche* has managed to climb, and that he has the means of settling there for good. Ostentation was important, not the consumption; those practicing it could be, and in many cases were, abstemious, ascetic puritans, abhorring luxury and waste, full of contempt for pleasure-seekers and hating those who indulged in sensual delights'. (cited in Rojek 2004: 294)

Does it then mean that consumption as an ideology is yet to make that fundamental transition from being instrumental to being 'autotelic', a value in its own right, pursued for its own sake, in the Indian case? Does consumption remain trapped in the interminable pecking-order duels Veblen was writing about and which, in any case, has historically been rendered more complex by the operations of a caste society? In any case, as Rohit Varman (2010) remarks, the place of consumption processes and practices in the construction of national identity is an under-researched area. Of late, researchers have been engaging with as to how consumptionscapes have come to frame the nationalist identity. In particular, Varman investigates the resurgence of oppositional neo-nationalist movements which regard global consumption practices as anti-national and unpatriotic echoing nationalist responses towards multinational products during the colonial era. Such movements not only privilege the use of local goods but also imbue them with values of authenticity, purity, tradition, and patriotism. Appreciably enough, his focus on the role of consumption in reinforcing/undermining the national identity in India and his careful attention to 'the elided relationship between consumption and national identity' (ibid.) has the potential to yield insights regarding the current debates on globalisation and its relationship with the middle classes in India. Students of society and culture in India can productively engage with these issues, which largely remain unexplored and untapped.

Conclusion: Decline of the Welfare State?

India today boasts a middle class of sixty to eighty million people whose 'craze for goods' turns out to be in sharp contrast to Mahatma Gandhi's vision of an India devoted to traditional crafts (Stearns 2001: 129). Gandhi's avoidance of the western-style consumerism in favour of spiritual and nationalist goals appears to have given way to a full-blown consumerism, which places premium on goods of higher quality whatever be their origins. If large number of middle-class Indians has come to define life through acquisition of goods and have started deriving better part of their identity in terms of what they possess and can exhibit, then their collective articulation of hopes and frustrations is bound to impact on the policy regime and the welfare character of the state. For instance, the intensifying appetite for various kinds of consumer goods among the middle classes has contributed to the dismantling of the policy of import substitution that was once an avowed nationalist goal.

In economic literature, there has been the usual profit-welfare-squeeze hypothesis. That is, globalisation exposes the nation-state to international competition arising out of the greater mobility of capital. Of necessity, the globally mobile capital seeks out the lowest levels of taxation and associated burdens to maximise its returns. Such dictates of internationally mobile capital in terms of short-term competitiveness, as a rule, reduces the room for manoeuvre for the competing nation-states, thereby, undermining its capacity for welfare policy measures. However, there are some observers who believe that 'increasing globalization and competitiveness create economic conditions which require the state or the public sector to play a more, not less, important role in social protection' (Mishra 1999: 33). In this reading, state's failure to appropriately respond to the demands of globalisation can lead to higher levels of unemployment and lower levels of welfare expenditure in the short term as capital exerts its market discipline. At the same time, the lower levels of funding of the welfare state leads to the long-term productivity slowdown. Any undermining of the welfare state is thus short-sighted, because the welfare state contributes to higher productivity in terms of long-term competitiveness at the international level. Moreover, there is a growing realisation to frame internationally recognised welfare standards to preclude the race to the bottom that the short-term competitiveness among nation-states may lead to. Such an understanding necessitates the reworking of the usual globalisation versus welfare state binary as state often promotes, rather than reluctantly accepts, globalisation (Fine 2002: 192–97).

All in all, it would be a trifle premature to write an obituary to the welfare state. True, it is being redefined but the reports of its death may appear to be a bit exaggerated. Yet, there are loud proclamations on the withering away of the welfare state. For example, Ulrich Beck writes,

> all fixed, fast-frozen relations, with their train of ancient and venerable prejudices and opinions are swept away... Today 'the fixed and fast frozen' is the welfare state and trade-union

> organization of labour, while the 'ancient and the venerable' are the bureaucratic prescriptions and fiscal extractions of the state. (2000: 2)

Undoubtedly, the welfare state has been subject to both inner national crises and constraints imposed by globalisation. It would be prudent to acknowledge that the policy outcomes of the welfare state depend upon the balance of internal forces as well. Such an acknowledgement in no way discounts the demands of long-term competitiveness that globalisation brings in its wake. The latter definitely circumscribes the supposed autonomy of state's policy regime(s). What is needed is a framework that examines how underlying economic and political interests are represented nationally and internationally. This framework imposes on us sensitivity not only to internal differentiation within the middle classes along usual sociological axes of caste, region, language, ethnicity, and religion, but also to increasingly salient differentiation between its 'diasporic' and the 'national' segments.

References

Abercrombie, Nicholas and John Urry. 1983. *Capital, Labour and the Middle Classes*. London: George Allen and Unwin.

Ahmad, Imtiaz and H. Reifeld (eds.). 2003. *Middle Class Values in India and Europe*. New Delhi: Social Science Press.

Bardhan, Pranab. 1989. 'The Third Dominant Class', *Economic and Political Weekly*, 24 (3): 155–56.

——. 1998. *The Political Economy of Development in India*. Delhi: Oxford University Press.

Beck, Ulrich. 2000. *What is Globalization?* Cambridge: Polity Press.

Béteille, André. 1989. 'Are the Intelligentsia a Ruling Class?', *Economic and Political Weekly*, 24 (3): 151–55.

——. 2003. 'The Social Character of the Indian Middle Class', in Imtiaz Ahmad and H. Reifeld (eds.): *Middle Class Values in India and Europe*. New Delhi: Social Science Press, pp. 73–85.

Bourdieu, Pierre. 1984. *Distinction: A Social Critique of the Judgement of Taste*, Cambridge, MA: Harvard University Press.

Brosius, Christiane. 2010. *India's Middle Class: New Forms of Urban Leisure, Consumption, and Prosperity*. New Delhi: Routledge.

Deshpande, Satish. 1998. 'After Culture: Renewed Agendas for the Political Economy of India', *Cultural Dynamics*, 10 (2): 147–69.

——. 2003. 'The Centrality of the Middle Class', in Satish Deshpande: *Contemporary India: A Sociological View*. New Delhi: Penguin Books, pp. 125–50.

Fernandes, Leela. 2000. 'Nationalizing "the Global": Media Images, Cultural Politics and the Middle Class in India', *Media, Culture and Society*, 22 (4): 611–28.

——. 2006. *India's New Middle Class: Democratic Politics in an Era of Economic Reform*. Minneapolis: University of Minnesota Press.

Fine, Ben. 2002. *The World of Consumption: The Material and Cultural Revisited*. London: Routledge.

Jaffrelot, Christophe and Peter van der Veer. 2008. *Patterns of Middle Class Consumption in India and China*. New Delhi: Sage Publications.

Johnson, Dale L. 1982. *Class and Social Development: A New Theory of the Middle Classes*. Beverly Hills: Sage Publications.

Kohli, Atul. 2009. *Democracy and Development in India: From Socialism to Pro-Business*. Oxford: Oxford University Press.

Lukose, Ritty A. 2009. *Liberalization's Children: Gender, Youth and Consumer Citizenship in Globalizing India*. Durham and London: Duke University Press.

Mathur, Nita. 2010. 'Shopping Malls, Credit Cards and Global Brands: Consumer Culture and Lifestyle of India's New Middle Class', *South Asia Research*, 30 (3): 211–31.

Mazzarella, William. 2003a. '"Very Bombay": Contending with the Global in an Indian Advertising Agency', *Cultural Anthropology*, 18 (1): 33–71.

——. 2003b. 'Critical Publicity/Public Criticism: Reflections on Fieldwork in the Bombay Ad World', in Timothy D. Malefyt and Brian Moeran (eds.): *Advertising Cultures*. London: Berg, pp. 55–74.

——. 2003c. *Shovelling Smoke: Advertising and Globalization in Contemporary India*. Durham: Duke University Press.

Mishra, R. 1999. *Globalization and the Welfare State*. Cheltenham: Edward Elgar.

Misra, B.B. 1961. *The Indian Middle Classes: Their Growth in Modern Times*. Delhi: Oxford University Press.

Nisbett, Nicholas. 2007. 'Friendship, Consumption, Morality: Practising Identity, Negotiating Hierarchy in Middle-Class Bangalore', *Journal of the Royal Anthropological Institute (N.S.)*, 13 (4): 935–50.

Osella, Filippo and Caroline Osella. 1999. 'From Transience to Immanence: Consumption, Life-Cycle and Social Mobility in Kerala, South India', *Modern Asian Studies*, 33 (4): 989–1020.

Panini, M.N. 1995. 'The Social Logic of Liberalisation', *Sociological Bulletin*, 44 (1): 33–62.

Radhakrishnan, Smitha. 2008. 'Examining the "Global" Indian Middle Class: Gender and Culture in the Silicon Valley/Bangalore Circuit', *Journal of Intercultural Studies*, 29 (1): 7–20.

Rojek, Chris. 2004. 'The Consumerist Syndrome in Contemporary Society: An Interview with Zygmunt Bauman', *Journal of Consumer Culture*, 4 (3): 291–312.

Rudra, Ashok. 1989. 'Emergence of the Intelligentsia as a Ruling Class in India', *Economic and Political Weekly*, 24 (3): 142–50.

Saavala, Minna. 2003. 'Auspicious Hindu Houses: The New Middle Classes in Hyderabad, India', *Social Anthropology*, 11 (2): 231–47.

Sheth, D. L. 1999. 'Secularisation of Caste and Making of New Middle Class', *Economic and Political Weekly*, 34 (34–35): 2502–10.

Sridharan, E. 2004. 'The Growth and Sectoral Composition of India's Middle Class: Its Impact on the Politics of Economic Liberalization,' *India Review*, 3 (4): 405–28.

Stearns, Peter N. 2001. *Consumerism in World History: The Global Transformation of Desire*. London: Routledge.

van Wessel, Marcel. 2004. 'Talking about Consumption: How an Indian Middle Class Dissociates from Middle-Class Life', *Cultural Dynamics*, 16 (1): 93–116.

Varma, Pavan. 1998. *The Great Indian Middle Class*. Delhi: Viking.

Varman, Rohit. 2010. 'Consuming Nationhood: Understanding the Role of Consumption in the Construction of Indian Nationhood' (Unpublished paper). Kolkata: Indian Institute of Management – Calcutta.

Voyce, Malcolm. 2007. 'Shopping Malls in India: New Social "Dividing Practices", *Economic and Political Weekly*, 42 (22): 2055–62.

Warde, Allan. 1994. 'Consumption, Identity-formation, and Uncertainty', *Sociology*, 28 (4): 877–98.

Weiner, Myron and Mary F. Katzenstein (with K.V. Narayana Rao). 1981. *India's Preferential Policies: Migrants, the Middle Classes and Ethnic Equality*. Bombay: Oxford University Press.

5

Gandhi and Globalisation

M.V. NADKARNI

Globalisation is a process, more than the state of a given situation. There can be a narrow, purely economic view of the process, a broader but still an anthropocentric view, and a still broader view comprising the whole global eco-system. These three views or dimensions of globalisation are first discussed briefly, before going into the question of how Mohandas Karamchand Gandhi (Mahatma Gandhi or Gandhiji) (1869–1948) would have looked at the whole process. The intention here is not to oppose either globalisation or economic growth totally, but to emphasise the need to be sensitive to their downsides, since these downsides may have serious repercussions on the poor and the deprived in whose name these two processes may be tried to be defended. This sensitivity is the essence of Gandhian approach to this or any problem. Unfortunately, such sensitivity is rare, or more formal than real, more said than done. It is found easier to dub honest Gandhians like Medha Patkar as anti-growth, than to address their real concerns. Gandhiji would certainly oppose reckless growth and globalisation, but support if these two processes were humane, poor-friendly, and environmentally benign.

In its narrowest, economic view, globalisation means an increasing integration of national economies through trade in

---

This chapter is an elaborated version the author's presentation at the panel discussion in the two-day National Seminar on 'Globalisation and the Management of Vulnerabilities' at the Institute for Social and Economic Change, Bangalore, 26–27 March 2008. The author is grateful to the seminar participants for the lively discussion.

goods and services, and freer corporate investments and other financial flows across countries. It involves accelerating international division of labour, in which multi-national or trans-national corporations play an increasing role. More significantly, it involves accelerating marketisation at two levels – goods and services, and money – both encompassing the whole world, almost breaking free of national boundaries.

When the earlier policy of import substitution gave way to a policy of export orientation and trade liberalisation in India in the early 1990s, the main justification given was that the earlier protectionist regime had spoilt Indian industry and made them indifferent to the need for constantly improving quality of their products. The so-called consumer sovereignty was crushed under the heels of industrial monopolists. It was hoped that throwing open our economy to fresh winds of international competition would compel these spoiled brats of monopolists to develop some quality consciousness and undertake responsibility for research and development activities in Indian industry which had been long ignored. It was also expected that trade liberalisation, competition, and globalisation in general would unleash the hitherto bound entrepreneurial forces, and bring in new technology on a wider scale, which, in turn, would step up the rates of economic growth. All this would make it possible to release more resources for poverty reduction and social security. It was emphasised that, while the earlier policy concentrated on distributing the given national cake, the new policy would increase the size of the cake itself, which would be more beneficial for all concerned including the poor. While this is a convincing argument when considered in isolation, it is good to remember that the beneficial results, particularly for the poor, would depend on the type of economic growth generated by globalisation, on whether the elite who control the process of economic growth would be willing to share the gains of growth with the less fortunate, and on whether the poor themselves are empowered enough to assert their rights.

This change in policy in favour of liberalisation and globalisation has attracted paeans of praise from many – economists and journalists alike (see Das 2000; Bhagwati 2004, for typical praise). There is also no dearth of detractors of globalisation; a very eminent example of which is Nobel laureate Joseph E. Stiglitz (2002). To illustrate the success of this policy in India, it has been usual to point out at the fantastic success of our passenger car industry. The consumer earlier had a choice of only three brands of petrol guzzling cars, and a long wait was unavoidable before getting a car (except, of course, for the powers that be!). In less than two decades, the scenario completely changed, where the consumer has not only a choice of many brands of cars of international standards with a lot more fuel economy, but the long wait also is no longer necessary. So, 'Competition *Zindabad*!', 'Liberalisation *Zindabad*!', 'Globalisation *Zindabad*!', and, 'State Control *Murdabad*!' But before an uncritical enthusiasm overwhelms our intellect, we need to put this example itself in a balanced perspective. This craze for private transport, which is mainly a consequence of globalisation directly and indirectly, has also led to traffic jams in almost all cities, terribly congested roads, and uncontrolled vehicular emissions. Secondly, has public transport witnessed a similar revolution as the private car industry? Yes, the railways have registered a remarkable progress both in passenger comfort and economic viability, but this is an area where there was hardly any globalisation of the level witnessed in automobile industry. And, ironically, the Indian Railways is also a prominent public monopoly, the dreaded enemy of liberalisers! In spite of being less globalised, the railways provide a sharp contrast to the general state of public road transport. This is only to show that globalisation by itself cannot yield miracles. On the other hand, it may result in unanticipated adverse consequences too. What matters more is whether the government knows what it should do, and is willing to exercise its intervention, when needed, in national or public interest.

While international trade in goods and services began much before, globalisation of financial capital and movements of hot money are a distinguishing characteristic of the present era of globalisation. Indeed, financial flows across countries in the form of foreign direct investments (FDIs) may give a boost to the economy through not only an increase in national income and employment, but also through product innovation, new technology, and quality improvement. But such investments form only a part of the total financial flows, often a small part, the magnitude of its proportion varying from time to time and from country to country. Marketisation of money in a globalised economy is a strange phenomenon! It goes much beyond giving credit for production or consumption purposes. A significant part of it is unrelated to either production or consumption, and may be unrelated also to any welfare consideration. It only serves the purpose of satisfying the speculative and the betting instincts in man, and serves hardly any other economic purpose. Yet it is common to welcome this dimension of globalisation, and to include inflows of hot money as part country's assets, however volatile they may be. This has no meaning, unless the governments of the countries concerned are strong and effective enough to control outflows. But, the moment the governments show some inclination for it, the inflows are also immediately and adversely affected! Even FDIs are adversely affected. Not to speak of political arm-twisting from governments that lead global capitalism, whenever the governments of developing countries dare to control financial flows. Globalisation of capital flows is an explicitly economic process, which does not eschew political factors either as a cause or as an effect. Economic instability, induced by hot money movements, could very well, and very quickly, lead to political instability as well.

A broader view would still be focused on the human dimension, but would go beyond purely economic activities, and would comprise a greater interaction between countries in the sphere of culture, language, and religion. In a sense, the process of globalisation began much before the modern era, in which military expeditions, traders, and missionaries played a major role. Earlier to the present modern phase of globalisation, it was more explicitly a political process, which included the economic, but mainly taking the form of colonialism. Migrations of people across continents also played an important role, often coupled with invasions, since the pre-colonial era itself. Even now, when the process of globalisation is more pronouncedly economic, it has not eschewed migration of people and cultural interactions. However, while migration of people was the major means of interaction earlier, it is no longer necessary now. Interaction takes place now mainly through media and communications and publicity campaigns. But the term 'interaction' in the present context of globalisation may well have become *passé*. 'Interaction' would have been more relevant in the pre-colonial days, but subsequently it has given way to dominance even in the sphere of culture. While invaders' culture dominated the affected countries in the colonial era, what takes place now is the dominance of market culture in the globalisation era and a replacement of most of the traditional way of life and culture in favour of a homogeneous market culture, where culture itself becomes an instrument of global capitalism. The colonial era permitted some cultural diversity, both because the colonial powers themselves had some distinct boundaries for their colonies and also because they showed some tolerance to local cultures to keep down discontent. The globalised market culture has no such boundaries, nor any inhibitions.

A still broader view of globalisation is about processes taking place in the global eco-system, in which human intervention – more accurately, market intervention – plays an increasing and often adverse role. Migratory birds may have been early 'agents' of globalisation, which started much before human intervention began to make an impact. But that was a part of nature's working, and certainly a harmless or innocent globalisation compared to the present which represents nothing short of marketisation or commoditisation of nature itself.[1] Under its auspices, destructive aspects of economic growth have been intensified significantly and at the global level, like fast shrinking drinking water resources, degradation of land, depletion of ozone layer, climate change, declining capacity of the oceans to absorb excess carbon from the air, depletion of bio-diversity, and increasing extinction of wildlife. Global eco-system knows no political boundaries of countries, since environmental impact of human intervention in one country spreads to other countries too in no time. Normally, however, globalisation is discussed mainly in terms of its narrowest, that is, economic view, but we can hardly afford to close our mind to other aspects.

Precisely because the process of globalisation, in all its three aspects, cuts across political boundaries, it becomes so much more difficult to tackle. Individual countries can always point an accusing finger at others and say: 'They have done it. Let them mend themselves first before we do!' Collective action, which is no easy matter even within a society or country, becomes all the more difficult at the international level. The major difficulty is not that it is impossible, but that political leaders have their fingers deep in the market pie!

Globalisation in the modern, dominantly economic, sense was not an issue of discussion during the days of Gandhiji. Instead, it was colonialism – also a globalising force, which, of course, Gandhiji challenged with all his might with significant success, through his own moral weapons of truth and non-violence. But how would he have looked at the present *avatar* of globalisation? Directly, he may not have commented on this process, but these is a lot in the Gandhian thought which is germane to the present process, and can help in better understanding globalisation through a Gandhian perspective. A Gandhian perspective would not only help us in analysing the nature of globalisation, but also factors and agents behind it, and its impact, and what is more, in finding a solution. The Gandhian perspective gives a set of useful criteria to analyse and assess, rather than *a priori* settled conclusions, leaving his followers to do their own analysis.[2]

Strictly speaking, a scholar ought to go through all 100 volumes of *Collected Works of Mahatma Gandhi* to know his views on any topic. His essential writings are, however, also available at least in two compilations (Iyer 1993; Mukherjee 1993), which have been mainly used for this paper.

It is important to dismiss in the first instance a naive view of Gandhian perspective on this issue. According to this view, since Gandhiji stood for *swadeshi*, *swaraj* and self-reliance, he would have opposed globalisation *per se*. This view offers a settled *a priori* conclusion about globalisation, and with it, about any mechanisation and international trade, particularly imports if not exports. We do not have to labour much to debunk this naïve view before we go to the more correct and sophisticated view of Gandhian thought on the matter. This is because Gandhiji himself debunked this naïve view, which had appeared in his own lifetime. His stand on globalisation *per se* can be summarised in his own famous words:

> I do not want my house to be walled in on all sides and my windows to be stuffed. I want the culture of all lands to be blown about my house as freely as possible. But I refuse to be blown off my feet by any one of them. (quoted in Rolland 2004/1924: 70–71)

Gandhiji conceded the literal meaning of *swadeshi* as using what is locally produced. But he also explained the more important, broader and overriding meaning of *swadeshi* as 'reliance on one's own strength' (cited in Iyer 1993: 362). What he meant was that so long as one relied on own strength, taking care that this strength is not eroded, one was free to use what was produced elsewhere. He warned his followers against making a 'fetish' of *swadeshi*:

> To reject foreign manufactures merely because they are foreign and go on wasting national time and money to promote manufactures in ones' own country for which it is not suited would be a criminal fully and a negation of the *swadeshi* spirit. A true votary of *swadeshi* will never harbour ill-will towards the foreigner, he will not be moved by antagonism towards anybody on earth. *Swadeshism* is not a cult of hatred. (cited in Mukherjee 1993: 78)

Gandhiji's stand on this was made clearer through his distinction between '*swaraj*' (self-rule) and 'independence'. He preferred the former as a better, more inclusive and positive term, which meant freedom of choice and freedom to act, whereas the latter term was rather negative and narrow. It could even imply isolation from the world, which could hardly be any country's goal. He made it clear that 'I do not want India to be a frog in the well, unaware of what happens outside the well' (cited in Iyer 1993: 409). Gandhiji wanted India to become a predominant member of the World Commonwealth (not so much to dominate, as to help other countries and uphold moral values in the world economy and politics) (Iyer 1993: 352–54; Iyer 2000: 348–49).

Gandhiji's first and foremost concern was with the freedom of the individual, since, for him, individual was the basic unit of the economy, polity, and society. A country's freedom has no meaning unless every individual in it has freedom, and this freedom was not just negative (such as freedom from the foreign yoke, freedom from hunger) but positive (to be a free moral agent, free to resist any abuse by authority, and exploitation by others). Gandhiji said,

'*Swaraj* of a people means the sum total of the *swaraj* (self-rule) of individuals' (cited in Iyer 2000: 353). The individual, of course, carried a responsibility not be selfish and be concerned about the welfare of others, as much as her/his own. In stressing the importance of the individual, Gandhiji did not mean an individual in isolation. The individual could freely associate with others in cooperative or collective action. Gandhiji asserted clearly:

> The sum and substance of what I want to say is that the individual person should have the control over the things that are necessary for the sustenance of life. If he cannot have such control, the individual cannot survive. Ultimately, the world is made up only of individuals. (cited in Mukherjee 1993: 289)

Gandhiji's emphasis on individual or on village *swaraj* did not mean exclusiveness and isolation. He made this clear more than once. For example, he said:

> ... every village will be a republic and panchayat having full powers. It follows, therefore, that every village has to be self-sustained and capable of managing its affairs even to the extent of defending itself against the whole world .... Ultimately it is the individual who is the unit. This does not exclude dependence on and willing help from neighbours and from the world .... Such a society is necessarily highly cultured in which every man and woman knows what he and she wants and, what is more, knows that no one should want anything that others cannot have with equal labour. (cited in ibid.: 83)

Gandhiji's insistence on decentralisation was mainly to take care of the individual. This decentralisation was as important in economics through following the principle of 'small is beautiful' as in politics through following the principle of village *swaraj*. Freedom of the individual certainly involved freedom to associate with others on equal terms and form groups, but the latter should not so dominate the individual as to be oppressive. This principle is pertinent in any discussion of globalisation, since multi-national corporations, which, in particular, are so much a part of globalisation, and global capitalism, in general, may well involve oppression of the individual. In a situation where not merely the state but even the civil society and its institutions make way for the market forces, the individual becomes simply a non-entity, despite the formal elections. Gandhian approach would require a check on this danger.

There is evidence to indicate that this danger is not just imaginary but real. For example, globalisation in India appears to have created more jobs in the unorganised or informal sector than in the organised sector, thereby pre-empting unionisation of labour. A more liberal hire-and-fire policy was allowed even in the organised sector. This has weakened trade union movement in India considerably. To the extent that this movement is an inherent part of democracy, democracy itself can be said to have become weak in the process. By curtailing labour rights, the possibility of labour asserting its right to an increased share in the growing national income is also pre-empted. An increase in inequality thus became inevitable. Real democracy is not just a political ornament to be worn only during festivals of elections. Real democracy protects the rights of the underdog and protects their interests.

Since every individual is important, no individual's deprivation can be justified by the enrichment of other individuals, even if they are more than the number of individuals deprived. That is why, in Gandhiji's village republic, there was no place for economic and social inequality or caste oppression. This stress on individual assumes significance in the processes of industrialisation, economic growth, and globalisation. These processes cannot ride on the back of exploitation or exploited individuals, because this would amount to violence. No economic and political or social process should be violent, whether it is industrialisation, mechanisation, urbanisation, or globalisation. And violence means not just injury, but also deprivation. If a process inevitably involves a gain for some and deprivation for others, those who are deprived have to be compensated for their loss of income, livelihood, or welfare, in such a way that they are not only not worse off, but even better off than before, so that all are equal gainers. Unequal gains also constitute injustice and violence, which have no place in a Gandhian system.

This Gandhian requirement or condition has an important implication for development projects as well as economic processes. A compensation mechanism is more easily implemented if those who are deprived are only a few but the gainers from the project/process are large in number, and if the amount of compensation required is smaller than gain. From out of the large gain, the small loss can be easily compensated, and the burden, if it can be so called at all, can be shared by the large number of gainers. If, however, the loss is huge and the gain is small, and if the losers are many and the gainers only a few, then such project has to be just given up. In such a condition, it is impossible to compensate the losers. Though this is economic common sense, with which anybody would agree, complications are introduced right at the planning stage when the few gainers have a political clout and mislead the government into believing that the gainers are large in number and the gains are huge from the project, underestimating deprivation significantly and deliberately. Only the direct economic costs are reckoned in such cases and social costs are ignored or highly underestimated. One has to be careful if this indeed is the case with globalisation too. Are the costs of globalisation, including ecological and cultural costs, borne by the large mass of people huge compared to the gains going only to the elite few? If this is the case, compensating mechanisms and income transfers to the poor and the losers can only be a farce.

To make the matters absolutely clear and simple, Gandhiji gave a criterion, which he called a 'talisman'. He said:

> Whenever you are in doubt, and when the self becomes too much with you, apply the following test. Recall the face of the poorest and the weakest man whom you may have seen, and ask yourself if the step you contemplate is going to be of any use to him. Will he gain anything by it? Will it restore him to a control over his life and destiny? In other words, will it lead to *swaraj* for the hungry and spiritually starving millions? (quoted in Mukherjee 1993: 91)

For Gandhiji and his eminent spiritual disciple, Vinoba Bhave, economic development meant *antyodaya*, the rise and the development of the marginalised and the poorest, and not a mere increase in the per capita income of the country as a whole. They would not mind economic development, but it had to pass this test. In the context of globalisation from a Gandhian view, it is crucial to check if it works mainly in the interest of the elite and the multi-national corporations, with only crumbs offered to the poor.

Globalisation would get Gandhian support only if it is the most effective tool to end poverty and deprivation. But globalisation by itself may not be of much help unless special efforts are made to empower the poor, by equipping them with not only formal literacy but also skills and knowledge, and access to productive assets, credit, and proper markets for their products and services. It will also depend on whether democracy and a voice for the poor is strengthened or weakened by globalisation.[3]

Gandhiji's advocacy for *swadeshi* has to be understood in the light of the above principles preached by him. Gandhiji felt that his test of whether the poorest of the poor are benefited, could have a palpable meaning only in *swadeshi*, as he understood it. He laid down what he called as the 'law of *swadeshi*' for its votary, which was to 'dedicate himself to the service of the immediate neighbours' (Mukherjee 1993: 76). If everyone took care of his immediate neighbourhood and ensured that it is free from injustice, poverty, and deprivation, the world would be a much better place to live in, he thought. He asserted: 'Pure service of ones' neighbours can never from the very nature, result in disservice to those who are remotely situated' (ibid.: 76). Not that he was against any altruism to benefit distant lands and people. The law of *swadeshi* is violated only if such altruism, or for that matter, any economic activity, involves 'a culpable neglect of immediate neighbours' (ibid.). This did not mean making a fetish of *swadeshi*, against which also he warned (ibid.: 78).

Gandhiji looked at the human problem in a holistic way. Economic was only one aspect, and he was equally concerned with the social, political, cultural, and the spiritual. It follows that the impact of globalisation on poverty and deprivation is only one dimension of the consequences to check. Other dimensions to check from a Gandhian perspective would be the impact on environment and the global eco-system, on the freedom of choice of the individual as well as village and a country, status of individual, impact on democracy, cultural diversity, and human rights.

One of the favourite arguments in support of globalisation has been that those who have adopted it, especially export-orientation, have done well in removing poverty, deprivation and illiteracy. A little deeper reflection, however, would show that countries who have made a success of globalisation were politically strong and did not suffer any loss of political strength in the process of globalisation. Countries which had already taken care to remove poverty through land reform, mass literacy, and universalisation of school education did better in this regard, and could thus make a success of globalisation as well. But countries, where local democracies were sabotaged by the vested interests of multi-national corporations, could not be a success story in globalisation. Countries, where their freedom of choice remained in tact, and which had the courage to control and even manipulate globalisation to their advantage, alone made a success of themselves. It is often said by its votaries that globalisation *per se* is benign, but unequal social structures and political strength of countries are another matter altogether, since the latter do not owe their origin to globalisation. Such an argument forgets that globalisation cannot operate in a vacuum, and that it not only can perpetuate but also accentuate inequality within and between countries, if this inequality is not effectively addressed.

The risk of globalisation adversely affecting global environment and the eco-system arises mainly from its inherent tendency to promote limitless consumerism, particularly on the part of the elite and the middle classes. The evidence that globalisation has been promoting widespread vulgar consumption, not so much to meet one's needs as to flaunt one's status, is conspicuous enough. In Gandhian view, unbridled consumerism is morally and spiritually degrading. It diverts the human spirit from nobler purpose of life, and deprives him/her of peace of mind which is necessary for real happiness. It has been promoting an intense rat race between corporations, and between countries, affecting adversely individuals' physical as well as mental health. This pernicious competition is producing impatience, unhealthy rivalry, intolerance, and perpetual discontent with what you have even if you become a billionaire. Increasing violence in the world in all spheres is only a reflection of this spiritual malady.

Consumerism is not spontaneous. It is often induced by business interests, promoting their products. It is the unbridled and unscrupulous variety of capitalism that has to take the primary responsibility for resource depletion. The state is often found to be inept and sometimes too corrupt to counter this. It has been, for example, widely alleged that political leaders are hand in glove with quite a few private mining interests in a particular district of Karnataka. Mining leases may be given for a specific area legally, but the allottees are allowed to illegally mine neighbouring areas also, with the political leaders enjoying a share in the spoils. When 'leaders', who are supposed to be people's protectors, become predators, who can protect ordinary citizens? This is widely believed to be happening. One can see wide ranges of hills levelled down, with the huge dust settled on agricultural fields and forests nearby, and converting the landscape almost into a desert. Most of the iron ore mined is exported, the price of which has increased by eight to ten times within half-a-dozen years. The case above is a concrete example of what globalisation can do to nature.

The crux of this example is that the social costs are largely, if not wholly ignored. The irony is that this is done often in the name of maintaining our competitiveness in the world market! Opencast mining, particularly on catchment slopes, which is environmentally the most destructive, seems to be more prevalent than better types of mining. As a result, rues *State of India's Environment – Citizens' Report 6,* that such mining has played havoc with the nation's water resources (Banerjee 2008: 10). Has it helped the local poor – the 'immediate neighbours'? Has increasing the size of the national cake by these means improved the share of the poor in the cake? The same *Report* also mentions the lands having rich mineral wealth also have rich forest cover, on which a significant number of forest dwellers depend for their livelihood. Ironically, lands with rich resources have also large concentration of poverty! Ironically again, the exploitation of these resources has done hardly anything to reduce this poverty. On the other hand, deprivation has only deepened and widened to cover many fronts. This would be hardly surprising for Gandhiji, because he always insisted that means cannot be justified by ends, and that violent means cannot lead to good results. He observed: 'They say "means are after all means." I would say "Means are after all every thing." As the means are, so is the end' (cited in Iyer 2000: 362).

Following the spread of a western variety of consumerism, globalisation also tends to homogenise culture and even attitudes to life. Individual 'national' cultures tend to obliterate numerous local cultures within a country, and the 'national' cultures themselves tend to conform to a uniform global elitist lifestyle and culture, suppressing diversity, artistic creativity and even freedom in the process. Even if the economic impact of globalisation in terms of employment, poverty, and deprivation is somewhat in dispute, its adverse impact on the global eco-system, on cultural diversity and attitudes to life, seems be so conspicuous as to be beyond dispute. Gandhiji made a trenchant critique of the modern civilisation as early as in 1909 through his booklet *Hind Swaraj* (reproduced in Mukherjee 1993: 3–66). Perhaps his critique of globalisation would have been even more forceful.

It is, however, pertinent to remind ourselves that Gandhiji would not have been against globalisation *per se*. If we could manage globalisation in such a way that we can avoid its adverse impact, he would not be against it. In particular, we need to check if globalisation (i) reduces or aggravates poverty and deprivation, particularly among the poorest; (ii) reduces or aggravates inequality, particularly between the poorest and the rest; (iii) suppresses or protects the individual and his control on his livelihood and freedom of choice; (iv) suppresses or protects democracy, self-rule, and the capacity of countries, represented by their governments, to take care of the welfare of their own citizens in national interest; (v) erodes or protects the cultural diversity of all people, their moral status and their spiritual health; and (vi) erodes or protects the environmental health of the earth, along with its diversity. In Gandhian perspective, all these tests are important.

But, do we have the competence and resourcefulness to control globalisation in a way that local initiatives, cultures, and freedom are not curbed, and the Gandhian individual would be in control of the process, rather than be its helpless victim? Our hope for this lies in strengthening the civil society which can stand up against a corrupt state and make it effectively play its duty-bound role of taming the market forces. And, who can strengthen the civil society except the committed Gandhian individuals, who will not be fooled by the empty promises of global capitalism? Gandhian teaching would require on the part of all individuals vigilance about what is going on around them, courage of conviction, and enough activism and institutional development to take up public causes and strive to enhance the welfare of all.

Interventions and Responses

A. Ramaiah: Are Gandhian teachings and principles relevant to solving the problems of dalits? Would not dalits benefit from globalisation, as it may help them escape from an oppressive local society?

Response: It depends on how far dalits can control the process of globalisation to their advantage and benefit from it. Gandhi opposed untouchability and discrimination against dalits with all his might. His village *swaraj* was based on the principles of equality and non-violence. Both these principles are against the oppression of dalits. Globalisation *per se* may not help dalits to escape from local oppression and inequity, if agricultural labourers and other informal labourers are excluded from its benefits, and if they have no escape from low-paid occupations.

Michael Walton: In emphasising the role of the individual, how did Gandhiji view the problem of reconciling individual freedom with group interests? Is not social action by groups a valid weapon for social change and reform?

Response: Gandhiji was not against collective action at all. In fact, all his life, he was busy mobilising mass opinion and mass action. He could see that group action or collective action is more effective than the actions of isolated individuals. But individuals' association with groups has to be voluntary, and group action should not rob the individual of his dignity as an individual, his creativity and livelihood, and be free from oppression. Gandhiji also emphasised duties more than rights, and the importance of sacrifice on the pant of individuals for the sake of collective welfare, but this had to be moral and voluntary, and not involving oppression and violence.

Notes

1. Michael Buraway (2007) speaks of three waves of marketisation associated with the commodification of labour, money, and land (read, Nature) respectively. In the third wave involving nature, 'every thing is up for sale', 'nothing is sacrosanct' (ibid.: 339), and marketisation is 'truly global in its causes and ramifications' (ibid.: 347), with 'no place to hide from the storm of marketisation' (ibid.: 346–47).
2. Narendar Pani (2001) speaks of the Gandhian method, which he also calls an inclusive method, and according to him, this method has to be distinguished from Gandhiji's theories and judgements. Whether his method can be wholly isolated from his theories and judgements is disputable, but there is something like a Gandhian method which can be applied to situation and problems which may not have prevailed during his times. It has some genorality or universality. The essence of the method is to include all aspects of the problem, and assess both the actual and logically anticipated consequences so as to have a holistic and balanced perspective. In order to minimise the subjective element in such an analysis, it is important to be conscious of and detach oneself from any selfish interests, irrespective whether they are personal interests or interests of the class one belongs to. The Gandhian method is not amoral, but is influenced and guided by his values of truth and non-violence and welfare of the poorest of the poor.
3. These are theoretical conditions. If they are fulfilled in practice, they should have an impact in terms of reduction in poverty. But has poverty actually declined? To test this, this author had earlier made an analysis of cross-country experience, and also of experience over time within a country – India. But the results were not conclusive in the former analysis. As for India, poverty has no doubt tended to decline, even while exports as per cent of GDP and ratio of exports over imports, have both tended to increase (Nadkarni 2002: 559–68). Subsequently, poverty may have declined even more, thanks to the introduction of the National Rural Employment Guarantee Scheme (since renamed as the Mahatma Gandhi National Rural Employment Guarantee Scheme). But, the decline in poverty on the whole has been painfully slow, and inequality has tended to accelerate. Even while absolute poverty may have slightly declined, relative poverty has increased. There is thus no room for complacency.

References

Banerjee, Souparno (ed.). 2008. *State of India's Environment: Citizens' Report 6 – Rich Lands Poor People – Is Sustainable Mining Possible?* New Delhi: Centre for Science and Environment.

Bhagwati, Jagdish. 2004. *In Defence of Globalisation.* New Delhi: Oxford University Press.

Buraway, Michael. 2007. 'The Future of Sociology', *Sociological Bulletin,* 56 (3): 339–54.

Das, Gurcharan. 2000. *India Unbound: From Independence to the Present Global Information Phase.* New Delhi: Penguin.

Iyer, Raghavan. 2000. *The Moral and Political Thought of Mahatma Gandhi,* New Delhi: Oxford University Press.

——. (ed.). 1993. *The Essential Writings of Mahatma Gandhi.* New Delhi: Oxford University Press.

Mukherjee, Rudraugshu (ed.). 1993. *The Penguin Gandhi Reader.* New Delhi: Penguin.

Nadkarni, M.V. 2002. 'Globalise and Grow? – An Empirical Probe', in Raj Kumar Sen and Biswajit Chatterjee (eds.): *Indian Economy: Agenda for the 21st Century.* New Delhi: Deep & Deep, pp. 559–68.

Pani, Narendar. 2001. *Inclusive Economics: Gandhian Method and Contemporary Policy.* New Delhi: Sage Publications.

Rolland, Romain. 2004/1924. *Mahatma Gandhi.* New Delhi: Publications Division, Government of India.

Stiglitz, Joseph E. 2002.*Globalisation and Its Discontents.* London: Penguin.

Part II
Analyses

6

Vulnerability and Globalisation

On Protection, Power, and Identity in India

MICHAEL WALTON

This chapter[1] concerns the interaction between globalisation and vulnerabilities, with a primary focus on what this implies for India. Globalisation is often reckoned to be a source of heightened vulnerabilities, with the poor and the weak most likely to be hurt. Is this true? Does this mean globalisation is a bad thing? Or can it be managed?

Two theses are explored here. The first draws from the core approaches from within economics, though it is not uncontroversial. Globalisation *can* be a source of increased vulnerability, but whether it is so in practice depends on interactions with domestic conditions. In either case, social provisioning for the management of vulnerabilities should be considered a *complement* to the greater dependence on markets, which is a central feature of globalisation, on both efficiency and equity grounds. Public action to manage vulnerability is of rising importance for a country such as India, since the stakes in participation in global markets are rising, with possibly irreversible consequences of stalled or incomplete participation. The state has a central role to play, but design is crucial: alternative designs can either improve or worsen both efficiency and equity. India has experience of both bad and good (or at least promising) designs.

The second thesis goes beyond economics, and argues that both the assessment of vulnerability and likely responses are linked to power and identity – at both the aggregate and local levels. Furthermore, the response to vulnerabilities (whether narrowly economic or linked to identity) is shaped by the structure of agency and associated power structures in a society. Unequal power structures are likely to lead to unequal patterns of neglect, or perverse responses that protect entrenched interests aligned with existing structures of identity or influence. Furthermore, the 'vulnerability of identity' can itself be a source of heightened anxiety and resistance, as support structures associated with existing group-based identities are threatened, even when the terms of recognition are initially unequal. From this general prism, effecting change requires developing the political basis and institutional supports for an efficient design. One interesting route is to move to a rights-based approach, with less emphasis on group-based identity as a mechanism for securing protections. Rights-based approaches have disadvantages, and can lead to new distortions if not well-designed. But they may have an important role in a society that is already highly distorted in terms of institutional functioning. This depends, of course, on how the state implements schemes, and respects (or fails to respect) rights.

This chapter is organised as follows. First, I state why the globalisation–vulnerability nexus is such a hot issue, providing one example – that of financial crises – to illustrate why there is surely *something* behind the prevailing concern. Second, I provide some analytical context in terms of the economics of vulnerability and markets, what this implies for public action and how this may interact with the structures of power and identity. Third, I turn to some history of how societies have responded to the issues raised by this context, suggesting that there are some useful lessons for India from the post-Second World War political consensus that laid the basis for the broadening of welfare states in industrialised countries. Finally, I discuss some design principles and look at the National Rural Employment Guarantee Act (NREGA) through the prism of the preceding analytical narrative.

Why is the Globalisation–Vulnerability Nexus a Hot Issue?

Globalisation attracts fierce proponents and detractors. It has many dimensions. Here, I am concerned primarily with the economic aspects of globalisation, and in particular the effect of increased integration of a country into international markets. In this sense,

India has indeed experienced a large increase in globalisation, especially since the beginning of the 1990s: there has been a large rise in integration with respect to product and capital markets, and, to a much lesser degree, for the labour market. Since 1991, there has been a sharp reduction in the barriers to international trade. As one indicator of effects, the ratio of total trade (exports plus imports) to GDP rose from less than the 15 per cent in 1990–91 to over 38 per cent in 2006–07 (see Figure 6.1). While the capital market is not fully open, there has also been a large increase in portfolio capital and foreign direct investment, with a rise in the share of associated flows from almost zero in the (crisis-affected) beginning of the 1990s to 3 per cent of GDP in 2006–07 (see Figure 6.2). One segment of the labour market has seen substantial international integration – that for the highest level of skills, especially amongst internationally mobile Indians.

Figure 6.1

The ratio of exports and imports to GDP in India, 1980–80 to 2006–07

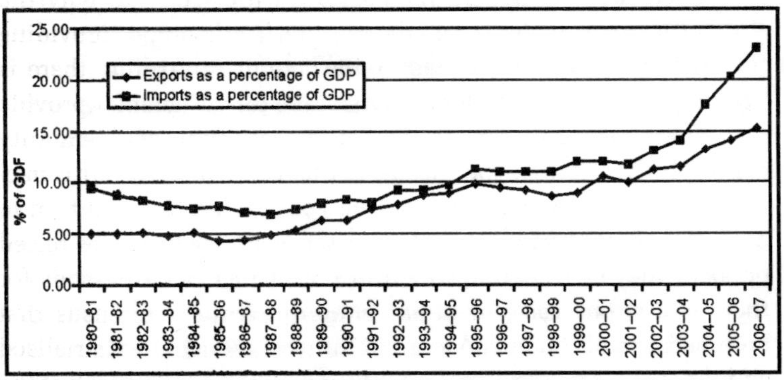

Source: Reserve Bank of India.

Is globalisation associated with increased vulnerability? It is hard to separate increased integration into international markets from the broader market-oriented liberalisation within the domestic market. In India, as in many countries, the processes were proceeding simultaneously. I do not seek to disentangle external and internal effects here, since the core debates of concern can be treated in relation to the joint effects of both processes. Take the following statements of a critical view on globalisation and vulnerability:

Figure 6.2
The ratio of foreign direct investment and portfolio investment to GDP in India, 1990–91 to 2006–07

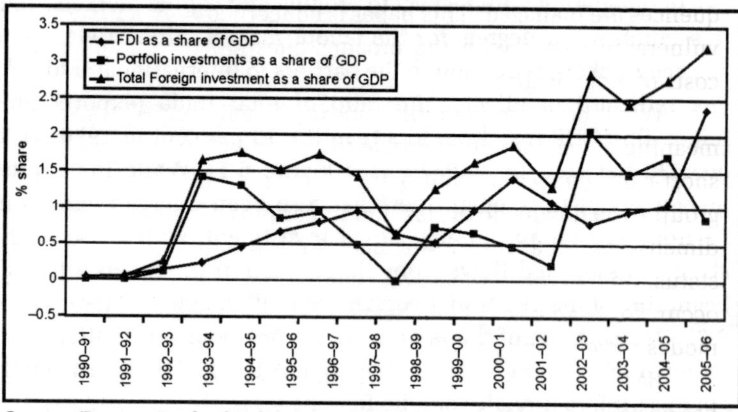

Source: Reserve Bank of India.

(a) Globalisation intrinsically increases vulnerability.
(b) There are pernicious interactions with social inequalities, with subordinate social groups suffering disproportionately.
(c) Globalisation causes a race to the bottom, rewarding countries and industries with less provisioning for vulnerable groups.

These are all present in the anti-globalisation discourse, and can usefully motivate the discussion here. I will argue that there are channels of change that can be *contingently* consistent with each of these statements, but there is no necessary link. Indeed, the opposite may be true. But, whatever the balance of specific effects, there is a strong case for public action to reduce vulnerability – both because of the intrinsic desirability of reducing vulnerability and because well-designed institutions for reducing risk (and design is crucial) are *complements* to the market-oriented development that is intrinsic to the aspects of globalisation of concern here. This matters a lot since increased integration into international markets is a central and powerful route to economic development. This is true of now-industrialised countries, and also vividly true of those countries that have experienced rapid, sustained growth in the more recent era, such as South Korea, China, Malaysia, and Thailand (see the Commission on Growth and Development, 2008, for a recent overview). Where there is variation is in the ways in which integration into international markets is designed, and the degree to which adverse consequences are managed. This paper is concerned only with effects on vulnerability, not with the broader question of the benefits and costs of globalisation.

What does vulnerability mean? I will focus on the core meaning of economic vulnerability: the probability of adverse short-run *changes* in well-being of an individual, household, or group – the downside of risk and uncertainty. This can have many dimensions: changes in incomes and wealth, losses in health status, and adverse effects on dignity and identity. The last may occur, for example, if globalisation leads to changes in traditional modes of work and social interaction.

Basic economic theory suggests insecurity bred of uncertainty has costs: under standard assumptions, individuals are risk-averse, in the sense that individuals put greater weight on changes in incomes at lower levels of wealth – that further implies that declines are more costly for poorer households and individuals.[2] And, for anyone, large declines have a greater welfare cost than the value of equivalent gains. This is consistent with the more immediately compelling perspective from poor people themselves: in the major collation of participatory assessment *Voices of the Poor* (Narayan et al., 2001) insecurity emerged as a pervasive and central concern of poor people. This is not only because adverse events are so costly when people are already suffering from chronic poverty. Adverse shocks can be a *source* of long-term welfare declines, when this leads to distress sales of land or cattle, pulling kids out of school and into work, or long-term effects of loss of work on the employability of workers.

What kinds of shocks matter in India? Some indications are provided by a recent survey in selected villages in Karnataka, Madhya Pradesh, and Orissa (see Figure 6.3). Amongst shocks common to communities ('covariate shocks'), weather-related ones dominate, notably droughts and cyclones. Amongst shocks specific to individual households ('idiosyncratic shocks') health-related shocks are clearly the most important. This study found that shocks affected all parts of the distribution of rural households. Indeed, weather-related shocks were *more* important amongst richer than poorer households, as might be expected from their greater landownership.[3] Health-related shocks are reported more amongst poorer groups. So, vulnerability matters across the distribution. Note, however, that this only refers to the incidence of shocks, not the severity of the consequences of shocks, that are likely to be greater for the poor.

Figure 6.3

Proportion of households reporting major shocks in the preceding year in selected villages in Karnataka, Madhya Pradesh, and Orissa

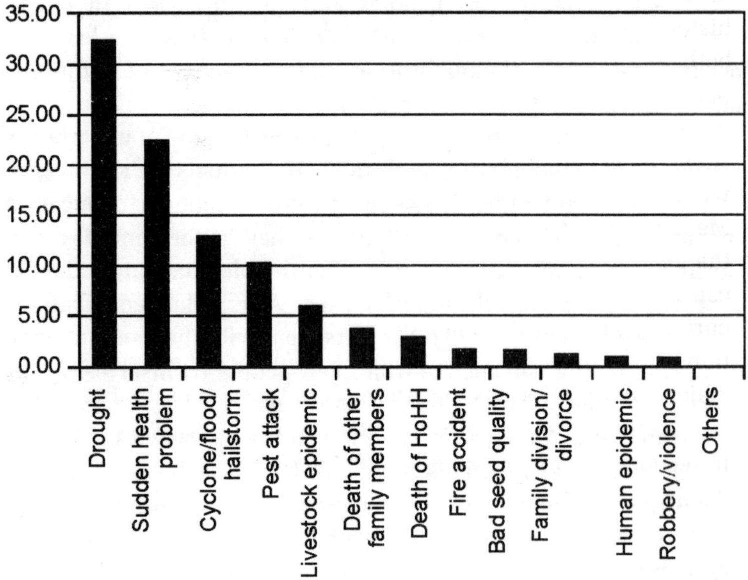

Source: Dev et al. (2007).

An Example: Financial Crises

To motivate the discussion of links with globalisation, let us look at the effects of a very different type of shock: the financial crises of the 1990s, that dramatically affected a range of countries, including, amongst larger cases, Argentina, Indonesia, South Korea, Mexico, Russia, Thailand, and Turkey. This was of particular interest in 2009 in light of the global financial shock that started in the United States, and has parallels with emerging market crises, only with much greater global reach. A financial crisis can be an acute source of vulnerability, both at the level of countries and at the level of households. All of the countries affected in the financial crises of the 1990s had been experiencing an intensification of globalisation through rising integration in both product and capital markets. At the time of its 1995 'Tequila' crisis, Mexico had recently joined the North American Free Trade Agreement (NAFTA), involving a major opening to its rich northern neighbours. The East Asian countries were coming off decades of extraordinary, transformative growth that had brought historically unprecedented reductions in poverty. In each case, both rising trade and growing financial market integration were part of the story. This interacted with domestic financial conditions: domestic financial systems often suffered from weak supervision and regulation, with lots of hidden bad assets and widespread connected lending (most notably in Indonesia in Mexico, but a feature of all cases). While specific channels varied, the general patterns were similar: a sudden stop in international capital flows, the emergence into the open of bad debts and currency mismatches, runs on the currency, and sharp deteriorations in the domestic banking industry, with many banks suffering major liquidity and solvency problems.

In the real economy, currency and financial crises led to falls in economic activities, rising inflation, job losses, real wage declines, and various combinations of rising unemployment or shifts of workers into lower-paying work in the informal sector and agriculture (with particular mechanisms depending on the workings of the local labour market – big rises in unemployment in Argentina, big shifts into informal work in Indonesia and Mexico).

There are plenty of debates over the nature of these crises, ranging from questions over whether greater capital controls can avert or mitigate their effects to the appropriate macro-economic response. Here I have a more limited focus: the interaction between the adverse shocks, distributional effects, the institutional structure of workout design, and the pattern of power in the affected society (see De Ferranti et al., 2004; Halac and Schmuckler 2004). Here is a characteristic sequence:

(a) Prior to the crisis there are weak *ex ante* resolution and protection mechanisms. Rules for deposit protection are often ill-defined, and safety nets are of limited reach. With the partial exception of Argentina and South Korea, there was no unemployment insurance, and other forms of safety nets were not designed to expand swiftly in response to large wage and employment shocks.

(b) As the crisis is brewing, richer and better informed domestic actors get their money out faster – and indeed this can be a catalyst for the crisis itself. This was clearly the case for Argentina and Mexico, for example (Halac and Schmukler 2004). Those who got their money out to Miami or New York before the currency and other asset prices tumbled actually stood to achieve substantial capital *gains* with respect to domestic asset values as the crisis unfolded. Money of the wealthy also fled from Indonesia.

(c) After the financial crisis occurs, substantial amounts of public money are spent on financial sector workouts – with estimates of the order of 19 per cent of GDP for Mexico, 27 per cent of GDP for South Korea, and 50 per cent of GDP for Indonesia for the crises of the 1990s (Honohan and Klingebiel 2003). This is undertaken ostensibly to save the banking system from systemic effects, which could hurt all kinds of economic activity. But these workouts benefit participants within the banking system – depositors and often owners – at the expense of those outside the system (Halac and Schmukler 2004). Financial sector participants are typically richer, and in the case of owners, very much richer, than the bulk of the population.

(d) A few workers who lose jobs may get severance payments (if the firms do not go bankrupt) or unemployment insurance (where it exists). But, for the most part, workers, and their families are hardest hit by the crisis in the short term, squeezed by job loss, falling wages, and rising prices. Indeed, crises can be seen as functioning as a mechanism for resolution of distributional struggles that are not effectively worked out in normal times (Diwan 2001). The bill for bailout costs comes in the form of higher taxes or lower public spending on goods and services, typically spread out over many years as the stock of bailout-related debt is paid down.

(e) The immediate shock to the labour market induces a range of individual, household and community-based adjustment mechanisms: movement to informal sector work (important in Mexico), back to agriculture (in Indonesia and Thailand), increased labour force participation of women and children, reduced spending on 'inessential' items, such as consumer durables, better quality foods, clothes, and even health and education spending.

What do we take away from this sequence of events? First, in this example, international integration (here in financial markets) is indeed part of the causal structure of the crisis. Countries that were weakly integrated in international financial markets – very poor African countries, for example – were little affected by this form of crisis. Those who retained significant capital controls, such as China and India, were also shielded from contagion effects. This does not mean international financial integration is a bad thing: both country cases and cross-country evidence support the view that such integration is an important source of long-term economic growth. But it raises questions over the timing and design of such integration. For example, you need a robust and well-regulated domestic financial system before full opening.

Second, in the absence of credible, politically supported *ex ante* loss-allocation mechanisms, the interaction between unequal structures of influence and a crisis is very likely to lead to inequitable *ex post* workouts. The wealthy have more information on the evolution of economic variables (in this case financial and currency values), more options to manage shocks through portfolio diversification (for example, through access to bank accounts in Miami or Singapore), and greater influence over domestic public support at a time in which public resources are declining and demands are rising. If there are no rules, the reaction of the government is a function of where short-run influence is most effective. Almost all scramble to strengthen safety nets, but, with the probable exception of South Korea, these were inadequate to the task of protecting those hurt.[4] The size of fiscal resources devoted to financial sector workouts were typically much larger than any spending on safety nets (as they will surely be in the workouts in rich countries in the wake of the 2008 financial crisis). There is a direct parallel with bankruptcy legislation. One of the motivations for the introduction of bankruptcy laws in the United States was to define *ex ante* the rules of the game when a firm became insolvent; otherwise, the powerful used their influence to extract most benefits, or minimise losses (Rajan and Zingales 2003).

Third, sophisticated household adjustment mechanisms do exist, but these are incomplete, and especially so with respect to common shocks that affect whole communities or countries.

Analytical Context: Economics, Power, and Identity

Let us start by placing the problem of vulnerability in the context of the analytics of market functioning and government responses. Economic vulnerability is a symptom of market failures, but both its nature and the responses depend on interactions with social structure and politics. Getting clear on this provides a useful basis for assessing the interaction with globalisation.

Vulnerability: (In Part) a Product of Market Failure

A central insight from economics is that economic vulnerability is linked to market failures. When a farmer suffers from a bad harvest, or a worker falls ill, with attendant costs of health treatment and lost wages, the underlying problem is of the absence of efficient insurance markets in a world of uncertainty. All households face the prospect of a range of possible outcomes: on the rains, prices, the health of household members, employment availability, and so on. Bad outcomes are disproportionately costly relative to equivalent good outcomes,[5] both because of their intrinsic impact on welfare, and because short-run shocks may lead to depletion of physical or human assets and have long-term effects. The standard view is that most people are risk-averse: they consequently pursue production and investment strategies that lead to lower risk, but also lower return, outcomes. This might, for example, involve choosing more drought-resistant crops, diversifying the occupational and schooling activity of kids, or the spatial location of family members.

If there were perfect insurance markets, in which households could purchase an actuarially fair insurance for bad weather, bad prices, or bad health outcomes, the cost of adverse shocks would be significantly lower. This is for two reasons: the well-being of households would be protected in the event of a bad outcome; and there would not be biases in favour of low-risk, low-return activities. But perfect insurance does not exist, for a set of reasons around imperfect information and limitations on contracting. Insurers may not be able to tell if a household is a good or bad risk (and so end up charging a premium that good risks would not pay, the problem known as adverse selection), insurance can lead to riskier behaviour (known as moral hazard), and transactions costs can be very high, especially in verification of small adverse events and catching false claims.

Households adapt to uncertainty through a variety of mechanisms. These can be put into three broad categories that I highlight here, since they are also useful for thinking about public action:

(i) *Ex ante* action to *reduce* risks. This includes actions designed to reduce the variability of incomes. It can include investing in risk-reducing assets, such as irrigation, choosing more drought-resistant crops, and diversification of individual and household activities across plots, occupations, spatial location, even marriage choices.

(ii) *Ex ante* action that *prepares for* shocks. In this category, income variability is not affected, but households take precautionary action that allows them to consume more, or (more broadly) achieve better outcomes, when adverse shocks occur. Savings in the form of financial assets, cattle, gold, or other assets are common mechanisms of 'consumption-smoothing' at the level of households. Insurance also falls into this category, with the important added feature of pooling of risks across individuals or households. It can involve the purchase of a formal insurance policy, or the informal community-based mechanisms, that may be implicit.

(iii) *Ex post coping* after shocks occur. Finally, when a shock occurs, households adopt a variety of strategies to adjust to the circumstances. This often involves selling assets, borrowing, getting help from friends and family, or increasing labour supply (especially of women and children).

All of these mechanisms have been documented for India. Households and communities have developed sophisticated mechanisms for managing risks. In some village studies, researchers have found that informal risk-management mechanisms seem to have a large impact, reducing the impact of income fluctuations on the consumption of individual households (Townsend 1994). However, these purely household- and community-based mechanisms have costs and are typically incomplete. Risk-reducing investment and occupational strategies are generally also lower return. Of course, some activities are higher return *and* lower risk. These are highly desirable – and particularly interesting from the point of view of directions for innovation – but these are not the difficult and interesting questions for the discussion here. Similarly, savings strategies intrinsically involve foregoing current consumption, and often in investing in low-return assets. Moreover, if a shock affects a lot of people at the same time, assets such as livestock are likely to experience price declines, or capital losses, precisely when most needed. Community-based insurance is particularly bad at handling such common shocks (bad rains that hurt all farmers, an aggregate price or employment shock) and catastrophic shocks (that have a drastic influence on wealth and livelihoods).

Market Failures around Risk and the Structure of Inequality and Deprivation

The costs of shocks and adaptation mechanisms vary systematically across wealth and socio-cultural categories. Households with less wealth and lower status are often systematically more vulnerable to adverse shocks. This is for several reasons. As they are poorer, the welfare cost is intrinsically higher. Sheer necessity may have led them to work in riskier occupations: many of the poor depend disproportionately on rainfed agriculture and irregular informal work. At the same time, personal and social mechanisms for managing risk have a weaker resource pool to draw upon, because social contacts are also likely to have less wealth. The poor have fewer savings to draw down or assets to sell. Informal insurance mechanisms may be less effective: while some poor communities have well-developed social networks (often termed 'social capital') with significant risk-sharing, the scope for mutual help is limited when it is amongst poor people. Furthermore, where risk management is embedded in unequal relations, this can have high implicit costs: borrowing from traders or moneylenders to manage shocks can carry high explicit or implicit interest rates; or a long-term labour relationship with an employer (say a local landowner) can reduce risk, since employment is more reliable, at the cost of lower bargaining power and the potential humiliations of an asymmetric relationship.

Inequalities in both exposure to risk and the capacity to manage risk can thus be a source of the *perpetuation* of inequality, and so of poverty – poorer and subordinate groups with greater vulnerability to risk consequently also have weaker prospects for improving their livelihoods through pursuing higher return activities and investing in their human or other economic assets. There are many other reasons for the persistent of inequalities; vulnerability is part of the mix.

The Structure of Vulnerability and the Structure of Identity

Inequalities between different *groups* are often of keen interest. Economic vulnerability can differ between groups with distinct social identities – for example, across castes, language, religion, or gender. The historical restriction of scheduled castes to lower-status occupations not only reduced their returns but also increased risk, since it reduced possibilities for occupational diversification, often confined these groups to more hazardous work, and made economic relations with employers systematically and fundamentally asymmetric in terms of power. The nature of social networks and norms of sharing or helping is often linked to group-based identities –with greater reciprocity and risk-pooling within groups. Of course, what constitutes a group will itself vary: it may extend to an extended family, a broader kinship group, a village.

This relates to a further point: it may be tempting to take identity as given in looking at identity–vulnerability interactions. However, identities are intrinsically socially formed, products of group-based interactions, and the nature of vulnerability can itself shape the nature and functioning of a social identity. This has been extensively documented for the evolution of social norms amongst societies that have to manage common pool resources (Baland and Platteau 1996). In many cases –fishing, for example – these also involve occupations with high levels of risk, with associated norms of mutual help. These internalised norms are constituent elements of the identity structure. I come below to the question of how globalisation can influence this, and how the vulnerability of identity itself can shape behaviours.

The Case for Public Action on Vulnerability

So, the point of departure is an uncertain world with inadequate options for precautionary savings and insurance, bred of market failures, that typically hurts poorer and subordinate groups more and can be a source of the persistence of inequalities. This, surely, provides a classic rationale for public action, but one in which the choice between making markets work better or substituting for markets should be a pragmatic one: what works best, including on grounds of equity, to deal with the problem at hand? And, indeed, there is a long tradition of government effort. We can use the categorisation from above, and apply this to public action:

(a) *Ex ante action* to *reduce risks*. There are many investments that are typically financed and undertaken by governments, because of their public good characteristics, in which risk reduction is a central element: irrigation schemes, other water management projects, and road networks, all fall into these categories. Note that these are often *complements* to market interactions.

(b) *Ex ante action that prepares for shocks*. As noted, household savings are an important adaptation mechanism, but one for which the costs and options may be inadequate, especially for the poor. This has an immediate corollary: a central, *market-thickening* mechanism to support better risk management is the broadening and deepening of financial systems. Broadening matters, since the reach to poorer households is crucial. Depth matters in the specific sense of having the liquidity, regulatory, and supervisory structures such that financial system is itself resilient to shocks – as vividly illustrated in the case of financial crises, including the 2008–09 financial implosion in rich countries. This also can involve specific action to protect poorer and middle groups, such as deposit insurance for small depositors, and support for the expansion of the microfinance institutions (that are often not deposit-takers, but can be a source of borrowing to smooth consumption). Insurance is trickier: getting market thickening through private insurance is fine, but runs into the classic problems of adverse selection, moral hazard, and transaction costs that intrinsically bedevil this sector, making market-based solutions for higher risk and poorer groups harder to devise. This is why industrialised countries mostly developed solutions with greater reliance on public enforcement or delivery, especially for unemployment, health and old age.

(c) *Ex post coping after shocks occur.* Public action can, finally, support coping after shocks occur through a variety of transfer schemes, including feeding programmes, subsidies, workfare, and cash transfers. Take Indonesia after the 1997–98 financial crisis: it introduced a range of 'safety net' programmes, which included subsidies to keep the price of low quality rice down, school-based transfers to keep poorer kids in school, and public works programmes (Pritchett et al. 2003).

This is fine in principle: there is a strong rationale for public action, and an array of instruments available, many of which have been tried in India. So, why are there such pervasive concerns, in India and throughout the developing world, that vulnerabilities are unacceptably high, even before we get into the globalisation debate?

Public Action Embedded in an Unequal Political Economy of Policy Choice and Implementation

The real problem is that governments also typically do a bad job of provisioning for security. This is sometimes framed in terms of the intrinsic likelihood of 'government failure'. Governments are not run by rule-bound Weberian bureaucracies, implementing the policies of politicians, who in turn faithfully represent the interests of all the people. But that only pushes back the question of why governments fail to effectively act in an area where there is a compelling rationale for extensive action. The Indian state does have significant capacity. Think of the impressive performance in running elections. Or take a more mundane example of the railways: trains are typically crowded and often late, but, to first order, the railways delivers on its aims, of transporting an extraordinary quantity of people and goods to their intended destinations, employing over 1.5 million staff to do so. If India had a social protection system that delivered as well as the Indian railways, the household level security of the bulk of the population would be radically different from now. Providing risk-management services is undoubtedly more complex – in part for some of the reasons that private insurance is hard, that were noted above. But, as argued by Jean Drèze and Amartya Sen (1990) amongst others, the international experience displays substantial variation in the extent to which governments do and do not take effective action in provisioning for security.

The core issue lies in the political economy of delivery of public services in an unequal society, and how this interacts with, and helps shape, state capacity. I highlighted above the links between inequalities and the capacity of different groups to manage risk. Political and economic elites usually have many options for managing the risks they face: either because of the assets they hold, or because they are in a better position to extract discretionary support from the state when shocks occur, as in the example of bailouts in financial crises. The two big questions are: (i) under what circumstances are political elites willing to choose policies and institutions that provision for security?, and (ii) what does this imply in terms of organisational designs that ensure the associated services actually get delivered?

The answer to the first question is closely linked to the political salience of demands from middle and poorer groups for provisioning. Under democratic auspices, this essentially amounts to the question of how effective democratic processes are in capturing and aggregating the interests and preferences of these groups, and then matching the demands with technical analysis of alternative policy and institutional designs. India presents a highly mixed picture here. On the one hand, it became a democracy at an unusually low level of income, and the poor are disproportionately more active voters. But, on the other hand, it has also been described as a 'patronage democracy' (Chandra 2004), in which political processes are dominated by the provision of goods and services to particular groups (sometimes on identity-based lines) in return for political support.

The answer to the second question is more complex, and depends on the functioning of the state. 'State capacity' is not a free-floating feature of governments, but a product of the interaction between organisational schemes within the state, including internal checks and balances, and societal functioning. Delivering front-line services, where officials have discretion of who to deliver services and how much, presents particular challenges (World Bank 2003). The prevalence of patronage structures leads to fundamental distortions in this, especially where there are substantial incentives for corruption, that is especially when internal and societal structures of accountability are weak. This is clearly the case for India.

The political economy of social security provisioning in an unequal society can thus be a source of malaise. Two malaises are common: 'neglect' and 'distortion'. Both are relevant to India and flow directly from her political and social characteristics.

By *neglect* I mean the failure to effectively deliver well-designed services where these are justified on either efficiency or equity grounds. Here, India again presents a mixed picture. As a democracy in which the votes of middle and poorer groups count – and, furthermore, a country born with the ideological aspiration of assuring equal opportunity for all – there has been plenty of action, and spending, across all three categories of risk-related policy areas: (i) risk-reducing measures such as irrigation systems; (ii) efforts to get banking services to the rural poor; and (iii) a long list of social protection programs that seek, at least in part, to reduce the vulnerability of the poor (even though some are really focused on chronic poverty.) But there remain massive areas of neglect. The bulk of rural households remain outside the formal financial system. Politically-driven *ad hoc* measures, such as the 2008 loan waiver, suffer from fundamental design flaws that will perpetuate financial exclusion. The state has a dismal record on providing for health risks. And, prior to the National Rural Employment Guarantee Act (of which more later), measures to deal with the high level of employment and wage risk in rural areas were inadequate, with some partial exceptions, such as the Maharashtra Employment Guarantee Scheme.

Distortions in the many programmes that do exist is a more typical feature of India's efforts (though neglect is often the consequence, when programmes fail to reach their intended beneficiaries). Distortion flows from the interaction with structures of patronage and local corruption, and can be sharpened by design flaws, in which poorly designed programmes are sustained because of entrenched interests and populist pressures. Take two cases from different categories of risk management action: water management and provision of food.

Water management is one of the most important areas for reducing weather-related agricultural risks – the major source of covariate risks for rural households from the survey work reported above. Investment in large-scale irrigation has been a major element of agricultural strategy, and the management of the irrigation system is an important activity of the Indian government. But there are significant failings in this process. In an in-depth study from the 1980s, Robert Wade (1985) documents how behaviour of government officers is shaped by considerations of maximising private returns from bribes (derived from discretionary delivery of water to farmers), and seek more lucrative posts on this basis. This, in turn, supported informal market for jobs, based on the expected returns to the position. It is unsurprising that there have been inadequacies in the provisioning and management in irrigation, and essentially private provisioning of water, through drilling of wells for groundwater, has become the major source of expansion in managed water use for agriculture. (This has led to a new set of common pool problems, with major problems of falling water tables in many parts of India, and thus new vulnerabilities for the future.)

In terms of direct provisioning of food, the Public Distribution System (PDS), by far the largest programme, is a genuinely massive effort to provide subsidised food through dedicated shops throughout the country. This programme may provide some security against food price inflation, but is otherwise weakly designed to deal with shocks, is highly ineffective at reaching the poor, and suffers from large-scale leakage (Radhakrishna and Subbaro 1997).

There is not the space here to provide details: the point is to highlight the sharp contrast between major governmental effort, oriented toward different aspects of the risk management policies framed above, and the very poor job of real risk reduction or management. The designers – and many of the managers – were, and are, undoubtedly sincere in their intentions, but effectiveness has been undercut either by poor design, or, more systematically, by distortions in the functioning of government.

Globalisation and Vulnerability

This may have seemed a lengthy detour from our core interest in interactions between globalisation and vulnerability, but it is precisely the interaction between global forces and domestic institutions that is of interest. There are essentially two questions: (i) does globalisation lead to increased vulnerability?, and (ii) does globalisation change the capacity of the state to effectively provision for vulnerability? The answer to both is: it depends. This answer is not a cop-out, for we can now put some more structure on it. In particular, there is a case for what might be termed a strong, but contingent, *complementarity* between globalisation and the provisioning of social security. It is contingent in two ways: on effective design; and on the interaction between globalisation and the structure of power and social identity in a society, here argued to be an underlying driver of the state's willingness and capacity to provision.

Writing in 2009, it may seem patently obvious that globalisation is a source of larger adverse shocks. International markets for oil and food have been a source of big increases in import bills and prices of essential commodities, that only fell when the global recession got under way. And, the credit crunch, which originated in the sub-prime mortgage market in the United States, spread viciously around the world, either through direct effects on financial institutions who had to write down assets linked to the crisis, or through indirect effects on both economic activity and increased risk aversion in international financial markets. India was relatively shielded from direct effects, but felt the indirect effects both through international financial market channels and lower demand for exports from rich countries.

However, recall the two main sources of shocks reported by rural households in India are weather- and health-related (see

Figure 6.3). Neither of this is directly affected by globalisation.[6] Indeed, the big concern in 2009 was, correctly, the effects of the delayed monsoon. Nor was price volatility an invention of more integrated markets. Indeed larger markets lead to lower price volatility, other things equal, though greater integration can lead to faster transmission of international price changes.

What of outcomes? Let us look at India's macro numbers, and take 1991 as the year in which the process of opening received a big, initial push. There is no evidence to support the view that opening led to increased vulnerability at the macro level: total output continued to grow rapidly in the 1990s (consolidating the growth acceleration that occurred in the 1980s) and then increased again in the 2000s. There was no year of negative growth. Or, if we take either general or food inflation, the story is of steady decline in the average rate of change and lower fluctuations around this average (see Figure 6.4 for general inflation; food inflation displays a broadly similar pattern). Some of the success in avoiding increased fluctuations at the macro-economic level is due to the avoidance of premature capital account opening, and reasonably prudent macro management (though there is a case for arguing that the biggest faults of the macro policy are too tight a monetary stance, inducing excessive slowdowns [see Bhalla 2009]). This highlights the complementarity between opening and domestic policy and institutions, and the need to tailor sequencing to domestic conditions – especially the depth and resilience of the domestic financial system.[7]

Figure 6.4

India's Inflation Rate, 1970–71 to 2006–07

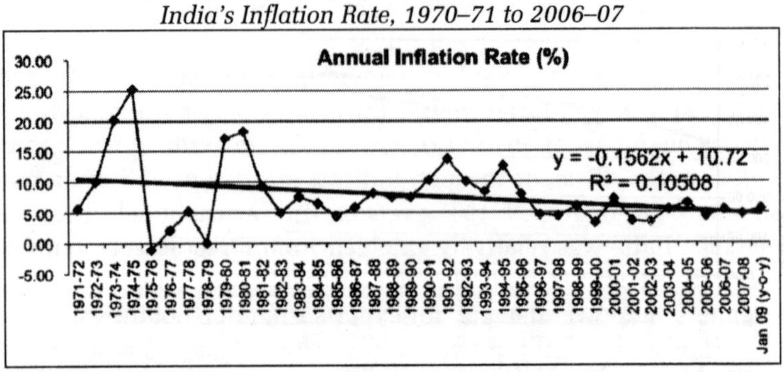

Source: Reserve Bank of India.

These indicative macro-economic numbers do *not* mean all is well. One issue concerns the management of external shocks when they do occur. But I would emphasise two more fundamental issues. First, vulnerability manifests itself at the micro and local level. Occasionally, an economy-wide shock occurs that has society-wide consequences. But, more commonly, the shocks captured in villagers' responses in Figure 6.3 are individual or local.

Second, it is *desirable* to support the creation and destruction of activities as an intrinsic element of the process of economic transformation. Globalisation is likely to accelerate this – and indeed led to shakeouts in some industries in India in the 1990s, alongside positive aggregate industrial growth. Here, there is indicative evidence of significant labour market adjustment in the organised industrial sector in the restructuring of the late 1990s. Both real wages and employment in this sector peaked around 1996–98 and then fell significantly, to levels prevailing a decade earlier (see Figure 6.5). We do not know where laid-off workers moved to, but this is *prima facie* evidence of significant welfare losses for both those who retained and those who lost jobs. The implication is that openness leads to an increased case for some risk management instruments, both on welfare grounds, since there can be transition costs when jobs or activities contract, and on political economy grounds to maintain support for the process of economic change.

Figure 6.5

Real wages per worker and employment in India's organised industrial sector, 1981–82 to 2004–05

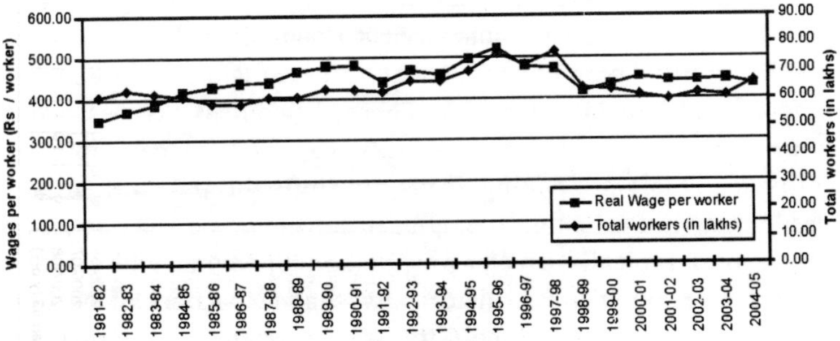

Source: Annual Survey of Industries Data Base.

This brings us to the second question: does openness reduce the capacity of governments to provision for risks? This is part of the broader question of whether openness implies smaller governments. Here, there is a striking empirical result from the cross-country patterns. Dani Rodrik (1998) finds that more open economies tend to have *larger*, not smaller, governments, and interprets this in terms of the greater need (welfare or political) to provide social insurance with greater openness, to the extent the latter is associated with either higher shocks or a more intensive process of creation and destruction. There is also evidence that this relationship is causal.[8] Peter Lindert (2004) cites evidence that this relationship also held in the historical evolution of industrialised countries, with those countries exposed to more external risks undertaking greater state-mediated provisioning for risks.

This empirical result is consistent with the specific experiences of developing societies that have been integrating into the global economy. South Korea, for example, a case of major insertion into international markets, increased central government spending from 14 per cent of GDP in 1995 to over 21 per cent in 2005 (World Bank 2008). The government had already embarked on expanded social insurance in the 1990s and undertook major *extensions* on provisioning for short-run vulnerabilities in the wake of the 1997–98 financial crisis.

How then does globalisation and vulnerability interact with local structures of power and identity? The relationship is ambiguous. Opening may undermine established political and social structures or those with more initial power, wealth and social status may benefit the most.

Let us focus on the question of unequal, culturally shaped identities, in relation to caste, tribal status, religion, and often also language and region of origin. These differences are associated with inequalities of work, education, asset ownership, and influence. Market opening leads to shifts in the structure of production and consumption, greater movement between jobs and places, and, typically, greater rewards for education. This can be a force for breaking down historically shaped barriers of occupational and educational mobility across groups. Examples are changes in the caste composition of new entrepreneurs, with Other

Backward Castes, and Brahmins for that matter, entering business activities from which they were historically excluded (Damodaran 2008). It is also reflected in *dalits* moving into activities from which they were previously excluded.

However, new market activities can also become an additional field in which those with initially greater influence, status, or wealth gain most. This has the potential to lead to further rounds of domination and difference, along the lines of group-based inequalities. There is evidence of continued discrimination in the private sector against individuals from both lower caste and Muslim backgrounds: this comes both from in-depth interviews, and from the research technique of sending equivalent resumés to the same employer, except for names signalling caste or religious status. Applicants with lower caste and Muslim names were significantly less likely to be called for interview (Thorat and Attewell 2007).

A further example of the complexity of interactions between market-driven change and social structure comes from Kaivan Munshi and Mark Rosenzweig's (2006) analysis of the interaction between educational expansion and gender in Mumbai. Traditionally, caste-based networks were linked to traditional occupations, especially for working class boys. These were in turn linked to education in local language schools. Munshi and Rosenzweig examine the effects of the increases to returns to English education in non-traditional, white-collar jobs in the 1990s. They find that boys tended to continue to be channelled into local language schools, in line with traditional, caste-based network patterns, but that lower-caste girls, who had not benefited from such networks in the past, took much greater advantage of English education. In this case, increased marketisation – indirectly of globalisation – was breaking one kind of traditional social differentiation, around gender, even while the caste-based system was impeding change for boys.

Then, what is interesting is the potential intersection of two kinds of vulnerabilities. First, there is the overlay of economic vulnerability on the structure of social differentiation. One way that this can happen is if a more marketised economy leads to a decline in informal, insurance mechanisms that are related to the group-based identity. This is potentially either insurance amongst households within a particular group, or embedded in labour, credit, or land contracts between individuals in different groups. While the latter can be asymmetric in terms of power and status they are often structured to provide (implicit) insurance: for example, on a guarantee of work from a landlord, in return for a lower wage; or, in the provision of credit for consumption, in return for a higher, explicit or implicit, interest rate. If such informal contracts decline in importance, households could become more vulnerable to adverse shocks – and this can map on to the pattern of group-based identity. Similar considerations apply when greater marketisation leads to increased variance in income in response to a shock, as when greater input-intensity, especially if credit-financed, leads to large declines in net returns in the face of drought. This has been a source of rise in suicides in some parts of India in recent years – though the incidence of suicides has been mainly amongst farmers, rather than landless labourers.

Second, there can be interactions between market opening and the pattern of identity itself. Social identities are not static phenomena, but are shaped by social interactions. As already noted, this can sometimes lead to a reduction in the salience of historically shaped patterns of social differentiation, where markets are 'blind' to patterns of identity. However, this is not necessarily the case. Markets are also socially embedded, and market participants often use group membership as a sign of a particular type – and this can potentially become self-enforcing. Glenn Loury (2002) discusses this in the context of race for the United States, though he argues that questions of stigma are even more important in perpetuating difference. But, the point here is that the interaction can lead to identity changes, and these can potentially lead to sharpening of identity structures, as opposed to softening of social differentiation. Manuel Castells (1997) develops the concept of 'reactive identities', in which seemingly traditional patterns of identity are actually highly contemporary phenomena, shaped in response to new developments. As one example, he uses the Zapatista movement in the southern Mexican state of Chiapas – an identity formed in response, he argues, to the combination of social exclusion and political neglect, and one that took as part of its structure resistance to globalisation, symbolically initiating its revolt on 1st January 1994, the day that Mexico joined NAFTA. While every movement is different, there are probably parallels with the identity of Maoist/Naxalite movements in India, which also have an anti-market ideology. I refer below to how the design of NREGA can be seen as supporting and more universal conception of citizenship, and so of identity.

Following this brief review of issues, let us revisit the three 'anti-globalisation' statements introduced earlier:

(i) *Globalisation intrinsically increased vulnerability.* There is no *intrinsic* link with vulnerability, but there can be channels of causation in which this occurs. Indeed, it is actually highly *desirable* that globalisation be associated with domestic processes of creation and destruction in order for the growth benefits to be realised. Social provisioning to manage vulnerability always matters, but is even more important with greater international integration.

(ii) *There are pernicious interactions with social inequalities, with subordinate social groups suffering disproportionately.* This is far from clear, and may go in either direction, where demands of the market help break down entrenched, unequal structures of social difference, especially when combined with the influence of ideas and information from globalising forces. However, it *is* often the case that the greatest gains from globalisation are reaped by those best equipped to respond, in terms of education, physical capital, and connectivity. This reinforces the case for public action to level *up* the playing field. There can also be unexpected interactions with the structure of identity with heightened anxiety from economic vulnerability.

(iii) *Globalisation causes a race to the bottom, rewarding countries and industries with less provisioning for vulnerable groups.* There is no general evidence that this is the case, though there are specific examples. An important example of negative interactions comes in mining experiences, where there is extensive anecdotal evidence that mining is associated with substantial displacement of poor groups and environmental degradation. There is evidence for this in India; in the extreme, this can lead to heightened violence (Bhushan and

Hazra 2008). However, the more striking correlation is of the complementarity between social provisioning and greater openness. This is further supported by looking at the experience of industrialised countries, to which I now turn.

What did Industrial Countries Do? Are there Lessons from History?

Can history provide insights for India? The story of social provisioning for now-industrialised countries is one of a large, long-term increase in both reach and associated public spending, especially in the 20th century (Lindert 2004). It is also a story in which the rising voices of middle and poorer groups were a central driver of change. And it is one in which the extension of the state into supporting risk management went hand in hand with the deep increase in international integration. Take the most extreme example: by the end of the 20th century the Scandinavian states ranked around the top, *both* on the social spending scales amongst industrialised countries (and so in the world) *and* on competitiveness scales by bodies such as the World Economic Forum, that are far from being socialist in inclination! There are indeed plenty of specific debates over the efficiency costs of particular designs, and periodic significant reforms, but this has occurred within the broader context of a first-order *combination* of expanded social provisioning to manage risks *with* globalisation.

The contemporary Scandinavian benchmark is interesting, since it shows that even massive spending and tax involvement can be consistent with high levels of openness and high productivity. But more immediately relevant to India and other developing countries is earlier history. Bismarck is often credited with being the original designer of measures to manage the risks faced by workers, with the introduction of accident, sickness, and old age insurance during the 1880s. Two things are interesting about the Bismarckian reforms. First, these were a reformist response to the revolutionary threat from Germany's Marxist Social Democratic Party – such a threat is one way of expressing voice. Second, they were tied to labour contracts: sickness, accident, disability, and old age insurance were all mandated benefits, shared by employers and employers. This much-copied model is highly problematic for most developing countries, both on equity grounds, since it confines benefits to workers with such formal labour contracts (that applies to many, but not all, workers in India's 'organised' sector) and on efficiency grounds, since it tends to raise the costs of formalisation, and increase resistance to job losses for those who have a formal sector job. This has become a central problem for middle-income countries, such as Mexico, significantly complicating the politics and economics of both social policy and labour market reform. When formal sector protection is tied to the labour contract, the – otherwise desirable – extension of social protection to the informal sector amplifies the incentives to stay informal, with potentially significant static and dynamic efficiency costs.[9]

An alternative model that emerged in the first half of the 20th century involved directly government-mediated social provisioning. A good example is the United Kingdom. The Beveridge Report (Beveridge 1942) was conceived and written in the middle of the Second World War, and formed the basis for the post-war settlement, at a highly propitious moment for a new social compact: the right to vote had been extended to all women only in 1928, and this combined with the unusually high degree of solidarity bred of the war itself, including between the working and middle classes. Also relevant was the fact that the measures were partly sold on the basis of the need to support the competitiveness of British industry, through the state taking care of social provisioning. Note, for example, the principles on which the report opens:

> Proposals ... should not be restricted by considerations of sectional interests .... Organisation of social insurance should be treated as one part only of a comprehensive policy of social progress .... Social security must be achieved by co-operation between the State and the individual. The State in organising security should not stifle incentive, opportunity, responsibility... (ibid.: 1)

Actual provisioning included the universal National Health Service, unemployment insurance and old-age pensions. All of these were revenue-financed and involved generalised rights of all citizens.

While there was a wholesale expansion in social provisioning to manage risks across the industrialised world, there were differences. Scandinavia and then Continental Europe developed the highest level of provisioning, followed by the United Kingdom, and then, some way behind, the United States and Japan. In exploring the reasons for both the generalised increase and the variation, Lindert (2004) emphasises five factors:

(i) increased voice – with the consolidation of democracy,
(ii) need – with the aging of the population,
(iii) globalisation – with the rise in felt needs to manage change,
(iv) rising income per capita – providing resources for provisioning, and
(v) social affinity – especially between middle and poorer groups.

He also gives a supporting role to ideology and religion, for example, Catholic countries, since the Catholic Church and affiliated parties 'shed their economic conservatism after World War II' (ibid.: 189). The big difference, especially between the United States and Europe, lies in lower social affinity between middle and poorer groups in the former country. In an extensive review of potential economic and political sources of this difference, Alberto Alesina and Edward Glaeser (2004) emphasise the lack of identification between middle and poorer groups, associated, in part, with social differentiation on racial lines. This is supported by belief systems, and especially the stronger belief in the United States that the poor could enjoy upward mobility if they exerted effort. In the World Values Survey, 60 per cent among the general public in the United States believe the poor are 'lazy' compared with 'only' 26 per cent of Europeans – though in reality there is no systematic difference in work hours across countries. There is indeed a difference in mobility at the bottom – but with *lower* upward mobility of the American poor (contrary to the myth of opportunity) and especially amongst blacks, and conversely, lower downward mobility into poverty of the middle classes.

How does India compare with this list? Voice is clearly high, given the vigorous democracy, with disproportionately high voting amongst poorer groups (contrary to the pattern in most countries). India is also relatively open, compared with the historical position of industrialised countries. Needs are also clearly high, if with a different structure – and there is a case for arguing that with increased political pressure the now-industrialised countries would have responded more vigorously to the patterns of vulnerability of earlier times. What of income per capita? Is not India at a starkly lower level of income? In fact, at purchasing power parity, India's 2007 income is around 40 per cent of the United Kingdom's in 1946.[10] This is lower, but not dramatically so. By contrast, social affinity is more complex and almost certainly lower in India than in European countries. The heritage of the caste system, the socio-cultural differentiation and generally lower de facto status of scheduled tribes, has bequeathed greater social distance between middle and (some) subordinate groups. Sadiq Ahmed and Ashutosh Varshney (2007) argue this is a source of the weakness of pro-poor political coalitions. This is an issue that needs to be taken account of in the design of social provisioning for risks.

So what happened to all the costs of expanded social provisioning in industrialised societies? Why have massive increases in spending not been associated with big impacts on effort and large costs from the associated taxation? There surely are some distortions, and there are continuing debates on the need to reform 'sclerotic' continental European social systems. These matter for future dynamism. But it is hard to argue that these have had *first order* effects, which have held down past growth for the now-richest group of countries in history (outside a few oil states), or on any differential performance of, say, the Scandinavian countries. Lindert (2004) argues that an important part of the explanation lies in smart design: with respect to the inter-country comparison, Scandinavian countries have paid much more attention than the United States (or much of continental Europe) to reducing the disincentive of both social provisioning and taxation. I would also suggest that the complementarity between broad-based systems of social provisioning and the process of creation and destruction also underpinned the long-run productivity increase that lies behind current wealth.

Some Implications for India

So, for a country such as India, rapidly integrating into global markets, fast-growing and undergoing major internal economic and social transformations, what makes sense? This is not the place to review the wide array of existing programmes (see World Bank, forthcoming, for a review). I rather conclude this chapter with some general remarks on design principles, the current policy mix, and a specific look at NREGA.

The first, overall message is that social provisioning for risk is a central element of the process of economic growth and structural transformation, and not an add on. Theory, experience, and history all support the view that government-mediated action to support management of risks faced by households is desirable on efficiency and equity grounds, is likely to be more important with globalisation, and can be done.

In the design of social provisioning, both the policy mix and technical design can make a major difference. A sound policy *mix* involves action in all three areas: of risk reduction, *ex ante* risk-management, and *ex post* coping. Risk reduction includes areas from macro-economic management to flood control. Supporting *ex ante* risk management includes broadening of the financial system and design of insurance options (for example, for health, weather, old age). Supporting *ex post* coping includes a range of what are traditionally termed safety-net measures (or, at least, those aimed at vulnerability rather than chronic poverty.) While the primary focus of most assessments of systems of social provisioning lies in the performance of the set of *ex ante* insurance and *ex post* instruments, it is important that these be considered within the broader mix of risk management policies and institutions.

Turning to technical design of the insurance and coping-related instruments, the central issues concern the relationship between the structure of risks, the nature of market failures, and instrument design. Instrument design, in turn, concerns the mix, targeting (who uses the scheme) and effects on behaviour. On mix, it is almost certainly the case that a range of schemes will be required (though undoubtedly smaller than the number of schemes that exist now), since design and delivery questions are quite different for dealing with health, weather, employment, and price-based risks. With respect to targeting, the question is often framed in terms of how effectively a scheme reaches the poor, that is the extent to which it covers only and all the poor. But this is not the right question for vulnerability: the issue is whether the instrument mix reaches all uncovered *risks*, and at what economic cost, in terms of changes in behaviour and market-based outcomes. This applies to both poor and non-poor households prior to a shock.

Of course, what matters most are (uncovered) shocks that are both large and hit the poorest households, since losses in well-being are greater the lower the initial wealth, as noted above. There are also questions of the extent to which insurance is financed by charges or general tax revenues. But there are sound economic reasons for comprehensiveness, as well as political economy ones.

A final general comment concerns the effects on behaviour and markets: this is central to an evaluation of any scheme, since it defines the counterfactual of what would occur in the absence of the policy. Often there will be costs. A classic example is unemployment insurance, which reduces welfare-declines when a worker loses his job, but typically also reduces efforts in finding a new job. There can also be benefits. To take an example from an area involving a largely non-risk-based transfer: 'conditional cash transfers', in which cash is provided to a poor household if a child goes to school (or other human capital related activity), induces behavioural changes that *offset* market imperfections linked to financing school attendance, that are the basis for the intergenerational transmission of inequality.

Of equal importance to technical design is the interaction with functioning of the state. As discussed above, the Indian state typically works as part of a patronage democracy in which the bureaucracy and politicians manage programmes with the objectives of increased political influence and personal enrichment, as well as the intended goals of the programme. The evaluation of social provisioning needs to take this into account: how far is the design of schemes aligned with clientelist and personal enrichment, relative to efficient risk management? And, assuming some degree of policy autonomy and some weight to broad social welfare goals of policy framers, exactly the same question needs to be posed with respect to new schemes.

So how does the Indian policy mix look relative to these considerations? A broad brush assessment would be: quite high with respect to overall effort, but low with respect to both mix and design (though I come to NREGA below.) Here is a summary assessment.

(a) *Risk reduction:* Avoidance of macro-economic fluctuations has been reasonably good. But action on efficient sectoral and micro-economic mechanisms for risk reduction has been varied, and often poor. The expansion of irrigation has undoubtedly had large impacts on farmers affected, but actual management was bedevilled by corruption, when carefully analysed in the 1980s (Wade 1985). It is unclear whether it has improved. Management of common pool resources, notably groundwater, has been dismal. Private wells have led to large medium-term benefits of reduced water variability, but this is likely to be a source not only of water shortage, but also greater water-related vulnerability in the future. Subsidies to power have exacerbated overexploitation.

(b) *Finance:* There has been substantial effort on the first leg of provisioning of mechanisms for *ex ante* risk management, that of broadening financial access, for example, in the push to expand rural banking. But results have been weak, with the bulk of rural households still without access to the formal financial system in the early 2000s (Basu 2006). It is too early to judge the recent push for financial inclusion.

(c) *Social provisioning for ex ante insurance and ex post copying:* Effort has been quite high: over 2 per cent of GDP on government spending for social safety nets is a substantial outlay for a low income country; health spending and emergency relief for disasters is on top of this. But results have been weak, because of both the mix and design issues. Here are the main features:

    (i) Until the introduction of NREGA, total outlays were dominated by the PDS of subsidised food and kerosene through dedicated shops. While this can have benefits in reducing price fluctuations, it is intrinsically a weak instrument for most state-contingent risks, and is riddled with problems of inefficiency and diversion, making it a very-high-cost instrument (Radhakrishna and Subbarao 1997).

    (ii) The health system does remarkably poorly in providing for catastrophic risks – especially in poor rural areas (see

Banerjee et al., 2007, for an account of part of the health system in rural Rajasthan).

(iii) Beyond these core areas, there are a wide range of smaller schemes, including mid-day meals for children, local public works, pensions for widows and disabled, and school stipends. Many of these bring positive benefits, though many are not directly linked to vulnerability, and many of those aimed at transfers to the chronic poor have well over half of their beneficiaries amongst the non-poor.

(iv) Some of the major Indian social transfer programmes, including the PDS, make use of the Below Poverty Line (BPL) categorisation, that is, a form of asset-based proxy means test, as the eligibility criterion. This is likely to be a poor measure of cost of shocks, since it reflects longer-term wealth – in addition to its intrinsic weaknesses in categorising the poor (Jalan and Murgai 2008) and susceptibility to administrative corruption.

(v) All programmes are embedded in state delivery systems, and subject to the vagaries of patronage and diversion. Some observers (Kapur et al. 2008) see this as a fatal weakness given the ways in which state systems operated.

This brings us to NREGA, probably the most ambitious scheme for risk management ever developed for a poor country. As is well-known, it involves a guarantee of up to 100 days of work per rural household within 5 km of residence at the state's agricultural minimum wage.[11] Targeting is by self-selection, that is, purely by the willingness of a person to undertake unskilled work. Public works schemes are implemented by local governments, and not contractors. It is backed by an extensive set of rights to infromation, requirements on transparency and other social accountability mechanisms. It was launched in 200 districts in February 2006, and has since been extended throughout India. It has been controversial, especially in the wake of the 2007 report of the Comptroller and Auditor General (CAG) of India. This found significant deficiencies in implementation – though, as argued by Siddartha and Anish Vanaik (2008), the CAG's assessment was a very partial one, which was extensively misinterpreted in the public debate. In mid-2008, there were further concerns with the murder of activists who were working to ensure that the required accountability measures were followed.

There are undoubtedly important issues in implementation, but it is too early to form an overall assessment on impacts. Here I only seek to place the scheme in the context of the issues raised in this essay.

(i) *Technical design.* The scheme has a set of design attributes that make it highly attuned to risk management for rural areas. The guarantee is crucial to this. It implies that households with able-bodied workers can systematically get access to wage work, in response to the full array of either idiosyncratic or common shocks. It is thus appropriate for weather or other agricultural shocks or to health-related shocks – provided, in the latter case, there is still available household labour supply. In this respect, it is a complement to health insurance, which only pays for health costs, not for foregone income. In terms of effects on household behaviour and markets, there is likely to be diversion from other, lower-paying uses of labour (that reduces the net transfer benefits, see Murgai and Ravallion 2005). But this has additional welfare benefits when it strengthens the local bargaining position of labour-surplus households in local labour markets, and puts an effective floor on local wages.

(ii) *Governance design.* The design for governance can be seen as both a well-articulated response to the functioning of the Indian state, and a gamble. Taking contractors out of the system reduces incentives for distortions, while the innovative range of transparency and social accountability mechanisms makes malfeasance by local officials more difficult and the right to the programme more likely to be meaningful. As the CAG report and field investigations reveal, in some states, there is considerable abuse. This is especially so in poorer states such as Jharkand (see Bhatia and Drèze 2006). There is also concern over lack of governmental staff support for planning and managing the public works. It is too early to assess how effectively these will be resolved. It is in these respects that the scheme is a gamble with respect to implementation. The objective of NREGA being a permanent, institutionalised programme, and a central pillar of a broader set of risk-management programmes, depends on it not being distorted by the functioning of the Indian state, that is, not becoming yet another badly implemented poverty programme.

(iii) *The role of rights.* NREGA seeks to change the way the state functions. At its core is a conception of universal citizenship – linked to a rights-based approach unrelated to either influence or identity. This potentially changes the dynamic of interactions between individuals, groups, and state actors. If the Act works on the ground as it is intended to, the natural alliance is with other workers, and with those who can support the claims, including through the social audit mechanism – precisely because of the universality. Thus, the right is essential. Does this mean that social mobilisation is unimportant? Not at all: indeed NREGA worked best when it has been in areas where there has been a history of social mobilisation, and this is sometimes on identity-based grounds, for example, around a local tribal identity. However, unlike the pre-existing system, the access to resources, in this case work, should not be a function of discretion, or patronage, of politicians, bureaucrats, or contractors. This potentially has psycho-social effects, since a right is associated with an affirmation of the dignity of those seeking that it be executed, as opposed to the subtle or not-so-subtle humiliation of seeking patronage from those in positions of social advantage.

(iv) *Political alignment.* Passing NREGA was a product of a concerted process of social and political action. A final question concerns the extent to which NREGA is aligned with underlying political processes. At one level, there is a parallel with the broadening of systems of social provisioning to manage risks in now-rich countries – as in the support for the Beveridge Report in the United Kingdom, and, more generally, in the wake of the expansion of the franchise. India has, in principle, a political structure supportive of such broad-based provisioning, especially in light of the salience of the rural vote, and the fact the poorer citizens have a higher propensity to vote. Furthermore, the choice to make NREGA an act was intended to provide some resilience to shifting political winds. But politics still matters. There is a range of contingent factors, around budget allocations from the centre and the states, and, especially, around the effectiveness of implementation of the scheme on the ground, and the protection of rights. This will be influenced by political considerations, perhaps especially at the level of state governments. So far, the signs are that NREGA is evolving into a scheme that has broad political support. It was strongly associated with the Congress-led United Progressive Alliance (UPA) that put forward the Act in 2005, and was expanded to the whole country under this government and featured in its election campaign for 2009. But implementation was by no means confined to UPA-run states. It has been particularly strong, for example, in Rajasthan, which was run by the opposition coalition until the recent elections. More broadly, NREGA appeared to be increasingly accepted across the political spectrum throughout India, with even competition over raising the wage – for example, in Uttar Pradesh. There remains the risk that political and administrative processes of patronage and corruption will undermine some of the core principles of the scheme, but this is a separate question from whether it is broadly self-enforcing politically.

Thus, on efficiency, equity, governance, and political alignment, NREGA has attractive design properties. There are important open questions on implementation, deeply linked to whether it can work against – and indeed contribute to changing – the functioning of the Indian state. Is it only a handout, supporting current consumption as opposed to the investment needed to equip workers for change? There are important consumption benefits. However, if the scheme effectively provides guarantee, it will help poor rural households to escape from high-risk traps, allowing them to invest, in addition to reduce the need for households to sell off their capital when adverse shocks occur. This has, of course, to be complemented with a whole set of other programmes around education, health, infrastructure, and so on. And is it affordable? Globalisation requires substantial investment in infrastructure and skills to support India's structural transformation, and has a substantial public debt burden. But NREGA should be financeable over the medium term from a combination of reallocation from other social programmes and increases in taxes. There are many other programmes that are worse on *both* efficiency/growth promoting grounds and equity grounds than a reasonably well-implemented NREGA. PDS and energy and fertilizer subsidies are just a few of the examples. Over the long term, NREGA should gradually decline in importance as urban-based mechanisms for unemployment insurance rise in importance.

Conclusion

Globalisation is here to stay. It brings potentially large opportunities. Failure to make use of the economic opportunities would severely hurt India's growth and structural transformation process. By itself globalisation is likely to have little or no impact on the most important sources of current vulnerability faced by Indian households, notably health and weather-related shocks. But, the global market developments of the past few years vividly show how international turbulence can be transmitted across borders. India has been partially protected from the sub-prime crisis by the incomplete integration of her financial system. A relatively slow pace of integration in the reform process of the past quarter century probably led to foregone gains in efficiency and productivity, but also provide a degree of protection against adverse events.

More fundamentally, reaping the benefits of globalisation depends on domestic structures that support the creation and destruction of activities that are central to long-term growth. This paper has argued that institutionalised risk-management structures are a *complement* to globalisation. This is for reasons of efficiency – given the widespread failures in the market for insurance; of equity – given the highly unequal distribution of the capacity to manage shocks; and of political economy – since the powerful have greatest leverage to influence discretionary policy when a crisis hits.

Of course, there are good and bad designs. But the international and historical evidence provides support for the view that such comprehensive provisioning is feasible as well as desirable. India has made some important innovations – with NREGA potentially the most significant – but has a long way to go to build such a system. It also has a host of ineffective programmes, embedded in patronage and rent-seeking structures.

A particular aspect of the nexus between vulnerability and globalisation lies in the functioning of social identities. Globalisation has complex interactions with the structure of identity: it may contribute to reducing the salience of hierarchical and exclusive patterns of identity, for example, through expanding market opportunities for groups who historically suffered adverse terms of recognition, that is, social identities subject to discrimination or humiliation in India society. But there can also be adverse interactions, when globalisation creates opportunities for economic change that are aligned with established power structures and when social groups with weak influence suffer attacks to their economic, social, and cultural positions – as in some of the interactions between mining ventures and *adivasi* groups. Identity is dynamic, and changes induced by globalisation can be both a source of affirmative change and of anxiety – and this may add to conflicts around economic designs.

Building a comprehensive, institutionalised system of social protection in India will involve confronting all these issues: of the relationship between design, efficiency, and equity; of the political economy of securing support for an institutionalised system; and of recognising the interactions with the structure of social identity in India society. This will involve transforming the functioning of the Indian state, which is significantly embedded in historically shaped structures of power and identity.

Notes

1. I wish to thank Ms Anusha Nath for her excellent research assistance.
2. This is intuitively very likely to be true for given absolute changes in wealth; it is often assumed that this is also true for the same proportional changes.
3. Dev et al. (2007) comment that this may have been influenced by the respondents' interpretation of the question, in particular that local employment and wage declines consequent on bad weather – that disproportionately affect the poor – were not counted as a shock.

4. South Korea is also interesting in view of the political salience of middle and poorer groups for the government, and high degree of solidarity across all groups in the face of the crisis.
5. In economic parlance, people have diminishing marginal utility of income.
6. There may, of course, be second round effects from the cost and availability of drugs, for example. In India's case, the dramatic growth of the pharmaceutical industries – that has greatly increased access to drugs – is positively linked to the globalisation.
7. There is an important question over how to design the process of opening of the financial sector to induce deepening, but that is not the focus of this chapter.
8. Rodrik (1998) explores this through use of the exogenous component of trade (as calculated from measures of distance and population size) in the regression equation explaining government size.
9. See Levy (2008) for a full discussion of the Mexican case.
10. This is based on calculations derived from Angus Maddison's data series, updated for recent Indian growth (see Maddison 2009).
11. This was increased to 100 days per person in the 2009 drought. But here we are concerned with the general principles.

References

Ahmed, Sadiq and Ashutosh Varshney. 2007. 'Battles half won: political economy of India's growth and economic policy since independence.' Background paper for the Commission on Growth and Development; accessed at www.growthcommission.org on 29 September 2009.

Alesina, Alberto and Edward Glaeser. 2004. *Fighting Poverty in the US and Europe: A World of Difference*. Oxford: Oxford University Press.

Baland, Jean-Marie and Jean-Philippe Platteau. 1996. *Halting Degradation of Natural Resources: Is There a Role for Rural Communities?* New York: Oxford University Press.

Banerjee, Abhijit; Esther Duflo and Rachel Glennerster. 2007. 'Putting Band Aid on a Corpse: Incentives for Nurses in the Indian Public Health Care System', *Journal of the European Economic Association*, 6 (2–3): 487–500.

Basu, Priya. 2006. *Improving Access to Finance for India's Rural Poor.* Washington D.C.: The World Bank.

Beveridge, William. 1942. *Social Insurance and Allied Services* (The Beveridge Report). London: His Majesty's Stationary Office.

Bhalla, Surjit. 2009. 'Lazy Banking at Its Finest', *Business Standard* (New Delhi), 21 January.

Bhatia, Bela and Jean Drèze. 2006. 'Employment Guarantee in Jharkhand: Ground Realities', *Economic and Political Weekly,* 41 (29): 3198–202.

Bhushan, Chandran and Monali Zeya Hazra. 2008. *Rich Lands Poor People: Is 'Sustainable' Mining Possible?* New Delhi, Centre for Sciences and Environment.

Castells, Manuel. 1997. *The Power of Identity: The Information Age (Economy, Society and Culture, Volume II).* Malden, MA: Blackwell Publishing.

Chandra, Kanchan. 2004. *Why Ethnic Parties Succeed: Patronage and Ethnic Headcounts in India.* Cambridge and New York: Cambridge University Press.

Commission on Growth and Development. 2008. *The Growth Report: Strategies for Sustained Growth and Inclusive Development.* Washington D.C.: The World Bank.

Damodaran, Harish. 2008. *India's New Capitalists: Caste, Business and Industry in a Modern Nation.* New Delhi: Permanent Black.

De Ferranti, David; Guillermo Perry, Francisco Ferreira and Michael Walton. 2004. *Inequality in Latin America: Breaking with History?* Washington D.C.: The World Bank.

Dev, S. Mahendra; K. Subbarao, S. Galab and C. Ravi. 2007. 'Safety Net Programmes: Outreach and Effectiveness', *Economic and Political Weekly,* 42 (35): 3555–65.

Diwan, Ishac. 2001. 'Debt as Sweat: Labor, Financial Crises, and the Globalisation of Capital' (Processed). Washington D.C.: The World Bank.

Drèze, Jean and Amartya Sen. 1990. *Hunger and Public Action.* New York: Oxford University Press.

Dutta, Puja Vasudeva. 2008. 'Poverty and vulnerability in India' (Processed). New Delhi: The World Bank.

Comptroller and Auditor General of India. 2007. 'Performance Audit of Implementation of National Rural Employment Guarantee Act, 2005 (NRÊGA)'. New Delhi: Government of India.

Halac, Marina and Sergio L. Schmukler. 2004. 'Distributional Effects of Crises: The Financial Channel.' *Economíc,* 5 (1): 1–67.

Honohan, Patrick and Daniela Klingebiel. 2003. 'The Fiscal Cost Implications of an Accommodating Approach to Banking Crises', *Journal of Banking and Finance* 27 (8): 1539–60.

Jalan, Jyotsna and Rinku Murgai.2008. 'An Effective 'Targeting Shortcut'? Analysis of the BPL Scheme in Reaching the Poor' (Mimeograph). New Delhi: The World Bank.

Kapur, Devesh; Partha Mukhopadhay and Arvind Subramanian. 2008. 'The Case for Direct Cash Transfers to the Poor', *Economic and Political Weekly*, 43 (15): 37–43.

Levy, Santiago. 2008. *Good Intentions, Bad Outcomes: Social Policy, Informality and Economic Growth in Mexico.* Washington D.C.: Brookings Institution Press.

Lindert, Peter. 2004. *Growing Public: Social Spending and Economic Growth since the Eighteenth Century.* Cambridge and New York: Cambridge University Press.

Loury, Glenn. 2002. *The Anatomy of Racial Inequality.* Cambridge, MA: Harvard University Press.

Maddison, Angus. 2009. *Statistics on World Population, GDP and Per Capita GDP, 1-2006.* Accessed 29 September 2009, at http: //www.ggdc.net/maddison/

Munshi, Kaivan and Mark Rosenzweig. 2006. 'Traditional Institutions Meet the Modern World: Caste, Gender, and Schooling Choice in a Globalizing Economy', *American Economic Review.* 96 (4): 1225–52.

Murgai, Rinku and Martin Ravallion. 2005. 'Is a Guaranteed Living Wage a Good Anti-Poverty Policy?' (*World Bank Policy Research Working Paper No. 3640.* Washington D.C. The World Bank.

Narayan, Deepa; Robert Chambers, M.K. Shah and Patti Petesch. 2001. *Voices of the Poor: Crying Out for Change.* New York: Published for the World Bank by Oxford University Press.

Pritchett, Lant; Sudarno Sumarto and Asep Suryahadi. 2003. 'Safety Ropes or Safety Nets? Dynamic Benefit Incidence of Two Crisis Programs in Indonesia', *World Development,* 31 (7): 1257–77.

Radhakrishna, R. and K. Subbarao. 1997 *India's Public Distribution System: A National and International Perspective* (World Bank Discussion Paper No. 380). Washington D.C.: The World Bank.

Rajan, Raghuram G. and Luigi Zingales. 2003. *Saving Capitalism from the Capitalists: Unleashing the Power of Financial Markets to Create Wealth and Spread Opportunity.* New York: Crown Business.

Rodrik, Dani. 1998. 'Why do More Open Economies have Bigger Governments?', *Journal of Political Economy,* 106 (5): 997–1032.

Siddhartha and Anish Vanaik. 2008. 'CAG Report on NREGA: Fact and Fiction', *Economic and Political Weekly,* 43 (25): 39–45.

Thorat, Sukhadeo and Paul Attewell. 2007. 'The Legacy of Social Exclusion: A Correspondence Study of Job Discrimination in India', *Economic and Political Weekly,* 42 (41): 4141–44.

Townsend, Robert. 1994. 'Risk and Insurance in Village India', *Econometrica,* 62 (3): 539–91.

Wade, Robert. 1985. 'The Market for Public Office: Why the Indian State is not better at Development', *World Development,* 13 (4): 467–97.

World Bank, The. 2003. *World Development Report 2004: Making Services Work for Poor People*. New York: Oxford University Press.

——. 2008. *World Development Indicators.* Washington D.C.: The World Bank.

——. Forthcoming. *Social Protection for a Changing India* (Draft Report). New Delhi: The World Bank.

7

Vulnerability of Cities to Globalisation

Towards a Conceptual Framework

NARENDAR PANI

An intriguing aspect of several debates on the vulnerabilities of globalisation, especially the more popular ones, is that we cannot always be sure we are talking about the same thing. In a general, rather vague, sense, we seem to be referring to the changes in communication technologies since the 1980s that have dramatically affected our economies, our polities, our societies, our criminal networks, our environment, and much else. Once we go a little deeper, though, we often find that we could, in fact, be talking about a variety of very different things. Are we talking about only the recent spurt in technological change or are we referring also to other inventions, like the telephone, that too changed the way people across the world related to each other? Should our concepts focus on capital flows or should they look at the effects the process has had on local communities?

Conceptualising globalisation in a way that showcases what each analyst thinks is the most important dimension of the process has led to a multiplicity of definitions of the term. It is not uncommon for textbooks to begin by acknowledging that 'no generally accepted definition exists' (Mcgrew 2005: 279). Nor are these differences merely a matter of semantics. The definitions, sometimes not even explicitly stated, often determine the conclusions we reach. If we define globalisation as the emergence of a new comprehensive global system, all changes would necessarily be attributed to it. All the vulnerabilities we have noticed since the 1980s would necessarily be attributable to globalisation. On the other hand, if we look at it more narrowly, as just the flow of capital across national boundaries, there are a large number of local changes, especially cultural ones, which would fall beyond the purview of the term. In this perception, the vulnerabilities exist despite globalisation. Indeed, some who take this view may even argue that globalisation offers fresh opportunities to reduce vulnerabilities.

This definitional quagmire is, if anything, even worse when we look at the relationship between globalisation and cities. While we might all accept that cities are places where a large number of people are concentrated, there is not much agreement on anything else. Each city has its own social, economic, and political processes working at any given point of time. In order to reduce the vast diversity that exists across different cities over both time and space, there have been efforts to categorise them as Third World cities, developing cities, and the like. Such classifications serve to reduce the diversity into what are supposed to be more manageable categories. But to insist that the common ground that is used to create these categories is necessarily more important than what is left out can itself be contentious. The criteria we use to define our common ground may well decide what we want to see. Lists of 'world cities' or 'global cities' may have their uses in deciding the command and control centres of the new world order; but they are not of much use in understanding the impact of globalisation on cities that are not a part of these hierarchies.

It is important then to spend some time confronting the challenges posed by a multiplicity of definitions available for globalisation as well as the diversity of concepts used to understand cities. In this paper, we first explore the reasons for this problem of abundance, before going on to suggest the broad contours of a conceptual framework that will help understand the relationship between globalisation and cities. We then go on to extend this framework to help us understand the vulnerabilities of cities to globalisation.

Globalisation

The most important reason for the multiplicity of definitions of globalisation is a perceived need to capture the defining aspects of a situation that has arisen from globalisation. When our concern about globalisation is prompted by developments in stock markets, it is difficult to come up with a definition that looks at very much more than the flows of capital across continents. When our concern is with the influence of foreign cultures on domestic social practices, it is futile to come up with a definition that does not put the changes in the entertainment industry up front. When our concern is about the impact of globalisation on the poor, it is impossible to function with definitions that ignore the local social, economic, and political milieus. Our definitions of globalisation tend to emphasise the aspects of specific situations that interest us the most. The multiplicity of definitions is then no more than a reminder of the many different effects this process can have. And, since very few of these different dimensions can be dismissed as trivial, we need a definition of globalisation that allows us to capture all of these concerns; a definition that allows for a multiplicity of effects, if not pluralism.

To find a definition that explicitly captures all the effects that can be linked to processes cutting across nations or even continents can be a daunting task. The tendency to be preoccupied with individual concerns rather than the whole is compounded by two self-imposed restrictions on those seeking to understand globalisation: the hesitancy to look beyond a particular discipline and the continuing effects of ideology.

The specialisations of each discipline can determine the very questions that are asked about globalisation. The preoccupations of economists have been largely around the extent to which national economies are being integrated into the global economy. They tend to see globalisation as the 'removal of barriers to free trade and the closer integration of national economies' (Stiglitz 2002: ix). Consequently, many of the studies of the economics of globalisation are focused on flows of capital across national borders and the degree of autonomy a national economy has in a globalised world economy. These studies are generally not too concerned with what happens to the local as a result of this change. Sociologists, on the other hand, tend to be much more concerned with local changes that could be attributed to globalisation. This is particularly true of those who are concerned primarily with social relations, as when

Anthony Giddens sees globalisation as 'the intensification of worldwide social relations which link distant localities in such a way that local happenings are shaped by events occurring many miles away' (1990: 21). Even those sociologists who provide a more critical role for economic links prefer to understand them in their local context. Saskia Sassen, for example, conceives of 'economic globalisation not just as capital flows, but as the work of coordinating, managing and servicing these flows and the work of servicing the multiple activities of firms and markets operating in more than one country' (2001: 347). Since servicing the capital flows and other activities of firms and markets happen in local sites, exploring the local remains a key to understanding the global. Political scientists are rather more interested in what the process does for international relations, and other social scientists have their own list of priorities. And we can go on.

To this discipline-based diversity we need to add the differences generated by varying ideological perspectives. These perspectives have been so diverse that they do not lend themselves to easy classification. There are a wide variety of terms in use including neo-liberalism, Marxism, statism, mercantilism, realism, economic nationalism, radical, critical, structural, dependency, world systems, and several more. The vast diversity in the effects of globalisation and the perception of these effects makes it virtually impossible to come up with a definition of globalisation that focuses on the effects of this process and is acceptable across both disciplines and ideologies.

Fortunately, focusing on the effects is not the only way to address the task of defining globalization. Our task becomes much easier if we shift the focus from the effects of globalisation to its causes. There is a fairly wide recognition that the effects that we perceive of globalisation are the result of the reduction of the effects of distance. In popular discourse globalisation has sometimes been taken to mean the death of distance. And, it is true that, in some cases, distance has been largely taken out of the equation. Jobs that had to previously be done in the vicinity can now be outsourced to points on the other side of the globe. But this is certainly not true for all jobs. We are still some time away from having our breakfast cooked in another continent. While the impact on the effect of distance may not be as comprehensive as some of the 'death of distance' exaggeration would suggest, there is little doubt that it has fundamentally altered the way a variety of activities ranging from business to entertainment are carried out. There has been a striking increase in what Robert O. Keohane and Joseph S. Nye call 'networks of interdependence at multicontinental distances' (2000: 105). We can then take globalisation to mean *a process that reduces the effects of distance across continental boundaries.*

This simple definition serves one basic requirement of being useful across disciplines. The specific consequences of a reduction in the effects of distance that interest a researcher are bound to be influenced by her/his discipline. An economist may choose to focus on capital flows, while a sociologist may prefer to look at the effects on the institution of marriage. Even when they choose to look at the same broad activity, they could be preoccupied with different dimensions. An economist may be interested in the financial viability of outsourcing, while a sociologist may choose to focus on the sociological implications of persons living in one culture providing services to those living in another. But to the extent that the same definition of globalisation can be used in all these cases, it will make it easier to piece together the analysis of globalisation emerging from different disciplines. All disciplines should benefit from a clearer conceptual demarcation between the process of globalisation and its effects.

The value of this definition in bridging ideological divisions is, unfortunately, less substantial. It is, no doubt, possible for individuals from different ideological persuasions to use this definition. This reduction in the effects of distance could well appeal just as much to some Marxists as it could to some who believe in free market economy. But, if we use the term 'ideology' to imply a worldview, our definition of globalisation is based on a worldview that will not be shared by some across the ideological spectrum. There are those who see globalisation as a system. Typically, they see globalisation as the latest stage in the development of capitalism. They believe, 'The essence of globalisation is global capitalism, which has superseded the nation-state stage of capitalism' (Robinson 1998: 563). From this perspective globalisation refers to the developments following the communication revolution of the last decades of the twentieth century. The essence of this system could, potentially, be captured in a model. And, the variations in the effects of globalisation would have to be treated as approximations to that model.

Treating globalisation as the reduction in the effects of distance, on the other hand, implies that it is a continuous process. The changes over the last two decades of the twentieth century have undoubtedly been dramatic, but this is not the first time that there has been a reduction in the effects of distance. This is a process that began many centuries back. The invention of boats that could cross the seas was a major step towards reducing the effects of distance, as was the development of advanced shipping, air travel, and telephony. Even if we were to argue that the current phase of globalisation is the most important one – a point that is not entirely beyond debate – we would still need to recognise earlier phases of the same process. This is not just for reasons of comprehensiveness or consistency. Even as the long periods of time between the different phases may well ensure that each phase of globalisation is very different from the other, we cannot rule out the possibility of earlier periods of globalisation having lessons, even if they are miniscule, for those seeking to understand its current phase (Pani 2009).

As the process of globalisation works itself out, it could unleash several other processes. In the current phase, the reduction in the effects of distance has made outsourcing of business processes possible. This, in turn, sets in motion economic processes that mobilise labour for this activity; social processes as the cultures of the resource providing city interact with those of the command and control centres of globalisation; and so on. These processes interact with each other as well as with other elements that already exist in the arena where globalisation is having an impact. As these conditions and their precise interactions with globalisation will vary from place to place, the nature of each interaction could well be unique to each place and each point of time. What we would get of a place at each point of time would be snapshots of particular situations. These snapshots are bound to vary not just across time and place but also across the perspectives from which they are viewed. This variability in the situations that the snapshots capture would be underestimated if we were to treat them as just approximations to a preconceived system. But once we treat globalisation as a process that throws up different conditions at different places at different points of time, we will be able to capture the situational dynamics of the process.

The distinction between processes and conditions is, of course, not entirely new. Political scientists have travelled some way down this path. The need to distinguish between 'balance of power' and bipolar systems led Morton Kaplan (2005/1957) to explore the role of process and system in international politics. Closer to our concerns in this paper, Keohane and Nye make a distinction between the process of globalisation and the condition of globalism. In their words, 'Globalism is a state of the world involving networks of interdependence at multicontinental distances .... Globalisation and deglobalisation refer to the increase or decline of globalism' (2000: 105).

Starting with the condition of globalism in order to define the process of globalisation is not without its difficulties. It requires the conditions listed in globalism to be comprehensive, so that we do not miss any change that is a part of globalisation. Keohane and Nye do provide a fairly comprehensive list, ranging from flows of capital and goods to that of biologically relevant substances. But given the diversity of the situations that globalisation can create, it is difficult to come up with a list that could cover all situations. And to the extent that globalisation throws up new, previously unknown, conditions, there is every chance that even a list that appears comprehensive at one point of time could be found wanting at another. At the same time, the more we expand our list in the search for comprehensiveness, the greater the tendency to list elements that are only occasionally relevant. It does seem more consistent, and certainly convenient, to begin at the other end by understanding the process of globalisation to be a reduction in the effects of distance. There is then no limit on the variety of different conditions that can be thrown up by that process. Nor is it necessary to predict these conditions in advance.

Defining globalisation in terms of the cause, rather than the effect, also brings to the fore at least two important aspects of the process of globalisation that are not always adequately emphasised. First, it provides greater clarity to the role of technology in globalisation. There is little doubt that phases of globalisation are enabled by the development of new technologies. From the primitive boats to the most advanced communication technologies, it is technological change that enables the reduction in the effects of distance. But whether, as well as when and where, these technologies are actually utilised would depend on a variety of other factors. Technology may have made it possible to set up call centres addressing customer complaints in the United States on the other side of the globe. But, if tapping the labour on the other side of the globe is more expensive than it is to do so in the United States, this technology will not be used. Even when the labour itself is less expensive, it would have to be equipped with language and other skills that a customer in the United States has come to expect. In other cases, the reduction of distance may not be culturally viable. The same technology can provide Swahili language programmes from Africa to an audience of Indians in Mumbai as well as Indian films to an audience of Indians in London. While the second is known to be viable, it is somewhat unlikely that the first will be so. The availability of technology, whether it is shipping, telecommunication or any other innovation that reduces the effects of distance, is then a necessary condition for globalisation, but it is not sufficient.

This difference, in practice, between what technology enables and the technology that is actually utilised, has its implications for our conceptions of globalisation itself. It adds another argument to the case against globalisation being seen as a homogenising phenomenon. If the new technologies are to create a single homogenous global village, then they must, at the very least, be implemented uniformly across the world. But once we take into account the difference between what is technologically possible and what we actually get, there is no reason for such a uniform implementation of the new technologies. The technologies of globalisation will be utilised to link only those points across the globe that suit those who command and control the processes of globalisation. They will only utilise the technologies that reduce the effects of distance, when and where it suits them. Colonial powers developed shipping links with colonies that provided them the greatest supplies of the commodities they wanted to control. They were not committed to providing links to every part of the globe. In the current phase, the spread of the technologies may be relatively more evenly distributed, and may require a greater degree of consent from all those who are affected by it; but it will still tend to be activated only in linkages that are considered viable. The degree of connectivity across the globe need not then be even. Some individual points will be better connected than others. Thus, even in the extremely unlikely event of the mere availability of new communication technology being enough to override all aspects of local cultures, the sheer fact of the technological linkages not being evenly spread would prevent homogenisation.

Second, defining globalisation in terms of a reduction in the effects of distance also influences our perception of the relationship between the national, the regional, and the global. The reduction in the effects of distance may have its most dramatic consequences across continents. But the same process works within regions as well as within countries. The same technologies that enable connectivity across different parts of the globe can also enable closer connectivity and between countries in a region. The mere fact that such connectivity is possible does not, of course, automatically imply greater integration within the region. Neighbours who have poor relations with each other may do little to maximise the utilisation of the new communication technology. But where such barriers do not exist, the same forces that support globalisation also encourage regionalism among neighbouring countries.

This underestimated compatibility between the regional and the global was perhaps most evident in the case of the World Trade Organisation (WTO). The coming into existence of the WTO followed the setting up of the North American Free Trade Agreement (NAFTA). The same processes do work within a nation too. The impact of technologies that reduce distance within nations may not be so substantial in small nations in that distances in these nations were not great to begin with. But, in large multi-ethnic and diverse countries, the increase in communication between different parts of the country can also act as a force of greater awareness of each other, and possibly integration. Large countries like India and China have moved towards globalisation even as their sense of national identity has grown stronger. Globalisation, regionalism, and nationalism are then not mutually exclusive. As they get a fresh impetus from the same technological possibilities, it is quite consistent to see all three tendencies increasing together.

Cities

An interesting dimension of the current phase of globalisation is the prominent place it provides for cities. In the colonial phase of globalisation, cities did have prominent roles as the ports through which commodities were transported to the colonial power or as local administrative centres. Yet a substantial part of the process of colonialism involved rural areas, whether it was in terms of the production of commodities or the collection of land revenue. In the current phase, as globalisation builds specific linkages between points across the world, these points are almost always cities. It is hardly surprising then that globalisation has seen the evolution of hierarchical concepts such as global cities and world cities.

These concepts do not break out of the well-established practice of understanding cities in terms of what we believe are its most important features. A demographer seeking relevant numbers may want to recognise them as no more than large urban settlements. Urbanisation is then, by definition, a simple matter of not being rural. This could be captured by, say, the Census of India's three criteria for an urban area based on the size of the population, its density, and agriculture not being its major occupation. But cities are more than just a concentration of non-agrarian population. They have a number of dimensions from the esoterically cultural to the more materialistic worlds of finance and economy. Understanding the dynamics of a city then implores us to look beyond the population figures, at the aspects that determine what it is and what it is going to be.

Here again, we face the challenges posed by disciplinary specialisations as well as individual preoccupations. Our understanding of the city is sometimes based only the element of the city we are concerned with. There was a time when the term 'city', especially in popular discourse, referred to no more than its financial districts. The 'City' section of a newspaper dealt with only its financial markets. Beyond the realm of popular discourse too there is a tendency to be preoccupied with specific aspects of a city that are of interest to a specific discipline. Urban economics sometimes gives the impression of a city being no more than a set of economic relationships. Architects, on the other hand, can sometimes look at a city entirely in terms what it does with its space.

This is not to suggest that there have been no efforts to break out of the shackles placed by one's discipline or immediate interest. In her highly influential work, *Global Cities*, the urban sociologist Saskia Sassen (2001) provides a pivotal role for economic relationships. Similar interdisciplinary efforts can be seen in other concepts that have emerged to capture the character of cities after globalisation, such as John Friedmann's 'world cities' (1986) or Peter Marcuse and Ronald van Kempen's 'globalising cities' (2000). But even as these terms explore important new dimensions of a city, they implicitly suggest that a city can be understood essentially in terms of its most dominant dimension.

In reality, this is rarely the case. At a mundane methodological level, there are a variety of criteria that could be used to decide dominance, and it is by no means certain that the dominance established by one criterion would match that generated by another. A high-end industry could dominate the city's economy in terms of the income generated, but a lower-end labour-intensive industry could be the most dominant one in terms of employment. The problem is not one of numbers alone. Even if a vast majority of the population of a city can be identified with one of its dimensions, can we ignore the possibly significant numbers who are associated with other aspects of the city simply because they are in a minority? If our concern is not just with some average number, but with the individuals that go to make a city's population, it would be difficult to do so. A prosperous city may like to flaunt its wealth and perhaps even the fact that a majority of its population has a meaningful share in that wealth. But, if that city includes the homeless or slum dwellers, the picture is not complete until we include them as well.

The need to look beyond the dominant dimensions has led some scholars to emphasise the uniqueness of individual cities.

Jennifer Robinson chooses to abandon all labels and come up with the concept of 'ordinary cities' that sees them as 'dynamic and diverse, if conflicted, arenas for social and economic life' (2006: 1). This approach allows us to capture the diversity of situations in different cities, and go beyond a preoccupation with their most dominant features. This celebration of uniqueness does, however, come with a cost. It severely restricts our ability to recognise common patterns across cities. We could, for instance, see globalisation creating pockets within cities that are more closely related to global financial centres. But as long as this relationship varies across cities in terms of scale or even the extent to which it is influenced by local customs, we would tend to underestimate the common trend.

There is thus a tendency when understanding cities to either get lost in the detail or to get into excessive generalisation. One way around this dilemma would be to go back to our distinction between processes and conditions. At the core of urbanisation is a demographic process that leads to the creation of large settlements with a density of population that is considered significant for the time. This process is accompanied, and at times sets off, several other processes. There are economic processes that influence the pace of urbanisation as well as the occupations that emerge in the urban settlement. There are social processes that emerge among individuals and groups that are thrown together. There are also political processes that can lead to greater or less democratisation, other processes that have a direct impact on the environment and the use of space, and so on.

The city is the arena where the processes of urbanisation play themselves out. The processes interact with the conditions that already exist in the city, as well as with each other, all the while creating new sets of conditions.

The conditions that are thrown up at each point of time then present a photographic view of a city that is in reality in a continuous transition. The nature of transition would depend on the conditions the city finds itself in. In agrarian economies that are in the process of moving towards a non-agrarian future, the economic process would tend to make them less rural. This need not however be a smooth process or indeed always be in the direction of becoming less rural. It could take years, even generations, for a rural population that moves into cities to break away from its rural roots. It is not unknown in Indian cities for the temporarily migrant population to continue to be a part of village politics, at least to the extent of exercising their franchise in their village. Similarly, when entire villages are engulfed within a rapidly expanding urban centre, they may lose their traditional occupations like agriculture, but continue to celebrate village festivals that have agrarian origins. At any given point of time, the conditions reflect the multitude of transitions a city is going through at varying paces. If, as Hiraclitus said over 2,500 years ago, we never step into the same river twice, we also never step into the same city twice.

Circuits

In our conceptualisation of globalisation and cities we have tried to ensure that we capture as much of the wide variation as is possible. Our focus on the process of globalisation allows us to deal with the entire range of effects this process could have. Our view of the city as an arena also allows us to relate to the entire range of urban processes that interact with each other. When we look at the interaction of the process of globalisation with the urban processes that are already at work in cities, there is potentially an even larger number of effects possible. This approach may suggest an open-ended system where nothing can be said with certainty. Such a view would, however, be quite misleading. While it is true that it is difficult to come up with a common generalisation for all cities, it is equally evident that not all possibilities are equally likely in each city. In each city some interactions between globalisation and local processes will be more prominent than others, and some other interactions may not exist at all. Within each city some interactions between different processes develop deep roots and even influence the character of that city. If we were to look at flows of goods and services both within a city and between those in the city and those outside, some consistent patterns could well become discernible. *A particular flow of goods and/or services can then form a circuit that tends to reinforce itself.*

Of all the many possibilities that exist in the interaction among urban processes, among the processes thrown up by globalisation and each other, it is those that develop into effective circuits that tend to influence the dynamics of a city. Each process has the potential to generate a specific circuit of its own. Industries could have their own circuits that link the producer of raw material to the consumer of the final product. A marriage bureau that arranges marriages, or a dating agency, could emerge as a circuit in social relations. These processes and circuits interact with each other in a city. The circuits may exist entirely within a city, may provide links between the local and the non-local within a country, or might provide links across nations.

There is then much to be said for Sassen's unpacking the global economy

> into a variety of highly specialized cross-border circuits corresponding to specific industries, more precisely, those components of industries operating across borders. Among these are a variety of financial sub-sectors, accounting, legal, advertising, construction, engineering, architecture, telecommunication services, and others. Each of these may have its own specific geography of networks, even though there will tend to be strong overlap in the case of some of these, notably finance and its sister industries. (2001: 347)

In terms of our more inclusive view of the impact of globalisation on cities, we would need to modify this definition in at least two ways. First, it is important to recognise that the circuits that are developed need not be confined to the economic dimension. There are well-established social circuits that can be relied upon to provide services though not for a price. Family networks can be very effective in facilitating the movement of labour and entrepreneurship across national boundaries. They also play a critical role in some social processes such as the globalisation of the Indian arranged marriage system. To the extent that these networks provide an established flow of goods or services, and reinforce themselves with their effectiveness, they can be treated as not just a network of contacts, but an effective circuit. Second, in keeping with our earlier contention that the reduction in the effect of geographical distance occurs not just across national boundaries, but also within countries, the circuits of globalisation would tend to develop alongside other circuits that work across the dividing lines between the local and the non-local. To the extent that globalisation is not an economic process alone, we would unpack not just the global economy but also all other circuits of globalisation, including military, social, cultural, environmental, and even criminal.

The process of globalisation can be unpacked into a number of different, economic, social, political, cultural, environmental, criminal and other circuits. These circuits of globalisation may be accompanied by the development of circuits within a region that cut across national boundaries as well as circuits within a nation that cut across the local and non-local. The circuits of globalisation, and the circuits that link the regional as well as the local and the non-local within a country, interact with conditions in the different arenas in which they operate, as well as with each other, in the process generating even newer conditions. And cities are among the most prominent of these arenas.

Vulnerabilities

Viewing globalisation as the reduction in the effects of distance has its implications for our understanding of its vulnerabilities as well. The definition based on the cause of globalisation allows for a multitude of effects. Some of these effects may be universally positive or universally negative. The ability to communicate across the world is a universally positive effect. On the other side of the coin, the use of the technologies of globalisation to spread terrorism is a universally negative effect. The positive or negative character of other effects can be more local. The benefit of globalisation in terms of generating opportunities for business process outsourcing tends to be concentrated in cities and not, usually, in rural areas. In yet other cases, the nature of the effects of globalisation can be so closely linked to place that it is positive in one place and negative in another. The outsourcing of a job is a negative effect of globalisation in the place it is outsourced from, while it is a positive effect in the place where a new job is created.

The wide range of effects has at least two important implications for our understanding of the vulnerabilities to the process of globalisation. First, it ensures that we cannot make a blanket statement about globalisation being a positive or negative process.

It can have both positive and negative effects. And since these effects come from the same source – that is, the reduction in the effects of distance – they may well come together. In such cases, the vulnerabilities created by the process of globalisation will be accompanied by fresh opportunities. To the extent that this package would vary from place to place, the assessment of globalisation has to be studied locally. Second, the wide range of inter-connected effects also makes the process very difficult to resist. Those who strongly dislike one effect of globalisation may be tempted to adopt another. The successful mobilisation of international protestors against globalisation at the Seattle ministerial of the WTO owed a great deal to some of the technologies that reduced the effects of distance, particularly the Internet.

The role of the local in understanding the effects of globalisation as well as the fact that it may not be realistic to expect to be able to stop the entire process determines our approach to understanding the vulnerabilities that arise from this process. Any suggestion that we could reduce the vulnerabilities of globalisation by simply stopping the entire process would be unrealistic. The variation from place to place and situation to situation implies that we cannot have a common approach to reduce the vulnerabilities of globalisation. What we could develop is a common method of looking for potential vulnerabilities before we can develop situation-specific responses to the pressure. Our purpose in this paper is to outline a broad framework that will help us identify potential vulnerabilities in the arena of the city.

The first step towards developing such a broad framework would be to identify the interactions, both positive and negative, between the process of globalisation and the processes that are already at work in a city. The interaction between the process of globalisation and the existing circuits can benefit a city in at least two distinct ways. It can lead to the creation of new circuits that add to the strengths of the city. The most obvious of these cases is that of information technology. The development of communication technologies in the 1980s opened up entirely new flows of information technology products and services. These circuits were able to tap manpower resources available in cities that were geographically distant from the command and control centres of that circuit. Cities like Bangalore first found their technical manpower getting opportunities that were far better than what was generally offered before the communication revolution. Later, the development of business process outsourcing (BPO) saw opportunities grow for a wider spectrum of the workforce, including accountants and those who operated call centres. A second source of benefit to cities from globalisation emerged when this process enhanced the opportunities for manpower in circuits that already existed in cities. A city with a well-established education circuit, for instance, could gain from the opportunities provided by improved communication technologies. The quality of education could be enhanced through the use of communication technologies that provide access to academic events taking place elsewhere in the world. It also allows for interactive teaching by faculty situated on the other side of the globe. These advantages are so substantial that cities move to tap them, thereby opening themselves out to the forces of globalisation, if not actually wooing them.

Attracting these forces of globalisation may have its benefits for a city, but it brings with it several other effects that can make the city vulnerable. These vulnerabilities tend to fall into at least three broad categories. First, there are the vulnerabilities that result from the circuits of globalisation competing with the circuits that already exist within a city. Second, we have vulnerabilities that exist within the circuit of globalisation itself. And third, we have the vulnerabilities that arise from the pressure the process of globalisation exerts on the economic, social, cultural, and political infrastructure that exists within the city.

Vulnerabilities from Competition

Competition between the circuits of globalisation and the circuits that already exist in a city can occur on various fronts. The common example is competition in the market for the final product. A product produced through a process of globalisation may be able to threaten the market for products that are the result of more local circuits, especially if they can tap the cost advantage of parts of their products being produced wherever in the world it is cheapest do so. The competition is, however, not restricted to the final product. There can be competition for inputs as well.

This could be true of any input from raw materials to skilled manpower. The globalised production and marketing of food products could reduce the availability of agricultural inputs for local circuits. The emergence of an information technology industry can attract engineers away from the more traditional engineering-based products.

In listing competition as a source of vulnerability, an impression must not be created that competition from globalisation can only have a negative effect on domestic circuits. The advertising campaign for a global product could easily expand the overall market, thereby creating space for similar products produced in domestic circuits. The difference between purchasing power parity and the higher market exchange rates could also be an advantage. The global product with imported components priced in dollar terms may well have to be priced higher than those produced locally. Thus, while competition can make domestic circuits vulnerable, they need not necessarily do so.

Vulnerabilities within Globalisation

The processes of globalisation can generate vulnerabilities from within. As these processes reach out to different parts of the world where costs of production are the least, they could easily prefer locations where this cost advantage is derived from lower official environmental or labour standards. This could lead to a rapid decline in the quality of the environment in the city alongside the establishment of sweat shops. The effect of these low standards can influence other cities as well. Once the cities with relatively better official standards are forced to compete with cities that have much worse standards, there is a temptation to find loopholes in the existing environmental and labour standards.

This process can affect traditional systems set up to protect labour interests. As workers seek to become a part of the circuits of globalisation, they would like to keep open as many employment opportunities as are available. This would make them less inclined to do anything that will reduce such opportunities, including joining a union. They would prefer to try to protect their interests by keeping open the option of moving from one job to another. In such a situation, many, if not most, of the rights that the trade union movement has developed could become just laws on paper that are not made use of.

Vulnerabilities from Pressure on Infrastructure

Beyond the competition between circuits and the vulnerabilities within them there are also the vulnerabilities that arise from the pressure that are exerted on the infrastructure available in a city. The establishment of a part of any new circuit in a city, irrespective of whether it is related to the process of globalisation or not, will exert pressure on the infrastructure. It will increase the demand for transport, power, water, and other resources that the city provides. There are, however, aspects of the circuits of globalisation that could accentuate these pressures. As cities compete with each other on a global stage, they feel compelled to invest heavily in infrastructure as a means of attracting the capital released through the processes of globalisation. The pressure to build new airports is particularly intense. These pressures gain an additional boost in cities that are the resource providers of globalisation as opposed to the command and control centres. There is little reason for those who command and control the forces of globalisation to be committed to a particular city that provides resources for the circuit. Indeed, the bargaining power of the forces of globalisation is derived, at least partially, from the fact that they can choose other options. The entire pressure on the infrastructure would then have to be met from local resources. This could divert resources from basic infrastructure like water for the poor to infrastructure that makes the city attractive to foreign investors.

The precise nature and extent of these vulnerabilities would vary from situation to situation. The ideal responses too can be quite different. In some cases the objective of the response may be only to ease the pressure, in other cases the emphasis may be on developing the ability to withstand the pressure, in yet other cases it may be necessary to develop alternatives to make the pressure irrelevant, and in still other cases there may be a need for a combination of these and similar objectives. All that we have tried to do in this paper is to develop a simple framework that tells us where to look when we try to understand the vulnerability of cities to globalisation.

References

Friedmann, John. 1986. 'The World City Hypothesis', *Development and Change,* 17 (1): 69–83.

Giddens, Anthony. 1990. *The Consequences of Modernity.* Cambridge: Polity Press.

Kaplan, Morton A. 2005/1957. *System and Process in International Politics.* Essex: ECPR Press.

Keohane, Robert O. and Joseph S. Nye Jr. 2000. 'Globalisation: What's New? What's Not? (And So What?)', *Foreign Policy,* 118 (Spring): 104–19.

Marcuse, Peter and Ronald van Kempen. 2000. 'Conclusion: A Changed Spatial Order', in Peter Marcuse and Ronald van Kempen (eds.): *Globalizing Cities: A New Spatial Order?* (pp. 249–75). London: Blackwell.

Mcgrew, Anthony. 2005. 'The Logics of Economic Globalisation', in John Revenhill (ed.): *Global Political Economy* (pp. 277–313). Oxford: Oxford University Press.

Pani, Narendar. 2009. 'Resource Cities Across Phases of Globalisation: Evidence from Bangalore', *Habitat International,* 33: 114–19.

Robinson, Jennifer. 2006. *Ordinary Cities: Between Modernity and Development.* New York: Routledge.

Robinson, William I. 1998. 'Beyond Nation-State Paradigms: Globalisation, Sociology, and the Challenge of Transnational Studies', *Sociological Forum,* 13 (4): 561–94.

Sassen, Saskia. 2001. *The Global City: New York, London, Tokyo* (Second Edition). Princeton, NJ: Princeton University Press.

Stiglitz, Joseph. 2002. *Globalisation and its Discontents.* New Delhi: Penguin Books.

8

Rural Communities in a Globalising World

Vulnerability, Opportunities and Prospects

V.M. RAO

The recent thinking and debates on globalisation in India have remained confined to the phase of economic reforms being implemented since about the mid-1980s. This paper[1] looks at globalisation from the broader perspective as a societal process bringing the countries in the world closer to each other and putting pressure on them to create mechanisms for collaboration and conflict resolution to cope with the growing global interdependence and its fallout of compulsions for global cooperation and collective action.

The focus of the paper is on the rural communities in India which are passing through a churning process, breaking down the traditional structures and processes and leaving them exposed to fast and unpredictable changes. Globalisation is one stream in this process interacting with urbanisation, spread of markets, and accelerated growth that is not inclusive. The total impact on the community is multi-dimensional: loss of traditional livelihoods, shifting from relatively self-sufficient and familiar face-to-face community to the unfriendly wider world, distant markets and impersonal social and economic processes, and having to cope with vulnerabilities resulting from the lag between rapid changes around them, on the one hand, and information, knowledge, and capacities needed to adjust to these changes, on the other.

A complicating factor is that the extent and pace of adjustment differ sharply across rural communities and across the strata within them like labourers, farmers, and rural elites. The adjustment process in India is far from complete. As a result, vulnerability and distress are widespread in rural communities and, while a few rise from rags to riches, millions struggle, barely managing to keep their nose above the water.

This scenario is not inevitable, as right strategies and policies could transform the adjustment process into one of inclusive growth and more harmonious society. The scenario so far has been discouraging, but improvements in future seem plausible. In a democratic polity, the vulnerability and distress typical of the adjustment process operating now in India generates political pressures counteracting the negative fallout of the process. Understanding the adjustment process is of critical importance for both academics and policy makers. This would help in devising measures to remove vulnerability and distress in rural communities. Even more important, widespread rural vulnerability and distress can well become formidable barriers in achieving viable and sustained development of India and stability and robustness of its polity. The purpose of this paper is to present a broad and simplified account of the adjustment process relying mostly on stylised types, relations, and processes. We begin with a sketch of the globalising world highlighting the features relevant for understanding the adjustment process.

Globalising World: Some Features of Structure and Dynamics

A prominent feature of the globalising world is the growing interdependence among the countries in the world. Policies and actions in one country can have serious repercussions in countries near and far. It is frequently observed in India that changes in interest rates in the United States has the effect of sudden and unpredictable destabilisation of Indian stock exchanges leading to adverse impact on business confidence and investment climate. These are not long-term changes, but they do disrupt economic processes like growth and price behaviour. Growing interdependence implies that the countries have to coordinate their policies with those of other countries. When there are clashes and conflicts in policies across countries, it is the weaker country which ends up accepting compromises favouring the stronger countries. The point is that the interdependence among the countries in the globalising world is sharply asymmetrical and not mutual.

A particular note needs to be taken in India of the trends attributable to asymmetrical relations between the developed and the developing countries. The development gap between the two groups is widening and the developed countries continue to control large and growing proportion of world resources and incomes. The implication is that developing countries may be able to achieve increases in income, but they will remain second-class citizens in the globalising world. Among the developing countries, India has much better prospects for growth, but it has to guard against naïve prescriptions of free trade as a panacea for accelerated growth and development. Developed countries twist the rules of international trade to suit them, their rampant consumerism is a serious threat to equitable world development, and the aid they give to the developing countries is far too meagre compared to what they can or should give. Experts are cautioning that many among the developing countries are turning into 'failed states' in the sense of losing economic viability and political stability.

The consequence of the growing and asymmetric interdependence in the globalising world is increasing proneness of developing countries to economic instability. Technological changes, shifts in demand triggered by widening range of goods and services, competitive advertising campaigns and rising incomes generate unceasing waves of change – frequent, sudden, and unpredictable – allowing little adjustment time to producers, employers, employees, and consumers. Worrying about what comes next and how to deal with it is seen by them as an indispensable strategy. This turns later into a habit and, eventually, hardens into a complex, dominating one's thinking and behaviour during waking hours as well as in sleep! Instability can be moderated through control measures like monetary policy and supply and demand management. But far more menacing is an extreme form of instability which can trigger chaos and major breakdowns in a large interdependent system like a globalising world. Familiar examples are earthquakes, volcanoes, and tsunamis, which are regarded as acts of god. These are rare and non-targeted, and they usually leave enough time between two occurrences to restore normal operation of the system. But, now, a computer hacker as inconspicuous as a pin in a haystack can disable global online transactions or tamper with the crucial data bases of multinationals. This can lead to widespread panic, further intensifying the chaos. Interestingly, much of economics is based on the assumptions of instabilities which are self-correcting, stability of equilibrium, and inability of individual economic agents to affect behaviour of the system. Few economists seem to understand that the globalising world is a very different animal than the models they use to mimic the real world systems confronting them!

A clear implication of these features of the globalising world is that the growth-cum-development trajectory of developing countries will be far from uninterrupted and smooth. These countries are already handicapped by poor governance, and their getting dragged into the globalising world will impose further intolerable burden on their capacities for governance and policy making for development. As noted above, the prospects of becoming a 'failed state' are already casting a shadow on them. What is important to note is that 'failed state' does not mean that the developing countries will all disintegrate. The scenario is likely to vary widely across them. We take a stylised case reflecting the broad experiences and prospects of India. In this case, the developing country will have a shining core gaining further in lustre through globalisation. The elites in these countries who are co-opted by the developed countries will attain peaks of affluence. The beneficiaries of globalisation will also include sizeable middle classes participating in accelerated growth. Below them will be another chunk of lower middle classes, upwardly mobile and enjoying political clout as organised groups but with modest lifestyles typical of the relatively better-off in urban slums. These three strata may account for a third of the population. The remaining two-thirds are the unorganised poor depending on overcrowded agriculture and a growing informal sector offering casual, unskilled, and low-productivity jobs. However, these divisions in the society will be changing over time.

In open democracies like India, growth, even if it is not inclusive, will nurture upward mobility among all the divisions.

This trend will work along two mutually reinforcing paths: improvement in economic conditions in the intermediate and upper strata, and growing political militancy among the lower strata in which rising aspirations trigger protests and agitations. The stability of the system will depend on the balance between the space created by growth for upward mobility among the lower strata and the intensity and spread of their political mobilisation. Underlying the formation of these strata are historical processes of urbanisation, spread of markets, decline of relatively isolated, local-based village economies, and modern technology-based economic growth. Globalisation has the effect of accelerating these processes and intensifying vulnerability of all strata to rapid change and instability generated by growing global asymmetric interdependence and proneness of global systems to chaotic shocks. However, elites and middle classes will have mechanisms and networks to face instability and to benefit from growth opportunities. This is not true of the lower strata which will remain large in size for many decades to come. It is the adjustment of these strata to globalisation which will play a crucial role in the long-term development of developing countries. In the case of India, the critical test is the accommodation of rural communities in the globalising Indian economy, polity, and society. The next section takes a look at the globalisation of rural communities in terms of recent and emerging scenarios.

Globalisation of Rural Communities

The decades since independence in India have witnessed a virtual transformation of rural communities. By transformation we mean a thorough societal churning of these communities, a process which is still in progress. The rural communities are in different stages of adjustment to globalisation and it could be several decades before their structure and economy stabilise. The following are the main factors underlying the societal churning:

(a) There have been by now over half a century of government interventions to improve physical infrastructures (roads, schools, health centres, market yards, etc.) needed by rural communities and the supply of development services to improve education, health, nutrition, skills, and assets.

Viewed from the historical perspective, these have been unprecedented in scale and spread. Their direct impact in terms of benefits conferred on rural people has been modest and uneven across regions and communities. However, their indirect effects in the form of opening up rural communities and linking them with wider world have been impressive and laid the foundation for rural transformation.

(b) Based on this foundation, market forces and other economic processes penetrated rural communities widely and deeply. As an important outcome, there is now a substantial middle class in rural communities aspiring for and adopting urban middle-class lifestyle and increasingly resembling their urban counterparts in worldview, attitudes, and behaviour patterns. This has an important implication for rural transformation. Rural demand for goods and services typical of urban middle classes expands leading to increase in secondary and tertiary sector employment available to rural people. Thus, market-induced growth will gain in inclusiveness because of its demand and employment effects on rural communities.

(c) Urbanisation has been understood so far as growth of cities and towns and migration from villages to urban places. Rural transformation adds new dimensions to the process of urbanisation. As rural demand and economic activities get stimulated, some of the villages become larger villages and eventually small towns. Thus, urban boundaries expand and the rural boundaries shrink. The distance between a village and its nearest urban place decreases and commuting helps more and more rural people to avail of urban facilities and newly emerging urban opportunities.

(d) Improvements in transport and communications and accessibility almost everywhere to TV, computers, and telephones and mobile phones bring about greater awareness and knowledge of the wider globalising world and improve capacity to participate in their activities and networks. There also occurs a shift in the aspirations, attitudes, and worldview of the rural people. This can be described as urbanisation of rural people while they still remain in villages! The urbanisation in this sense far exceeds the extent of urbanisation as given by the conventional measures.

(e) The traditional isolation had kept the rural communities bound with the past while the urban people moved ahead towards modernity. This isolation is now dissolving along with the social, cultural, economic, and political gaps between the two. The rural communities are getting drawn into a new world full of menacing vulnerabilities but which also offers opportunities to break with the past of stagnation and deprivations. Rural transformation is not a gentle evolutionary process. It resembles violent churning, uprooting people, destroying their traditional livelihoods, and compelling them to adjust to changes much before they understand and get ready to accept the changes. The vulnerabilities and opportunities confronting rural people need to be viewed from this perspective.

It is helpful for this purpose to have a device which enables us to view the various changes above as a composite process of rural transition. We construct such a device based on two rural types which are polar opposites of each other. These are briefly described below.

Traditional Rural Community (TRC)

- Local based, survival-oriented, inward-looking with livelihoods, contacts, transactions, and economic and social relations all mostly confined within the community with little links with and support from the world outside.
- Rigidly hierarchical with the lower strata accepting their status – mutual dependence between the lower strata and local elites – the community could come together in facing famines, maintaining village tanks, etc.
- No economic growth, development, and new technologies.
- The poor traced their sufferings to destiny and not to the domination by the elites. Elites, in turn, were exploitative but also played the role of patrons towards the poor as clients. The community had only two strata: elites and the poor.
- The community was isolated from winds of change from outside. Further, there were no endogenous factors bringing about changes in community structure and its internal balance and stability.
- The community was vulnerable to droughts, floods, etc. and faced the risk of being wiped out. This did happen on a significant scale checking population growth.

Urban Layout (UL)

- A settlement of residents – a part of large organised city/town – with livelihoods, contacts, transactions, social and economic relations mostly outside the layout. UL is a neighbourhood, not a community.
- The intra-layout contacts mostly for festivals and celebrations.
- A layout usually consists of people roughly similar in socio-economic status leading to the dichotomy of posh areas and slums separating the upper and the lower strata and leading to alienation of the latter and indifference and even hostility among the upper strata towards the slums and its inhabitants.
- Changing and heterogeneous composition of UL due to continuing entry and exit of residents with different religion, language, and regional features.
- Residents have multiple identities and participate in several networks (religious, occupational, cultural, etc.) spanning large areas and some with even global spread!
- UL is a polar opposite of TRC. Directly or indirectly, it is linked to and integrated with global networks and is exposed to fast changes, instability, and chaotic shocks typical of globalising world.

Rural communities in India are moving from TRC to UL at different pace, with some reaching the terminal point and others settling at intermediate stages. We feel that probing this transition could bring out vividly the processes of rural change. TRC and UL are types to assist research, not development goals. They could be of help in conceptualising meaningful intermediate types to enable the modelling and quantification of processes of rural change and their implications for rural development.

Let us see a few illustrations of how this transition operates:

(a) Nagarabhavi, where the Institute for Social and Economic Change is located, was, until the early 1970s, a small hamlet with only a cart track connecting it to Bangalore city. The establishment of the Institute in 1975 led to the construction of a *pucca* road and later a blacktop road. This attracted residential layouts on both sides of the road along with numerous service activities. Today, Nagarabhavi is 'Bangalore – 560072' with two universities, a super-speciality hospital, and some high-profile institutes located within or nearby, an exploding population of migrants from outside and a perpetual traffic jam! All this happened in less than three decades. It is difficult to see any rural attributes in the present Nagarabhavi or in its inhabitants.

(b) Here is an interesting pen picture of Bajpe, a village about 15 km from Mangalore, a growing city in coastal Karnataka: 'Mangalore International airport is located at a distance of 2 km from the village which is one of the main reasons for its rapid development. It has also led to influx of population making it a transit point for many to commute to other places to seek employment. Non-Resident Indians (NRIs) and caretakers of their properties also constitute many households. The village is much urbanised with good access to infrastructural facilities' (a private communication received by the author).

(c) The spatial pattern of habitations in rural areas is marked by large villages providing a variety of services to neighbouring villages and serving as their link with the world outside. In the course of rural transition, these grow into towns with multiple linkages with towns and cities nearby and far. The neighbouring villages of such towns remain rural only in name and records. They become outlying parts of the town. Simultaneously, apart from migration to urban areas, relocation of rural people takes place within rural areas from small and remote habitations to large villages where markets and growth generate new economic activities. Rural people gain in accessibility to and visibility in the mainstream and acquire a deep urge for upward mobility. Rural transition along with the looming presence of rural people in the mainstream is both irreversible and unstoppable.

For considering vulnerability and opportunities arising in the wake of globalisation, the first step is to find out how the composition of rural communities changes. In our view, as the transition progresses, three identifiable strata emerge in the community:

(i) A gradually expanding creamy layer of elites living in the village but belonging to the wider urban world with active economic and social relations outside the village rather than within. They resemble lower-cum-middle classes in urban areas in lifestyle, and have similar livelihoods, attitudes, aspirations, and membership in mainstream networks. They are better-off than the rural poor, but not affluent. Only a few among them acquire enough political clout to bend government policies.

(ii) An intermediate strata of upwardly mobile people – mostly farmers – struggling to get out of subsistence agriculture to join modern, commercialised agriculture producing for distant markets and using purchased inputs coming from outside. Some succeed, many fail. The rural elites are their role model. Gradually, a rural middle class emerges with urban lifestyles and consumerist aspirations. They are eager to join the urban mainstream, their children leave village and agriculture, and those in the village shift to value-adding agricultural activities and other non-agricultural activities. Some of them join rural elites, and the creamy layer expands.

(iii) A large and heterogeneous lower stratum (about 75 per cent of people in the village) consisting of the chronically poor, deprived, and suppressed sections at the bottom; an enterprising section striving to move up; and those downgraded from the intermediate strata having failed in their efforts to become upwardly mobile. Our guess is that the lower strata also acquires urban perceptions, attitudes, preferences, and aspirations like the middle classes and elites, but get disaffected as they do not benefit from rural transition. The gap between what they are and what they want to become grows fuelling impatience, anger, and a deep urge to join extremist groups like the Naxalites. This numerically large stratum is potentially a major actor in the mainstream economic, political, and social spaces, particularly in the latter two. If they move up in the economic space, they graduate into relatively contended and orderly citizens in the mainstream at the level of lower middle classes in UL. The mainstream comes under increasing pressure from those gate-crashing into the economic space and those challenging the mainstream in the political space. The changing villages will unleash in India a phase of unrest, violence, some broad-based and inclusive growth and accommodative response from the presently organised groups in the mainstream which is likely to be 'too little, too late' in nature. Will this phase lead to a new equilibrium based on peace, harmony, and social justice? This will depend on how the policy makers help the people in this stratum to join and participate in the mainstream.

While all the three rural strata described above are likely to be overwhelmed by the rural transformation triggered by a host of change processes including globalisation, it is the strata of rural poor which would play a crucial role in the adjustment of rural communities to globalisation. If the rural poor achieve improvement in their economic and political status, it will give a powerful boost to inclusive growth in rural areas and in the economy as a whole. In this scenario, the other two rural strata would find it easier to adjust and add further thrust to economic growth and political stability. Ordinarily, the government policies would be biased in favour of the elites and intermediate strata. A crucial requirement for adjustment of rural communities to globalisation is that the government policies give priority to the needs of rural poor. The next section brings out the vulnerability of rural poor and their priority security requirements to enable them to protect themselves and to benefit from development processes.

Adjustment of the Rural Poor to Globalisation

In TRC, the rural poor were bound to their masters in a slave-like relationship. This had roots in the caste hierarchy and, hence, it was impossible to break it so long as the caste system survived. It is necessary to remember that TRC as a whole was poor in the absence of development and technological change and highly vulnerable to natural disasters owing to its isolation and absence of any mechanism from outside for providing aid during disasters. Very likely, the 'uninhabited villages' figuring in our census district handbooks are the scars of the devastations which occurred in the past. The transition from TRC to UL pushes the rural poor into a totally new world of opportunities, but which is hostile to those – like the rural people – uninformed and unequipped for the transition. This is the principal source of vulnerability in the new world. The rural elites and the upwardly mobile find it relatively easy to adjust – as indicated by the expanding urbanised rural middle classes and the rich. But, for the rural poor, the transition is like a fall from the frying pan into the fire. The breakdown of TRC removes the very foundation supporting their survival. They drift towards activities in the informal sector – also known as the unorganised sector – which is a euphemism for low-skilled, ill-paid casual employment with intermittent work for changing employers and with no security cover of any kind. However, the informal sector is an expanding part of the economy and, with accelerated growth in the mainstream economy, new semi-skilled and skilled avenues of employment originate and grow in the informal sector.

The rural poor thus get some opportunities, though very modest, for upward mobility. They are held back by three traps in their quest for upward mobility. First, lacking food and employment security, they operate with shortest time horizon having to survive from day-to-day without any assurance about the morrow. This constitutes the *hardcore poverty trap* driving them towards exploiters like moneylenders and employers. Dependence on these categories perpetuates their poverty, which often spills over to future generations. Second, investments in education, health, nutrition, skills, and assets need medium-term to long-term perspective, sustained investments, efforts and enterprise, and adequate capacity to bear risks and tide over crises. This may be called the *human development trap,* which the poor can hope to tackle after leaving hardcore poverty behind. Third, as a result of these two traps, the poor suffer from the *isolation trap* in the sense of poor political visibility in the mainstream and absence of political clout and bargaining power. The isolation trap makes the poor vulnerable to exploitative relationships in their dealings in the mainstream.

There are three forces which have a softening effect on these traps: (i) urbanisation in the broader sense described above, (ii) expansion and diversification in the informal sector, and (iii) the wide range of development interventions by the government, funding agencies, and the activists. However, currently and over the coming years, the rural poor are likely to remain extremely vulnerable. The spectre of economic and political destabilisation would loom large over India until the rural poor are helped through in time to come out of the three traps.

We draw upon a study conducted by the Centre for Development and Decentralisation, Institute for Social and Economic Change, Bangalore to describe in more detail and concrete terms the vulnerability of the rural poor.[2] This was a study of workers in the unorganised sector to which the rural poor turn as TRC disintegrates. The unorganised sector has strata ranging from semi-skilled and semi-organised at the top, like construction workers, to the casual agricultural labourers and domestic workers at the bottom. Our study was based on these three strata for two reasons. These strata provide insights into the heterogeneity within the unorganised sector arising from emerging of new activities with better skill content and more opportunities to the workers to get organised. We assume that this trend in the unorganised sector helps the sector to seek parity with the organised sector. This provides a path to those in the lower strata, like agricultural labourers, to move up in the scale of skilled employment with potential to get organised. Our study does not give a full view of this process, but provides suggestive glimpses of the process bringing out the vulnerabilities of the rural poor and the measures which the policy makers can take to help them along the path of upward mobility opened up in the unorganised sector.

A word about the methodology of our study is in order. Since we look at vulnerability in the unorganised sector in a comparative framework, including organised sector, we need to have a norm from the organised sector of secure status of worker and indices capable of reflecting the gap between the two sectors. Our choice of constructs for this purpose is briefly outlined below.

Regarding the norm, we look at the security characteristics of the class IV category of workers in government and public sector undertakings which are listed below. We consider this category as forming the lowest stratum in the organised sector.

(a) Full employment security and post-retirement benefits.
(b) Emoluments adjusted for price rise.
(c) Provisions to meet health needs and crises occasioned by sickness.

(d) Access to modest but reasonable amenities like housing, electricity, and drinking water.
(e) Adequate food security and affordability of balanced diet.
(f) Ability to provide schooling to children.
(g) Access to institutional finance for a variety of purposes.
(h) Work free from risks, hazards, and drudgery.
(i) Reasonable working hours and adequate leave facilities.

We consider these characteristics as constituting a reasonable norm to aim at for the workers in the unorganised sector. We call it the LOSW norm, as it is based on the characteristics of the category of the Lowest Organised Sector Workers. The reason for choosing the LOSW norm is that we consider it a reasonable norm to aim at in devising security measures for the unorganised workers. It would only be fair to admit that the LOSW category is not free from deprivations. We use the LOSW norm under the assumption that, once the unorganised workers reach this norm and enter the organised sector, they will acquire enough political clout and capacity for collective action to protect their interests as the present workers in this category do. It is the logic of our democratic polity that within the organised sector the relative position of groups depends on their political bargaining power. Regarding the indices to find out the gap between the two sectors, the gap is so wide that the indices which we use are much more modest than the LOSW norm. It was also necessary to keep in mind the data available as the indices had to be based on them. The three indices used in our study are indicated below:

(i) Livelihood Security Index (LIVS) assumes the value 100 for a household when it
    (a) has adequate access to the public distribution system (PDS),
    (b) is under no compulsion to borrow from informal sources to purchase food grains,
    (c) has access to owned land, and
    (d) has income greater than 125 per cent of poverty line income (PLI).
(ii) Human Development Index (HD) assumes the value 100 for a household when

(a) all children in the age-group 6 to 10 years attend school regularly,
(b) all adults in the household have completed secondary schooling, and
(e) the household has adequate access to primary health centre (PHC) or equivalent health facilities.

(iii) Lifestyle Index (LS) assumes the value 100 for a household when it
(a) has a *pucca* house,
(b) gets adequate drinking water throughout the year, and
(c) can afford a diet consisting of meat.[3]

Our findings suggest that there is a linkage between these three indices. Improvement in livelihood security provides the foundation for improvement in human development and lifestyle. However, we also get the impression that unless improvement in livelihood security is substantial, there will be no impact on human development and lifestyle. It is best to begin the story by noting that our indices would understate the gap between the unorganised worker and the worker in the organised sector getting the benefits mentioned earlier above. It may also be mentioned here that the highest values of the three indices over the entire sample were 72 for LIVS, 78 for HD, and 67 for LS. Thus, the unorganised worker usually having more skills, and working much harder and for much longer hours than a LOSW, suffers from a miserably low economic status as compared to his/her cousin in the organised sector. A worrisome implication is that the process of upward mobility of the rural poor, if at all operating, is slow and halting. Such societal processes can abort or get distorted if they are too slow or too fast. We also get the indication that disaffection is spreading among the rural poor, which in fact makes the prospects of their smooth and peaceful adjustment all the more problematic.

We now turn to the detailed findings of our study. It can be seen from Table 8.1 that the unorganised workers are mostly landless and belong to the Scheduled Castes, Scheduled Tribes, and backward castes – the enslaved categories in TRC. An interesting clue is that the construction workers are a little better off than the other two categories. Construction work is typical of urban growth and large developmental schemes. The last two rows in the table suggest that the rural poor benefit from 'trickle down' from mainstream growth and from development schemes, though the latter was seen to be a minor contributor. It is usual for development schemes to dry up as they percolate down to the lowest rural strata.

Table 8.1
Key household indicators

Key indicators	*Categories of workers*		
	CW (301)	*DW (104)*	*AL (505)*
% of BPL households	22	41	34
% of landless households	88	95	94
% SC/ST households	43	46	42
% Backward Caste households	16	13	11
% katcha house households	16	13	27
% households where highest literate member has completed at least secondary school	80	75	68

Abbreviations: CW = Construction Workers; DW = Domestic Workers; AL = Agricultural Labourers; BPL=Below Poverty Line.

Note: Figures in parentheses are the total number of sample workers in each category.

The investigators also recorded their visual impression of the condition of the households they visited. The categorisation based on this recording is presented in Table 8.2. 'Near destitute' and 'Very poor' account for over 90 per cent of domestic workers and agricultural labourers. Again, the construction workers are seen to be marginally better off, though even among them over 70 per cent belong to these two categories.

Table 8.2
Distribution of households by visible indicators of poverty

(percentage)

Categories of workers	*Visible indicators of poverty*		
	Near destitute	*Very poor*	*Poor*
Construction workers	9	63	28
Domestic workers	23	70	7
Agricultural labourers	27	65	8

Table 8.3 shows the distribution of households by income. The income categories are based on poverty line income (PLI), which is the income level used by the government to measure poverty. The middle category consists of those whose income was between 75 per cent of PLI and 125 per cent of PLI. '–PLI' is the category of those with income less than 75 per cent of PLI and '+PLI' contains those with income more than 125 per cent of PLI. Construction workers have incomes higher than the other two categories. The more interesting point about Table 8.3 is that PLI – a norm that forms the foundation of measurement and analysis of poverty in India – is so low that even those who are visually assessed as poor fall above the line! The National Commission for Enterprises in Unorganised Sector (NCEUS 2006) has argued in favour of a much higher norm, which gives a poverty headcount of nearly 70 per cent as compared to the Planning Commission estimate of around 20 per cent! It may be mentioned here that unorganised workers form over 90 per cent of India's workforce. The NCEUS suggestion has still to be taken note of by the Government of India. In our view, the low PLI is indicative of an important limitation of the anti-poverty strategy in India: the strategy is relief-oriented and not development-oriented. It is driven more by an attitude of charity towards the poor than a firm commitment to free them from the poverty trap.

Table 8.4 helps in bringing out the linkage among indices mentioned above. While LIVS improves substantially across the income categories, HD and LS indices show little increase. It seems plausible that the higher levels of income achieved by the unorganised workers still remain below the threshold above which HD and LS get impacted.

Table 8.3

Distribution of households by income categories

(percentage)

Categories of workers	*Income categories*		
	–PLI	*PLI*	*+PLI*
Construction workers	9	28	63
Domestic workers	30	27	43
Agricultural labourers	17	35	48

Notes: PLI = Poverty Line Income; –PLI = those with income less than 75 per cent of PLI; +PLI = those with income more than 125 per cent of PLI.

Table 8.4

Average LIVS, HD, and LS indices by income categories

(percentage)

Categories of workers	*Income categories*		
	–PLI	PLI	+PLI
Average LIVS index			
Construction workers	28	38	56
Domestic workers	27	38	51
Agricultural labourers	29	40	51
Average HD index			
Construction workers	46	46	52
Domestic workers	48	48	52
Agricultural labourers	48	49	52
Average LS index			
Construction workers	41	42	45
Domestic workers	42	43	41
Agricultural labourers	37	39	40

Notes: PLI = Poverty Line Income; –PLI = those with income less than 75 per cent of PLI; +PLI = those with income more than 125 per cent of PLI; LIVS = Livelihood Security; HD = Human Development; LS = Lifestyle

Finally, consistent with the interpretations drawn from the tables above, Table 8.5 indicates that the primary concern of the worker remains with the interruptions in employment either due to lack of it or reasons like sickness. It is only logical that old age, when capacity to work declines sharply, looms as a threat in the perception of unorganised workers. It is difficult to think of a more revealing indication of poverty trap keeping down the unorganised worker than their perceptions contained in Table 8.5.

Table 8.5

Distribution of workers by top priority given to social security needs

(percentage)

Categories of workers	*Social security needs*				
	Sickness	*Employment/ Injury*	*Unemploy-ment*	*Old Age*	*Death*
Construction workers	13	24	31	26	6
Domestic workers	13	6	28	41	12
Agricultural labourers	11	7	36	39	7

Profiles of Rural Poor Households

We conclude the paper with two profiles of rural poor households: one, a typical agricultural labourer still in the poverty trap and, the other, a construction worker who is emerging out of the trap, but the improvement in his income is apparently too modest to enable him to kick it away fully. The profiles are slightly edited version of the notes prepared by the researchers in our study when they were engaged in fieldwork. The profiles help in adding a bit of flesh and animation to the pictures of rural poor emerging from the tables.

Agricultural Labourer

Hanuma is an agricultural labourer in Someshvarapura, who was earlier pursuing his caste-based occupation of mat-making, but because there was too much uncertainty in it, he quit it completely and started working as an agricultural labourer. His wife also works as an agricultural labourer.

Someshvarapura is a village in Mysore taluk in Mysore district. It is around 16 km away from the city of Mysore. There is a primary and secondary school in this village as well as a PDS outlet. The nearest PHC and the high school are in the neighbouring village of Devalapura, which is 2 km away.

The two main occupations in the village are agriculture and construction. Some other occupations that some people undertake are caste-based occupations like basket-making, mat-making, blacksmith, pig-rearing, etc., or driving, lorry cleaning, etc., for which the workers have to go to the cities. The distribution of occupations across the households is based on two important dimensions: landholding or landlessness, as the case may be, and caste. The landed people are involved in agriculture throughout the year, and in related farm activities such as poultry, cattle rearing, etc. The farmers with irrigated land grow mostly paddy, while the dry-land farmers grow ragi and jowar predominantly. The nearest market where they can sell their agricultural produce is Mysore city. Since there are around 60 landless households in the village, members of these households work as daily-wage earners. In this aspect, there is a gender divide. The men from landless households are mostly construction labourers (both skilled and unskilled) or other kinds of daily-wage earners such as drivers or lorry cleaners, etc. For all of these activities, they go to the urban areas, mainly to Mysore city. The women usually stay back in the village as agricultural labourers. Some women also go to the city for construction work, but only during the slack agricultural season (March to May).

One of the important features of the landless households is that a majority of them belong to various servicing castes, such as blacksmiths, mat-makers, basket-makers, pig-rearers, etc. (these are the four main service castes in this village). But not many of them choose to practise their caste-based occupations because it is not profitable for them. This means that, while some members of their households may still be involved in these occupations, they are no longer the *principal occupation of the household.* Other members are involved in wage labour such as agriculture, construction, etc., which accounts for the larger share of the household income.

Hanuma and his wife have two children. After their daughter had passed the seventh standard, they had to pull her out of school because Someshvarapura does not have a high school, and they cannot afford the bus charges to send her to the neighbouring village (Devalapura) where there is a high school. Hanuma mentioned that he would certainly like to have his children well educated, but since the family income is so unsteady, it is difficult. Currently, only their son Narayana is attending school, and Hanuma hopes that he will be able to at least send him to Devalapura for high school education, since he does not want his son to end up as agricultural labourer like himself. The household has always had a ration card and has full access to PDS in the village. Since the PDS operator in Someshvarapura is known to indulge in considerable diversion of food grains, the household does not always get the quantity of PDS items that it is entitled to, and during such periods, it has to depend on other shopkeepers. There is no problem of drinking water in the village as there is adequate water from both the bore-wells as well as the public taps.

Table 8.6
Hanuma's household socio-economic profile

Income category	75–125% of BPL income
Visible indicator of poverty	Poor
Imputed asset value of household	Zero
Livelihood security index	27.78%
Human development index	44.44%
Lifestyle index	33.33%

Neither Hanuma nor his wife is a member in any self-help group (SHG) or other organisations. His wife said that she was interested in joining a SHG in the village, but since they belong to the Nayaka caste, she was not permitted to join the group, which consists of only the richer and forward-caste people in the village. In addition, now, they do not have the money to contribute to such endeavours anyway.

Both Hanuma and his wife work as agricultural labourers. Hanuma said that, for both of them, there is usually more work in summer because they work for only the big farmers who have irrigated lands. During the monsoons, they seldom go out to work because when there is very heavy rain, they cannot work. Therefore, contrary to the usual employment pattern of agricultural labourers, this household claims that there is more employment during the slack agricultural season, and during periods of unemployment, they depend on borrowings. Hanuma gets a daily wage of ₹ 50, while his wife gets only ₹ 20. They do not have any other source of income, as they do not have any income-generating assets, nor has either of them undertaken any non-agricultural labour in the last one year.

Hanuma said that he has not learned anything new as far as his work goes in the recent past. Since the employment he gets is insufficient even to assure two meals a day, he has been looking for more and more employers, both within the village and in neighbouring villages. He said that there are no trade unions or other such worker-level organisations in the village. In 1996, Hanuma had taken out a post-office life insurance policy for a sum assured of ₹ 20,000 and a monthly premium of ₹ 99. He said that he paid one month's premium to the agent who was collecting it door-to-door, but after the first month, the agent did not come back.

About four years ago, the household had taken a loan of about ₹ 2,000 from a moneylender at the rate of 10 per cent interest per month to tide over their household expenses during a prolonged period of unemployment. They had taken the loan on the condition that they would repay it within one year. Since they could not repay it, the moneylender used to come banging at their door every single day and threaten Hanuma of dire consequences. Unable to take this strain, he ran away from the village for a period of one year. He went to Srirangapatna where he did all kinds of casual labour for that one year. Whatever he could save out of that, he sent home to his wife for the household expenses. On asking him how he left his family at the mercy of a moneylender who threatened them, he replied that he knew the moneylender to be a decent man. Much as he might threaten him, he was confident that he would never hurt the family in any way. It was with this confidence that he disappeared from the village for a year. In the meanwhile, during that one year, his wife tried to work as much as possible, and took another loan of ₹ 3,000 from another moneylender at ten per cent interest per month, and managed to repay the previous loan. Only after she repaid this did Hanuma enter the village. Though they have managed to somehow shake off one money-lender, the household is still indebted to the second one. They have for the last two-and-a-half years, paid nearly ₹ 3,600 by way of interest to him and no part of the principal amount has been repaid yet.

When Hanuma was asked to rank the social security needs, he gave the top priority to survivor benefits to his family in the event of his death, since he does not want them to suffer later. The second and third ranks were given to old-age pension and insurance against sickness respectively. He also said that he would be willing to contribute ₹ 20 per month towards a social security scheme that took care of his needs as he has ranked them. He was, however, skeptical at the mention of a scheme and the idea of contributing towards it. He said that since he has burned his fingers once with the life insurance policy, he would contribute towards a new scheme only if he was assured that it was cent per cent trustworthy and foolproof.

Construction Worker

Basava is a construction worker (painter), belonging to the Lingayat caste, who hails from the village of Huyilalu in Mysore district. On approaching the village people and asking them about the painters in the village, all of them unanimously pointed in the direction of his house and said that he is the most skilled painter (master-painter, they called him) in the village, and if we interviewed him, it was as good as interviewing all the painters in the village. We learned that Basava and his brother-in-law are the two most experienced painters in the village and have taught the art to all the others there.

Huyilalu comes under the jurisdiction of the Gram Panchayat of Nagavala, which is 20 km away from Mysore city, off the Mysore-Hunsur highway. It is well connected by roads and bus services. Huyilalu has 180 households and one of the chief features of this village is that along with a few more villages such as Nagavala, Udburu, Ilwala, etc., in Mysore taluk, it is known for the concentration of construction workers, and this has an important bearing on the social organisation of production in the village. Huyilalu is known for skilled workers, especially the painters. This implies that all the construction workers in this village are men. They are all daily commuters to Mysore city, and they get a daily wage of anywhere between ₹ 100 and ₹ 180 depending on their skill level.

The number of landless households in this village is small, and so the agricultural labourers are few and far between. But the small and marginal farming households also undertake agricultural labour during the slack seasons. Since it is only the women who undertake agricultural labour, the wages for agricultural labour in this village are very low. The village does not have a PHC or any private doctor or clinic. The nearest PHC for the people of Huyilalu is in Ilwala, which is about 8 km away.

Basava lives in a rented house in the village paying a rent of ₹ 200 per month. He purchased a house site close to the village in 1998, and he says that he will start constructing his own house there in the near future. His household assets, besides the site, include just a kerosene stove and a wall clock. His wife is a member of an SHG in the village, which Basava says has joined more because of community pressure than anything else. But now, she has realised that belonging to such an organisation has a lot of advantages. Basava was one of the workers in Mysore who said very vehemently that he will never go and live in an urban area. He said that he does not mind commuting every day, and being away for some time when he is working in far away place, but he will never migrate to the city. He said that the construction workers in the cities lead a pathetic existence, living in pigeonholes, and paying exorbitant amounts of money for everything.

Table 8.7

Basava's household socio-economic profile

Income category	>125% of BPL income
Visible indicator of poverty	Non-poor
Imputed asset value of household	<=Rs 1,000
Livelihood security index	55.56%
Human development index	33.33%
Lifestyle index	33.33%

Basava was a running a small tea-stall in the village till about thirty years ago, and on incurring too many losses, he shut it down and started working as a construction worker. Initially, he was a helper, but eventually learned the art of painting. In recent years, he has even learned how to work on a computer, especially with respect to mixing colours, etc. Even though he has attended school only up to the age of 9, he says confidently that computers have certainly simplified our lives. He explained that earlier, the clients would be very fussy about the colours they wanted, and the painters had to waste a lot of time, money and effort in mixing shades and arriving at the right one, and even that would only be an approximation of what was required. But now with the computer doing this 'dirty work', the required shades are readily available, and clients are easily pleased.

Basava has always been active on the trade union scene. About fifteen years ago, he initiated the Karnataka Kattada Karmikara Sangha in Bangalore, and within a short span of time, it had nearly 15,000 members. However, due to a 'big problem', which he did not wish to discuss, this movement was short-lived. Basava did not lose heart; he revived it in Mysore three years ago, and is now the president of a 300-member strong workers' group. He says that it is very important for workers to have these unions as a security against exploitative employers. All the members pay ₹ 15 per month and the money is used to fund any emergencies they may have, to pay their rents during difficult times, pay for accident expenses, etc. Basava was unwilling to discuss social security schemes. It was apparent he had little faith in them.

Notes

1. This paper is based on my papers listed in the References.
2. Tables 8.1 to 8.5 and the two profiles are from Rao, Rajasekhar and Suchitra (2006).
3. Generally, the unorganised workers belong to castes that are non-vegetarian in their food habits.

References

National Commission for Enterprises in the Unorganised Sector (NCEUS). 2006. *Report on the Unorganised Sector. New Delhi:* NCEUS.

Rao, V.M. 1998. 'Economic Reforms and the Poor: Emerging Scenario', *Economic and Political Weekly,* 33 (29–30): 1949–54.

——. 2000a. 'Mapping the Periphery: The Poor Communities in the Southern States', *Journal of Indian School of Political Economy,* 12 (2): 235–65.

——. 2000b. 'Where Reforms Do Not Reach: Rural Poor in the Vicinity of Bangalore', *Journal of Indian School of Political Economy,* 12 (1): 1–19.

——. 2004a. *Rainfed Agriculture* (Volume 10 in the Series *State of the Indian Farmer: A Millennium Study*). New Delhi: Academic Foundation and Ministry of Agriculture, Government of India.

——. 2004b. 'Towards Effective Poverty Reduction: A Global Perspective' (Working Paper No. 155). Bangalore: Institute for Social and Economic Change.

——. 2005. *Poverty Reduction in an Elite-driven Democracy.* New Delhi: Institute for Human Development and Daanish Books.

——. 2006. 'Farmers in Market Economy: Would Farmers Gain through Liberalisation?', in N.A. Mujumdar and Uma Kapila (eds.): *Indian Agriculture in the New Millennium: Changing Perspectives and Development Policy* (pp. 73–87). New Delhi: Academic Foundation.

——. (ed.). 1998. *The Poor in a Hostile Society: Glimpses of Changing Poverty Scenario in India*. New Delhi: Vikas.

Rao, V.M.; D. Rajasekhar and J.Y. Suchitra. 2006. 'Unorganised Workers: Deprivations, Social Security Needs, Policy Implications', *Economic and Political Weekly*, 41 (19): 1913–30.

Rao, V.M. and D.V. Gopalappa. 2004. 'Agricultural Growth and Farmer Distress: Tentative Perspectives from Karnataka', *Economic and Political Weekly*, 39 (52): 5591, 5593–98.

Rao, V.M. and H.G. Hanumappa. 1999. 'Marginalization Process in Agriculture: Indicators, Outlook and Policy', *Economic and Political Weekly* (Review of Agriculture), 34 (52): A 133–38.

Rao, V.M. and P.D. Jeromi. 2000. *Modernising Indian Agriculture: Priority Tasks and Critical Policies* (Study No. 21). Mumbai: Development Research Group, Department of Economic Analysis and Policy, Reserve Bank of India.

9

Liberalisation and the Agrarian Crisis in India

GAURANG R. SAHAY

It is an acknowledged fact that rural India was an extremely backward social formation and faced numerous development-related problems such as landlessness and lack of resources and assets, poverty and indebtedness, lack of educational facilities and illiteracy, malnourishment and poor conditions of health and sanitation, etc., during the pre-economic reform phase. India's official approach to resolve these problems was critiqued by many scholars, development agencies, and national and international financial institutions such as the World Bank (The World Bank 1986, 1991; Parikh 1993, 1997; Pursell and Gulati 1993). It was argued that the official approach did not lead to rural development because it created barriers to development in agriculture, which has always been the major source of livelihood in the villages, by skewing the terms of trade against agriculture through protectionist trade policies and an overvalued exchange rate. Therefore, it was claimed that economic reforms and the liberalisation of the agrarian sector would lead to higher prices for agricultural produce, resulting in incentive to agriculture and, consequently, the growth in agricultural production. Since India had major comparative advantages in diversifying its cropping pattern in favour of highly valued and universally sought-after crops such as fruits, vegetables, and flowers, free trade and openness would maximise efficiency and gains in the agrarian sector. It was also contended that the process of liberalisation would make terms of trade favourable to agricultural growth in the country by cutting down on subsidies and doing away with the policy of output support prices and procurement of food, which was fiscally unsustainable and had usually suppressed prices of agriculture produce and proved inefficient and costly to farmers. The process of economic reforms promised to make agrarian sector competitive, efficient, and productive through deregulating agricultural credit, contract farming, raising land ceilings or putting an end to state-led land reform programme, encouraging private sector agricultural research, and making NGOs partners in the agricultural extension system. Accordingly, the Government in India started liberalising its economy from 1991 by adopting the neo-liberal economic agenda, that is, Structural Adjustment Programme (SAP). Important domestic regulatory measures were either removed or slackened, thereby encouraging free trade, technology imports, and foreign direct investment.

However, the data on agriculture in the last two decades show that the SAP-based economic reforms did not live up to their promises. They, in fact, resulted in large-scale crisis in rural India by creating some new problems and exacerbating the existing ones, and by increasing vulnerability and insecure conditions of peasants and agricultural labourers. This was because, contrary to expectations, the process of reforms adversely affected agriculture – the main occupation in rural areas employing about 57 per cent of the country's population. This crisis manifested in different forms: the most glaring and the gravest form has been the large number of cases of suicides by farmers and peasants. In this chapter, based mainly on government reports and academic research, this observation is sought to be substantiated through an analysis of the agrarian situation in contemporary times.

Agrarian Situation in Contemporary Times

Increasing Landlessness and Inequality in Landholdings

Under the neo-liberal policy framework, crop diversification became a desirable policy objective. Therefore, the cropping pattern was shifted from less-remunerative food grains to the high-value and export-oriented cash crops. This required rearticulating the economies of scale in agriculture. Thus, the policy prescribed concentration of landholdings through purchase or leasing-in by big landowners. This inevitably increased the inequalities in landownership. Also, raising or lifting of land ceilings for privately owned firms accelerated land concentration and reduced the amount of surplus land available through ceiling laws for distribution among the growing number of the landless people. This trend has substantially increased the land price and ousted small farmers out of the land market. To quote S. Hirashima,

> If the land leased out from small and marginal farmers to progressive farmers or landlords, whose objective of renting in land is to take advantage of economies of scale, then it would be difficult to terminate such a contract when land has already become an integrated part of scale farming. The land would remain leased out, or ultimately sold out. (2000: 3884)

Declining Productivity in Agriculture and Increasing Marginalisation of Peasantry

During the post-reform phase, the sectoral distribution of Gross Domestic Product (GDP) in India has seen a consistent decline in the share of agriculture. However, the shifting of associated labour force from agriculture has been much less than proportionate. In 2004–05, the share of agriculture in GDP was 20.2 per cent, and the workforce employed in agriculture constituted 56.5 per cent of the total workforce (see Table 9.1). The burden of this high percentage of agricultural labour force, along with their much less inter-sectoral relative productivities, gets further compounded because of a steadily contracting cultivable land area and a huge increase in the proportion of marginal landholders. During 1960–2003, the cultivable land area declined from 133 million hectares to 108 million hectares, whereas the number of holdings doubled from 51 million to 101 million (see Table 9.2). This has led to a sharp decline in the average size of the holding, leading to increasing number of marginal farmers from 39.1 per cent in 1960–61 to 71 per cent in 2003. This category of farmers operates only 22.6 per cent of the total land. The number of small, medium, and large farmers[1] has declined consistently during this period (see Table 9.3). Such landownership pattern aggravates the agrarian crisis in terms of insecurity associated with cultivation of marginal landholdings and the associated practice of sharecropping, high input-costs, inadequate returns, difficulties in accessing credit, etc. (Assadi 1998).

Table 9.1
Share of agriculture in GDP and employment

Year	*Share of agriculture in GDP at 1999–2000 prices (%)*	*Share of agriculture workforce in employment – UPSS (%)*	*Ratio of worker productivity in agriculture to non-agriculture*	*Ratio of worker productivity in non-agriculture to agriculture*
1972–73	41.0	73.9	0.26	3.92
1993–94	30.0	63.9	0.24	4.12
1999–00	25.0	60.2	0.22	4.55
2004–05	20.2	56.5	0.20	5.12

Source: Central Statistical Organisation (CSO) and National Sample Survey Organisation (NSSO) cited in GoI (2007) and Posani (2009).

Note: GDP = Gross Domestic Product, UPSS = Usual Principal and Subsidiary Status.

Table 9.2
Characteristics of operational landholdings

	1960–61 (17th Round)	*1970–71 (26th Round)*	*1980–81 (37th Round)*	*1990–91 (48th Round)*	*2003 (59th Round)*
Number of operational landholdings (millions)	50.77	57.07	71.04	93.45	101.27
Percentage increase	—	12.40	24.50	31.50	8.40
Land area operated (million hectares)	133.48	125.68	118.57	125.10	107.65
Average land area operated (hectares)	2.63	2.20	1.67	1.34	1.06

Source: NSSO cited in GoI (2007) and Posani (2009).

Table 9.3

Changes in the size distribution of operational holdings and operational area

Category of holdings	*Percentage of operational holdings*					*Percentage of operated area*				
	Year (Round)					*Year (Round)*				
	1960–61 (17th)	*1970–71 (26th)*	*1981–82 (37th)*	*1991–92 (48th)*	*2003 (59th)*	*1960–61 (17th)*	*1970–71 (26th)*	*1981–82 (37th)*	*1991–92 (48th)*	*2003 (59th)*
Marginal	39.1	45.8	56.0	62.8	71.0	6.9	9.2	11.5	15.6	22.6
Small	22.6	22.4	19.3	17.8	16.6	12.3	14.8	16.6	18.7	20.9
Semi-medium	19.8	17.7	14.2	12.0	9.2	20.7	22.6	23.6	24.1	22.5
Medium	14.0	11.1	8.6	6.1	4.3	31.2	30.5	30.1	26.4	22.2
Large	4.5	3.1	1.9	1.3	0.8	29.0	23.0	18.2	15.2	11.8
All Sizes	100.0	100.0	100.0	100.0	100.0	100.0	100.0	100.0	100.0	100.0

Source: NSSO cited in GoI (2007) and Posani (2007).

Changing Cropping Patterns and Diminishing Food Security Status

With the opening up of the economy, expectations of export opportunities and higher world prices of agricultural commodities led many farmers to move away from food crops to cash crops (Menon 2006). Devaluation of the rupee made Indian exports cheaper and hence attractive in the world market, and further encouraged shifting from food crops to cash crops (Christian Aid 2005). On aggregate, the total area of the country's farmland growing food grains declined by 18 per cent in the decade after 1990–91, whereas areas growing cash crops of sugarcane and cotton increased by 10 per cent and 25 per cent respectively (Shiva 2005). This process led to a sharp decline in the production of food grains production and this is now threatening the status of India as a 'food secure nation'.

The proponents of economic reforms argue that the slowdown in food grain or cereal production after 1990–91 does not reflect on structural crisis in Indian agriculture, but on the changing consumption patterns, from cereals to high-value products like fruits and vegetables, milk and milk products, meat, eggs, and fish, driven by higher incomes across different sections of the society (Government of India [GoI] 2005; Gulati and Mullen 2003; International Food Policy Research Institute 2005). This is also supported by data from the National Sample Survey Organisation (NSSO) rounds, which show that along with the slowdown in food crop production in the 1990s, there was a fall in the per capita consumption of cereals and an increase in the per capita consumption of high-value products mentioned above. However, there are many who do not buy this argument, because this period has witnessed a sharp fall in the levels of per capita calorie consumption. The NSSO data also show that the per capita per day calorie intake in rural areas fell from 2,266 kilocalories in 1972–73 to 2,183 kilocalories in 1993–94, and 2,149 kilocalories in 1999–2000 (Patnaik 2001). This fall was more conspicuous among the poorer or weaker sections of society. Given the falling calorie intake, along with a high level of malnutrition in rural India, the fall in food grain consumption can only be seen as a signifier of agrarian/rural crisis. Abhijit Sen suggests that, among the relatively poorer sections, the share of income spent on food was increasingly compressed in the 1990s by the growing shares of expenditures on health, fuel, transportation, and education (cited in Chandrasekhar 2007).

Declining Growth Rates of Agriculture

In the post-reform period, production of food grains is diminishing along with the declining growth rate of agriculture. The growth rate of agricultural component in GDP fell from 3.08 per cent over the period from 1980–81 to 1990–91 to 2.57 per cent from 1992–93 to 2005–06 (see Table 9.4). This included the fall to 1.3 per cent in 1999–2000 and even a negative growth of –2 per cent in 2000–01 (Posani 2009: 22). The growth rate by yield of all crops taken together dropped from 3.19 per cent during the period from 1980–81 to 1990–91 to 1.58 per cent from 1990–91 to 2003–04 (see Table 9.5). State-wise disaggregation of the data shows that this slowdown has occurred in most states except Bihar, Gujarat, and Orissa. Even these states had a low base and the growth rates were very low (see Table 9.6).

Table 9.4
Growth of GDP, sectoral GDP, and per capita income

Year	Agriculture	Industry	Services	GDP at factor cost	Per capita NNP at factor cost
1980–81 to 1990–91	3.08	5.79	6.54	5.15	2.82
1992–92 to 2002–03	2.61	5.82	7.65	5.85	3.89
1992–93 to 2005–06	2.57	6.05	7.72	6.00	4.10
1950–51 to 2005–06	2.54	5.19	5.40	4.26	1.94

Source: CSO cited in GoI (2007) and Posani (2009).

Note: Growth is Compound Annual Growth Rate; GDP = Gross Domestic Product; NNP = Net National Product.

Table 9.5
Growth of area, production, and yield of major crops

Crop	1980–81 to 1990–91			1990–91 to 2003–04		
	Area	Production	Yield	Area	Production	Yield
Rice	0.40	3.56	3.47	0.15	1.14	0.99
Wheat	0.46	3.57	3.10	0.74	2.13	1.35
Coarse Cereals	–1.34	0.40	1.62	–1.58	0.25	1.87
Total cereals	–0.26	3.03	2.90	–0.25	1.32	1.58
Total pulses	–0.09	1.52	1.61	–0.87	–0.74	0.16
Food grains	–0.23	2.85	2.74	–0.44	1.16	1.11
Sugarcane	1.44	2.70	1.24	1.41	1.22	–0.16
Oilseeds	1.51	5.20	2.43	–1.07	0.18	1.26
Cotton	–1.25	2.80	4.10	0.82	0.15	–0.69
Non-food grains	1.12	3.77	2.31	–0.09	1.20	0.62
All crops	0.10	3.19	2.56	–0.25	1.58	0.90

Source: Ministry of Agriculture cited in GoI (2007) and Posani (2009).

Note: Growth is Compound Annual Growth Rate.

Table 9.6
Growth of agricultural GSDP and GSDP across states

State	1983–84 to 1993–94 (at 1980–81 prices)		1993–94 to 2003–04 (at 1993–94 prices)	
	Agricultural GSDP	GSDP	Agricultural GSDP	GSDP
Andhra Pradesh	3.05	4.58	2.80	5.63
Assam	2.12	2.69	0.51	2.93

Cont'd...

...Cont'd

Bihar	***–0.45	5.00	2.50	5.34
Gujarat	***0.84	6.18	***1.13	6.19
Haryana	4.86	5.89	1.77	5.96
Himachal Pradesh	3.08	5.86	1.30	6.53
Karnataka	3.54	5.21	3.12	7.10
Kerala	4.40	7.42	*-2.00	4.85
Madhya Pradesh	*2.82	3.39	***0.23	4.14
Maharashtra	*5.39	5.13	1.27	4.92
Orissa	***–0.57	6.19	***0.17	3.96
Punjab	4.62	5.13	2.15	4.13
Rajasthan	3.93	6.19	***1.21	5.32
Tamil Nadu	4.43	7.45	***-0.60	5.08
Uttar Pradesh	2.80	4.66	2.18	3.76
West Bengal	4.45	4.73	3.45	7.03
India	3.05	5.32	2.19	6.01
Coefficient of variation for states	58.72	25.43	102.88	22.75

Source: CSO cited in GoI (2007) and Posani (2009).

Note: Growth is Compound Annual Growth Rate; GSDP = Gross State Domestic Product. All growth rates are significant at 5 per cent but for *, which is significant at 10 per cent and ***, which is not significant even at 20 per cent.

Diminishing Profitability of Agriculture

The post-reform phase has witnessed a fall in profitability of agriculture, notwithstanding variations across crops and regions (Sen 2003; Sen and Bhatia 2004; Surjit 2008). Abhijit Sen points out, this trend has been caused by a general slowdown in the diffusion of yield-increasing technologies and inputs and a slow rise in the prices of crops (Sen 2003). To quote Sen,

> During the 1980s, when yield growth was higher and prices of most crops tended to rise faster than the cost of living, the real per hectare margin of gross value of output (GVO) over cost ... increased for all crops except maize... During the 1990s, with yield growth slowing down for most crops and prices of crops other than cereals and sugarcane rising slower than the cost of living, the real GVO-cost margin fell for most crops other than wheat, sugarcane, barley and tur... Across states also, increases in GVO-cost margins were less evident during the 1990s than during the 1980s. (ibid.: 38 cited in Ramakumar 2010: 53)

In his study of farm business incomes from paddy cultivation in seven most important paddy-growing states, V. Surjit (2008) shows that, in four out of seven states, the growth rate of farm business incomes, which was positive in the 1980s, became negative in the 1990s (see Table 9.7). In other three states, except Andhra Pradesh, the growth rate slowed down significantly in the 1990s.

Table 9.7

Growth of farm business incomes from rice cultivation, 1973–74 to 2002–03

State	*TE 1983–84 to TE 1993–94*	*TE 1993–94 to TE 2002–03*
Andhra Pradesh	0.5	3.5
Karnataka	1.8	–2.1
Orissa	3.7	–4.5
Punjab	1.6	0.4
Tamil Nadu	NA	0.9
Uttar Pradesh	3.3	–2.1
West Bengal	3.7	–8.0

Source: Reports of the Commission for Agricultural Costs and Prices cited in Surjit (2008).

Note: Growth is Compound Annual Growth Rate; TE = triennium ending; NA = not available.

Balamuralidhar Posani (2009) has reflected on the inter-sectoral terms of trade between agricultural and non-agricultural sectors (that is, the ratio of total prices received by the agricultural sector to the total prices paid by it to non-agricultural sectors) to spell out that agricultural sector as a whole has lost in the process of economic growth. Based on official data, he writes,

> Although the reforms in the 1990s with policies such as devaluation of currency and ending of protection to industry were expected to benefit agriculture and improve its relative terms of trade (ToT), this has not really been sustained. The barter and income ToT became favourable to agriculture from 1984–85 until 1996–97, but thereafter they more or less stagnated. Likewise, the Input-Output Price Parity (computed by comparing the index of prices paid for agricultural inputs with the index of prices received for the outputs), which was unfavourable to agriculture during the 80s and then turned favourable in the early 90s, has

since 1994–95 remained lower than one hundred, indicating declining profitability of agriculture (ibid.: 24).

Wearing Away of Real Incomes of Farmers

The empirical case of late 1990s and 2000s also militates against the argument that claims that, during the phase of economic reforms, the terms of trade will increase real incomes of farmers by leading to a significant increase in the prices of crops. However, there was, actually, an erosion in the real incomes of farmers, because prices of crops fell sharply after 1996–97, largely as a result of the sharp fall in the international prices of primary commodities. The comparative growth in the prices of primary commodities from 1990–91 to 1996–97 occurred primarily because of the rising administered (procurement) prices of food grains, particularly rice and wheat. This apart, in the post-reform period, when the prices paid by the farmers for consumer goods (that is, Consumer Price Index for Agricultural Labour) are compared with the prices they receive for their crops, it becomes obvious that farmers have been facing an erosion of real incomes, because the rise in aggregate price index for consumer goods has been higher than the rise in price index for agricultural commodities (Government of Andhra Pradesh 2007; Mishra 2007; Posani 2009). This has resulted in declining relative living standards of farmers, particularly among small and marginal farmers, whose incomes are clearly inadequate to meet consumption expenditure (see Table 9.8).

Table 9.8

Monthly per capita income and consumption by size-class of holdings, 2003

Size-Class (hectares)	*Income (Rs)*	*Consumption (Rs)*
< 0.01	1,380	2,297
0.01 – 0.40	1,663	2,390
0.41– 1.00	1,809	2,672
1.01– 2.00	2,493	3,148
2.01–4.00	3,589	3,685
4.01–10.00	5,681	4,626
>10.00	9,667	6,418
All sizes	2,115	2,770

Source: NSSO – 2005 cited in Mishra (2007) and Posani (2009).

Slowdown of Exports and Increased Uncertainty vis-à-vis Cultivation

Contrary to the promise of economic reforms, India has witnessed a major rise in imports, rather than exports, of agricultural commodities after the mid-1990s. This has significantly narrowed down the difference between the rupee value of farm exports and imports. According to the Planning Commission estimates, the ratio of dollar value of agricultural exports and imports fell from about 5 in 1996–97 to 2.2 in 2003–04. The share of agricultural exports in total merchandise exports declined from 21 per cent in 1996–97 to 12 per cent in 2003–04. The ratio of agricultural exports to GDP from agriculture also fell from 7.6 per cent in 1995–96 to 6.9 per cent in 2003–04 (GoI 2005).

The rise in the imports often led to a sharp fall in the domestic prices of many primary commodities such as cotton, tea, coffee, spices, and many fruits and vegetables. This happened due to greater integration of the country's agrarian sector with the international market, which has displayed a sharp fall in the international prices for most agricultural commodities after the East Asian crisis, absence of quota controls as in the pre-WTO (World Trade Organisation) period, and the ineffectiveness of low tariffs (Bhalla 2004). A sharp fall in the international prices made imports cheap and exports uncompetitive. Integration with the international market, which led to an alignment of domestic and international prices, also made, following the volatility of international prices, the prices of agricultural commodities in the domestic market volatile (Patnaik 2002). This created some serious problems in the agrarian sector such as an increase in the uncertainties vis-à-vis cultivation and prices of primary commodities that will significantly erode competitiveness of Indian farm exports in the post-WTO period.

The Reduction of Input Subsidies

The provision for state subsidies on inputs is meant to enable farmers to modernise agriculture by adopting new technologies and inputs, including seeds, and to bear the associated risks. State subsidies considerably contributed to the success of 'Green Revolution' (Sen 1992). They also proved to be inclusive, leading to significant benefits for marginal and small farmers (Acharya and Jogi 2004). However, with the fiscal reforms that followed liberalisation, there has been a decline in state subsidies on inputs. This has been considered to be an important reason for the erosion of profitability of agriculture and the consequent agrarian crisis during the phase of economic reforms. In the early 1990s, the government used 1.6 to 1.9 per cent of GDP for subsidies on inputs; this reduced to about 1.3 per cent during 2003–06. So far as the share of state subsidies on inputs in the agricultural GDP is concerned, there has been an increase in the share of subsidy on electricity, whereas the share of subsidies on fertilizer and irrigation has fallen since the late 1990s, and particularly in the 2000s (see Sen 1992; Acharya 2000; Acharya and Jogi 2004).

Since state subsidies on inputs rationalises the ratio between the output price and the input price in favour of farmers, any reduction in the subsidies adversely affects farmers, because they have to pay more for inputs. Some would argue that the adverse impact caused by the rise in input price can be compensated by raising the output or procurement price of primary commodities (see Parikh 1997). However, this argument is not sustainable because a large number of farmers in India are small and marginal farmers who hardly generate a marketable surplus; most of their production goes into household consumption. This apart, procurement operations of the government are limited to certain regions in certain states (Sen 1992; Acharya 2000; Acharya and Jogi 2004). Notwithstanding the above arguments, there is a genuine scope for reducing subsidies without raising input prices through an improvement in the efficiency of production and management in the fertilizer, power, and irrigation sectors that is ironically not being paid adequate attention to by the liberalisation regime in India.

Lastly, cultivation of cash crops, particularly of the high-yielding varieties, which has been a fast growing practice during the phase of economic reforms, requires much greater amounts of water, fertilizers, and pesticides. However, with the reduction of subsidies on these inputs, following fiscal reforms, farmers' reliance on the market for these inputs increased substantially. Since the market prices of these inputs have risen considerably in the recent past, there is a sharp rise in the overall cost of cultivation. For example, the price per tonne of urea, diammonium phosphate and muriate of potash were ₹ 2,350, ₹ 3,600, and ₹ 1,300 respectively in 1990–91, which increased to ₹ 4,830, ₹ 9,350, and ₹ 4,455 respectively in 2003–04. The prices of cotton and chilli seeds went up by 400 per cent (Rao and Suri 2006). This apart, the new Intellectual Property Rights (IPR) regime forbids the reuse of the seeds from the current harvest for the next planting, compelling farmers to purchase seeds anew each time (GoI 2006).

Declining Gross Capital Formation in Agriculture

Capital formation – an essential element of growth of any sector – is manifested in different forms in agriculture, such as development in irrigation system and rural infrastructure. Many studies have shown that a larger part of the post-reform period has seen a noticeable fall in gross capital formation (GCF) in agriculture (Shetty 1990; Chand 2000; Gulati and Bathla 2001; Sawant et al., 2002; Posani 2009). Table 9.9 shows that the share of agricultural GCF in total GCF and GDP fell from 16.1 per cent and 3 per cent in 1980–81 to 7.3 per cent and 2.4 per cent in 2005–06. This was mainly due to a sharp decline in the share of public sector GCF and the inability of the private sector to fill the gap. Posani also writes, 'Simultaneously, there was a big fall in the rural share of total development expenditure from 11.7 per cent of GDP in 1991–92 to 5.9 per cent in 2000–01. This translates into less state support and hence increased expenditure by rural families on things like health and education' (ibid.: 26).

Traditionally, in India, public investment in agriculture has encouraged private investment by farmers. This complementarity between public and private investments was visible till the 1980s (Shetty 1990; Storm 1993; Dhawan 1998). During the period of economic reforms this complementarity has been largely disturbed; though there has been an increase in private investment, public investment has noticeably declined. In fact, the rise in private investment in agriculture appears to have been caused by a significant fall in public investment. This observation is substantiated by the fact of falling public investment in canal irrigation and a rise in private investment in groundwater, such as in tubewells.

Table 9.9
Gross capital formation in agriculture at current prices

Year	*Total GCF (Rs crore)*	*Public Sector GCF (Rs crore)*	*Private Sector GCF (Rs crore)*	*Share of Public Sector (%)*	*Share of Private Sector (%)*	*GCFA as per cent of total GDP*	*GCFA as per cent of AGDP*	*GCFA as per cent of AGCF*
1980–81	4,342	1,876	2,466	43.2	56.8	3.0	9.2	16.1
1990–91	15,839	3,586	12,253	22.6	77.4	2.8	10.5	11.5
1995–96	17,392	5,952	11,440	34.2	65.8	1.7	6.9	6.3
1999–00	50,151	8,670	41,481	17.3	82.7	2.6	11.2	9.8
2000–01	46,432	8,176	38,256	17.6	82.4	2.2	10.3	9.2
2001–02	60,366	10,353	50,013	17.2	82.8	2.6	12.4	11.1
2002–03	61,883	9,564	52,319	15.5	84.5	2.5	13.1	10.1
2003–04	61,827	12,218	49,609	19.8	80.2	2.2	11.6	8.4
2004–05	70,786	13,610	57,176	19.2	80.8	2.3	13.2	7.6
2005–06	83,952	—	—	—	—	2.4	14.1	7.3

Source: CSO cited in GoI (2007) and Posani (2009).

Note: GCF = Gross Capital Formation; GCFA = Gross Capital Formation in Agriculture; AGDP = Agricultural Gross Domestic Product; AGCF = Aggregate Gross Capital Formation.

Decline in Public Investment in Agricultural Research and Extension and Irrigation

Historically, in India, public investment in agricultural research and extension in India has been seen as creation of 'public goods'. A. Vaidyanathan (2000) opines that the widespread specialised state-funded agricultural research centres under the Indian Council for Agricultural Research and the agricultural universities, working with and through the National Extension Service, have contributed to the growth of agricultural productivity by developing and diffusing knowledge, skills, better varieties of seeds, and practices. This trend reversed during the phase of economic reforms. Liberalisation led to a drastic decline in the growth rate of public spending on agricultural research and extension: from 6.3 and 7 per cent to 4.8 and 2 per cent respectively between the 1980s and 1900–2005 (see Table 9.10). To compensate the decline, private sector investment in research and extension was encouraged; 100 per cent foreign equity was allowed in the seed industry, and import of seeds was permitted for research purposes under the Open General License. The government withdrew subsidies on extension services to create a favourable field for private players in seed industry and biotechnology firms. The gradual decline of state support also means that many state-run agricultural institutions or corporations, which had provided support, including skills to farmers, particularly small and marginal farmers, disappeared or became largely inactive due to shortage of funds.

Table 9.10

Growth in real public expenditure on agricultural research and extension, 1960s to 1990–2005

Period	*Research and education*	*Extension and training*
1960s	6.5	10.7
1970s	9.5	–0.1
1980s*	6.3	7.0
1990–2005	4.8	2.0

Source: Balakrishnan et al. (2008).

Note: Growth is Compound Annual Growth Rate; 1980s* = figure for 1980s is for 1980–94 for 'extension and training'.

However, decline in public investment in agricultural research and extension, and consequent changes, have proved to be disastrous for agriculture in India. According to a Planning Commission review, the sluggish growth in agriculture during the phase of economic reforms was caused by 'unresponsive agricultural research, nearly broken down extension [and] inadequate seed production, distribution and regulation' (GoI 2005: 197). A commission, constituted by the Government of Andhra Pradesh, has also noted that the collapse of public agricultural extension services has been a contributory factor to the agrarian crisis in the state (see GoAP 2004).

Although there has been a clear shift in cropping patterns towards cash crops that requires more water for cultivation, the total net irrigated area remained stagnant (GoI 2007). Referring the situation in Andhra Pradesh, Posani writes:

> ... it actually declined from 43.5 lakh hectares in 1990–91 to 37.1 lakh hectares in 2004–05... Successive state governments have grossly neglected investment in surface irrigation infrastructure. Consequently, there has been an increase in private investment in exploiting ground-water sources (mainly bore wells), which have been growing relative to canal and tank irrigation. (2009: 29)

This has added heavily to the cost of irrigation or cultivation, made agriculture a highly risky enterprise, and 'led to overexploitation of groundwater and a falling water table, forcing farmers to deepen their wells every few years' (ibid.: 29).

Decline of Social and Development Banking and the Return of the Moneylenders

An essential component of economic reforms is financial liberalisation, which has altered the objective of the nationalisation of commercial banks in the country. The project of nationalisation of commercial banks (in 1969) included a supply-led policy of social and development banking in the rural areas. As a result, the nationalised commercial banks emerged as the main formal institutions of credit provision in rural areas, and tried to correct the deeply imperfect rural credit market by financing agriculture at an affordable, controlled interest rate (Shetty 1997; Ramachandran and Swaminathan, 2001; Chavan 2005). It helped farmers, particularly small and marginal farmers, in their attempt to adopt the costlier new technologies, high-yielding variety seeds, and farming practices, a critical component of the Green Revolution that largely solved India's food problems.

The national effort based on a supply-led policy of social and development banking to help farmers came to a rapid end with the implementation of the recommendations of Narasimhan Committee on Banking Reforms post-1991. The committee recommended the disconnection of monetary policy from the objective of redistribution, the decontrol of rates of interest, and allowing closure of rural branches to rationalise branch networks. The committee redefined priority lending and, thereby, squeezed credit lines to farmers. Many scholars have argued that the Narasimhan Committee report, based financial liberalisation after 1991, led to (a) large-scale closure of commercial bank branches in rural areas, (b) a broadening of inter-state inequalities in credit provision with a sharp decline in the proportion of bank credit in underdeveloped regions, (c) a sharp fall in the growth of credit flow to agriculture, and (d) an increased exclusion and marginalisation of the disadvantaged and dispossessed sections of the population such as small and marginal farmers from the formal financial or credit system (see Ramachandran and Swaminathan 2005; Chavan 2005, 2007; Shetty 2006; Posani 2009). To quote Posani,

> In Andhra Pradesh the proportion of bank lending to agriculture fell from 43 per cent in 1998 to 26.7 per cent in 2003, covering only one-third of the credit needs of the farmers. Even mandates of special lending to SCs [Scheduled Castes], STs [Scheduled Tribes] and very small farmers were revoked to pursue commercial viability and aggressive loan recovery. Tenant cultivators with insufficient titles are altogether denied access to formal credit'. (2009: 31–32; see also Christian Aid 2005)

Another noteworthy consequence of the financial liberalisation has been an increased hold of non-institutional usurious moneylenders on rural debt portfolios in different degrees across India. To quote Posani again,

> With this drying up of formal credit, the farmers are left with no choice than to depend on 'informal' sources for credit. An NSSO survey in 2004 revealed that 68.6 per cent of the total loans taken by farmers in Andhra Pradesh are from the informal credit market. This credit typically comes at usurious interest rates (anything between 36 per cent and 100 per cent compound), and worse, from the same entrepreneur who is selling the farmer the seeds and fertilizers. This stranglehold of the trader-moneylender has become the root of much exploitation and misery. Credit from these agents is almost never in cash form. It is inputs (his own brand of seeds, fertilizers) issued against the future output whose price, invariably low and exploitative, is fixed by the agent himself. (2009: 32; see also Christian Aid 2005; Suri 2006)

Though there has been a revival of agricultural credit in India in 2000s, its nature and objective is in consistent with the agenda of financial liberalisation; it is mainly targeted towards financing large-scale commercial, export-oriented and capital-intensive contract farming (Ramakumar and Chavan 2007).

Output Side of Agriculture: Uncertainty and Risk

Since 1990, the risk associated with the output side of agriculture has acquired new dimensions, which are detrimental to farmers. Referring the official data, Posani argues, 'To the conventional yield shocks associated with deluge or dearth of water, have been added shocks resulting from spurious seeds and adulterated pesticides from unregulated private dealers. The resulting crop failures have been one of the major factors pushing farmers into spiralling indebtedness' (2009: 30). Besides, shocks related to crop price resulting from India's accession to WTO have also been a major concern. With accession to WTO, state trading agencies were practically removed from participating in trade in agricultural commodities and, by 2000, all agricultural products were removed from 'Quantitative Restrictions' and brought under the tariff system or Open General Licensing. This development caused an unexpected increase in cheap agricultural imports that substantially depressed prices of domestic agricultural commodities: 'Import duty on cotton, for instance, was reduced to almost zero, leading to a sharp dip in the price of cotton which has been the crop of choice for many farmers in Andhra Pradesh.... A survey of cotton prices in Warangal district of AP [Andhra Pradesh] found the price of a quintal of cotton swinging wildly between ₹ 2,200 [and] ₹ 1,450 in a 45-day period, dipping at times to ₹ 1,200' (ibid.; see also Menon 2006). Traditionally, or before economic reforms, low yields were correlated with relatively higher crop prices; but, from the early 1990s, as P. Rao and K. Suri (2006) opine, the yield prices have depended more and more on the global rather than local supply and demand. Thus, the impact of low yield became grave because of low prices and the yield and price shocks together caused uncertainty and misery to farmers.

This problem is further compounded by a sharp decline in government procurement of agricultural produce over the years. Posani observes,

> There is no public procurement for commodities like chillies, pulses and oil seeds, and a very small percentage of the cotton produced is publicly procured. In addition, the minimum support price for many commodities is less than the market price. Since market prices revolve around the minimum support price, they end up reaching very low levels at the time of the harvest. (2009: 30–31)

Suicide by Farmers: Magnitude and Trends

The foregoing developments in the realm of agriculture in the post-reform period have brought about a crisis in rural India that manifests itself, among other things, in the increased incidence of suicide by farmers (see Assadi 1998; Parthasarathy and Shameem 1998; Shiva and Jafri 1998; Revathi 1998; Prasad 1999; Vasavi 1999; Bose 2000; Iyer and Manick 2000; Mohanty 2001, 2005; Deshpande 2002; Grover et al., 2003; Nirmala 2003; Sarma 2004; Mohanty and Shroff 2004; Rao and Gopalappa 2004; TISS 2005; IGIDR 2006; Mishra 2006; Sainath 2007). The official data show that the scale and spread of farmers' suicides in India are massive and the number and rate of these suicides have increased over the years.

The main source of official data on farmers' suicides is the annual reports on accidental and suicidal deaths published by the National Crime Records Bureau (NCRB) of the Ministry of Home Affairs, Government of India. These reports consist of a range of tables, and one of them is on the distribution of suicides by profession that includes a category for self-employed persons in farming/agriculture. All-India-wise consistent and complete data on suicides by persons employed in farming/agriculture is thus available for twelve years, from 1997 to 2008, covering the largest part of the economic reform period. However, as K. Nagaraj has argued, the rate among farmers (number of farmers' suicides per 1,00,000 farmers) 'can be calculated on a reliable basis only for the year 2001 because that is the only year for which we have reliable data on the number of farmers in country, and in different states, from the Census of India' (2008: 7). Given this, we have presented the data pertaining to farmers' suicide rates only for the year 2001.

Table 9.11

Farmers' suicides and all suicides, 1997–2006

Year	Farmers' suicides		All suicides	
	Number	% of all suicides	Number	Suicide rate
1997	13,622 (100)	14.2	95,829 (100)	10.0
1998	16,015 (118)	15.3	104713 (109)	10.8
1999	16,082 (118)	14.5	110,587 (115)	11.2
2000	16,603 (122)	15.3	108,593 (113)	10.8
2001	16,415 (121)	15.1	108506 (113)	10.6
2002	17,971 (132)	16.3	110,417 (115)	10.5
2003	17,164 (126)	15.5	110,851 (116)	10.4
2004	18,241 (134)	16.0	113,697 (119)	10.5
2005	17,131 (126)	15.0	113,914 (119)	10.3
2006	17,060 (125)	14.4	118,112 (123)	10.5
2007	16632 (122)	13.6	122,637 (128)	10.8
2008	16196 (119)	13.0	125,017 (130)	10.8
Total	199,132	14.8	1342,873	10.6

Source: National Crime Records Bureau (NCRB).

Note: Figures in parentheses give indices with 1997 as the base; Suicide Rate = Number of suicides per 100,000 population.

The NCRB data (see Table 9.11) show that, during 1997–2008, as 1,99,132 farmers committed suicide in the country. During this period, on an average, about 16,500 farmers committed suicide every year, and every seventh suicide in the country was a farmer's suicide. However, this distressful number is considered by many as an underestimation of the actual number of suicides by farmers in the country. Nagaraj observes,

These data published by the National Crime Records Bureau ... are put together from the police records from different states. Our experience during our field visits in Andhra Pradesh as [part] of the Farmers' Commission set up by the state government in 2004 was that the police often adopted a rather strict and stringent definition of a farmer in identifying a farm suicide. The title to land was taken as the criterion for identifying the farmer and this often left out a genuine farmer from the count. For example, a tenant farmer who leased in land and hence did not have a title to the land could be denied the status of a farmer; so also a farmer if the title was in his father's name (ibid.: 3–4).

Notwithstanding this, Table 9.11 shows that there has been an 18 per cent increase in the number of farmers' suicides in 1998 as compared to 1997, and the number remained more or less steady (between 16,000 and 16,500 suicides per year) during 1998–2001. The next sharp increase was in 2002 – about 10 per cent compared to 2001 – and the number has moved up and down (at around 17,000 to 18,000 per year) during 2002–06. However, the years 2007 and 2008 have seen a small decline in the number of farmers' suicides.

There is a high degree of variation in the number of farmers' suicides across the states. In Maharashtra, Karnataka, Andhra Pradesh, Madhya Pradesh (including Chhattisgarh), Kerala, Tamil Nadu, Pondicherry, and West Bengal, where the number of farmers' suicides is significantly higher, the problem is more acute. These states are followed by Assam, Gujarat, Haryana, Orissa, Bihar (including Jharkhand), Uttar Pradesh (including Uttarakhand), Himachal Pradesh, Punjab, Jammu and Kashmir, and Rajasthan, which account for a comparatively lower number of farmers' suicides. Moreover, in most of the north-eastern states and union territories, the number of farmers' suicides can be considered inconsequential (see Table 9.12).

To understand the patterns in farmers' suicides, Nagaraj (2008) has classified the states and union territories into four groups on the basis of number, rate, intensity, and trend of such suicides. In this classification, the states and union territories where the number of farmers' suicides is inconsequential have been excluded. Group I consists of Maharashtra, Karnataka, Andhra Pradesh, Chhattisgarh, and Madhya Pradesh. Kerala, Tamil Nadu, Goa, Pondicherry, West Bengal, and Tripura constitute Group II. Only four states, namely, Assam, Gujarat, Haryana, and Orissa, belong to Group III. And Group IV comprises Bihar, Jharkhand, Uttar Pradesh, Uttarakhand, Himachal Pradesh, Punjab, Jammu and Kashmir, and Rajasthan.

As can be seen in Table 9.13, of the four groups, it is in the Group I states the problem of farmers' suicides is most severe.

Table 9.12

Farmers' suicides in various states, 1997–2008

State	*1997*	*1998*	*1999*	*2000*	*2001*	*2002*	*2003*	*2004*	*2005*	*2006*	*2007*	*2008*
Andhra Pradesh	1,097	1,813	1,974	1,525	1,509	1,896	1,800	2,666	2,490	2,607	1,797	2,105
Assam	223	160	82	126	167	271	187	331	299	322	278	197
Bihar including Jharkhand	94	127	127	32	88	101	69	44	163	149	199	138
Goa	07	05	05	15	18	11	18	08	11	05	00	06
Gujarat	565	653	500	661	594	570	581	523	615	487	317	526
Haryana	45	185	205	238	145	190	207	160	140	190	179	150
Himachal Pradesh	23	28	39	35	22	25	34	52	22	22	15	188
Jammu and Kashmir	03	02	03	38	15	16	08	01	02	34	33	06
Karnataka	1,832	1,883	2,379	2,630	2,505	2,340	2,678	1,963	1,883	1,720	2,135	1,737
Kerala	1,204	1,514	1,431	1,295	1,035	1,533	1,583	903	1,118	1,124	1,232	820
Madhya Pradesh including Chhattisgarh	2,390	2,278	2,654	2,660	2,824	2,578	2,511	3,033	2,660	2,858	2,856	3,152
Maharashtra	1,917	2,409	2,423	3,022	3,536	3,695	3,836	4,147	3,926	4,453	4,238	3,802
Orissa	251	418	265	199	256	345	365	379	254	283	240	260
Pondicherry	40	128	133	230	91	88	23	145	147	175	197	17

Cont'd...

...Cont'd

Punjab	111	108	87	73	45	40	26	74	47	85	88	66
Rajasthan	659	705	724	736	505	587	636	749	461	395	618	796
Tamil Nadu	932	1,089	804	882	985	1,455	1,052	1,599	1,255	426	484	512
Tripura	18	241	97	14	41	41	04	15	29	07	00	50
Uttar Pradesh including Uttarakhand	568	727	845	735	709	559	428	518	546	462	514	773
West Bengal	1,539	1,457	1,240	1,377	1,246	1,518	1,036	822	965	1,187	1,102	759
Other States and Union Territories	98	87	65	79	79	112	84	109	100	67	110	136
All India	13,622	16,015	16,082	16,603	16,415	17,971	17,164	18,241	17,131	17,060	16,632	16,196

Source: NCRB.

Notes: 1. Other States and Union Territories include most of the north-eastern states (Arunachal Pradesh, Manipur, Meghalaya, Mizoram, Nagaland, and Sikkim) and Union Territories (Andaman and Nicobar Islands, Chandigarh, Dadar and Nagar Haveli, Daman and Diu, Delhi, and Lakshadweep).

2. The states of Chhattisgarh, Jharkhand, and Uttarakhand were formed in 2001 by bifurcating the erstwhile states of Madhya Pradesh, Bihar, and Uttar Pradesh respectively; hence, the data applicable to the states of Chhattisgarh, Jharkhand, and Uttarakhand, which have been available only from 2001, have been added to Madhya Pradesh, Bihar, and Uttar Pradesh respectively.

Table 9.13

Farmers' suicides and all suicides in different groups of states

Year	Group I States			Group II States			Group III States			Group IV States		
	FS	AS	FS as % AS	FS	AS	FS as % AS	FS	AS	FS as % AS	FS	AS	FS as % AS
1997	7,236 (100)	38,910 (100)	18.6	3,746 (100)	33,672 (100)	11.1	1,084 (100)	11,789 (100)	9.2	1,458 (100)	9,909 (100)	14.7
1998	8,383 (116)	43,453 (112)	19.3	4,434 (118)	36,003 (107)	12.3	1,416 (131)	12,443 (106)	11.4	1,695 (116)	11,217 (113)	15.1
1999	9,430 (130)	46,170 (119)	20.4	3,710 (99)	36,943 (110)	10.0	1,052 (97)	13,470 (114)	7.8	1,825 (125)	12,424 (125)	14.7
2000	9,837 (136)	47,157 (121)	20.9	3,813 (102)	35,905 (107)	10.6	1,224 (113)	14,034 (119)	8.7	1,649 (113)	9,843 (99)	16.8
2001	10,374 (143)	47,906 (123)	21.7	3,416 (91)	36,191 (107)	10.6	1,162 (107)	13,497 (114)	8.6	1,384 (95)	8,983 (91)	15.4
2002	10,509 (145)	49,341 (127)	21.3	4,646 (124)	35,418 (105)	13.1	1,376 (127)	13,742 (117)	10.0	1,328 (91)	9,876 (100)	13.4
2003	10,825 (150)	49,211 (126)	22.0	3,716 (99)	36,316 (108)	10.2	1,340 (124)	13,809 (117)	9.7	1,199 (82)	9,741 (98)	12.3
2004	11,809 (163)	51,482 (133)	22.9	3,492 (93)	36,939 (110)	9.5	1,393 (128)	13,912 (118)	10.0	1,438 (99)	9,495(96)	15.1

Cont'd...

...Cont'd

2005	10,959 (151)	49,754 (128)	22.0	3,525 (94)	37,870 (112)	9.3	1,308 (121)	13,865 (118)	9.4	1,239 (85)	10,492 (106)	11.8
2006	11,638 (161)	52,043 (134)	22.4	2,926 (78)	38,698 (115)	7.6	1,282 (118)	14,447 (123)	8.9	1,147 (79)	10,653 (108)	10.8
2007	11,026 (152)	53,538 (138)	20.6	3,015 (80)	39,125 (116)	7.7	1,014 (94)	15,383 (130)	6.6	1,467 (101)	12,349 (125)	11.9
2008	10,796 (149)	53,524 (138)	20.2	2,164 (58)	39,392 (117)	5.5	1,133 (105)	16,714 (142)	6.8	1,967 (135)	13,180 (133)	14.9
Total	122,822	582,489	21	42,603	442,472	9.6	14,784	16,7105	8.8	17,796	128,162	13.9

Source: NCRB.

Note: FS = Farmers' Suicides; AS = All Suicides; figures in parentheses give indices with 1997 as the base.

During the twelve-year period (1997 to 2008), 1,22,822 (21%) out of 1,98,005 cases of farmers' suicides occurred these states, giving an average of around 10,200 per year. The states in this group have also seen an almost constant increase in the number of farmers' suicides during most of the years between 1997 and 2008. In this context, Nagaraj writes, 'Considering the period 1997–2006 as a whole, farm suicides in this region increased at an annual compound growth rate of 5.4 per cent. This rate, if held, would mean doubling of the number of suicides every 13–14 years' (ibid.: 16).

Based on the data extrapolated from the 2001 Census, Table 9.14 tells that the farmer suicide rate in this group of states is around 25 per 1,00,000 farmers, which is almost twice as high as the all-India average. The general suicide rate in this group is around 16 per 1,00,000 persons, which is also significantly higher than the all-India average. Thus, these figures show a higher intensity of farmers' suicides in this group of states: the farmers' suicide rate is nearly 60 per cent more than the general suicide rate.

Table 9.14

Number and rate of suicides for general population and for farmers in different groups of states, 2001

Group of states	*Number of suicides*		*Farmers' suicides as % all suicides*	*Suicide rate (per 100,000 members)*	
	Among farmers	*Among all population*		*Among all population*	*Among farmers*
Group I	10,374 (63.2)	47,906 (44.2)	21.7	15.6	24.8
Group II	3,416 (20.8)	36,191 (33.4)	9.4	20.1	28.8
Group III	1,162 (7.1)	13,497 (12.4)	8.6	10.0	6.9
Group IV	1,384 (8.4)	8,983 (8.3)	15.4	2.4	2.6
All India	16,415 (100.0)	108,506 (100.0)	15.2	10.6	12.9

Source: Census of India – 2001 cited in Nagaraj (2008).

Table 9.13 further shows that 42,603 (9.6%) of the farmers' suicides took place in the Group II states, working out to an average of 3,550 suicides per year during 1997–2008. This period has seen two sharp increases in the number of suicides, one in 1998 and the other in 2002. Table 9.14, however, reveals that the farmers' suicide rate for this group of states in 2001 was around 29 per 1,00,000 farmers, which is the highest among all the groups. So far as the general suicide rate is concerned, this group of states has also witnessed a very high rate, i.e., 20.1 per 1,00,000 persons, which is nearly twice as high as the corresponding all-India rate. Consequently, the intensity of farmers' suicides, that is, farmers' suicides as a percentage of all suicides, is very low in this group.

In Group III states, the total number of farmers' suicides is 14,784, which is 8.8 per cent of all suicides, during 1997–2008. The number of farmers' suicides per year during this twelve-year period is around 1,200, which, comparatively, is not high. The period has seen two sharp increases in the numbers – one in 1998 and the other in 2002. Table 9.14 shows that the farmer suicide rate for Group III states is very low, i.e., 7 per 1,00,000 farmers, which is significantly lower than the all-India average. The level of general suicide rate in this group of states is also quite low, that is, 10 per 1,00,000 persons, which is nearly as high as the corresponding all-India rate. Thus, the farmer suicide rate here is lower than the general suicide rate. These figures delineate that the intensity of farmers' suicides in this group of states is also not very high.

Table 9.13 also shows that the total number of farmers' suicides in Group IV states is 17,796 (working out to an average of 1,483 suicides per year), which is 13.9 per cent of all suicides. Given the large number of states in this group, some of them being big, the figure of 17,796 suicides for this group is very low in comparative terms. However, this group of states, apart from two sharp increases in the numbers in 1998 and 1999, has also, unlike other group of states, seen significant increase in the numbers in 2007 and 2008. Table 9.14 reveals that the farmers' suicide rate for this group of states in 2001 was only 2.6 per 1,00,000 farmers, which is the lowest among all the groups. This is also the region where the general suicide rate is lowest, i.e., 2.4 per 1,00,000 persons. Thus, the intensity of farmers' suicides in this group of states is the lowest. It can be said that, though the phenomenon of farmers' suicides in this group of states has not been a major problem, the 2007 and 2008 figures show that the cases of farmers' suicides is on the increase in comparison to other groups of states in India.

Thus, the official data suggest that it is the Group I states where the problem of farmers' suicides is largely concentrated in terms of both number and rate. Though this group is populated by 30 per cent of the total population and 33 per cent of the total cultivators in India, every 6.3 out of 10 farmers' suicides during the twelve-year period under reference took place in this group. The extent of concentration of farmers' suicides in this group has increased during this period: in 1997, this group of states accounted for nearly half of the total farmers' suicides in the country; in 2006, this proportion increased to more than two-thirds. Farmer suicide rate is much higher than the general suicide rate, and farmers' suicides account for a very large proportion of total suicides in Group I states. This particular fact implies that, unlike in the Group II states, farmers' suicides do not reflect general suicides or they are not related with each other in the Group I states. Another significant fact about the Group I states, which can be considered as the graveyard of farmers today, is that the problem of farmers' suicides is mainly found in certain regions of the states such as the Vidarbha region in Maharashtra, Deccan and Hyderabad Karnataka regions in Karnataka, and Telangana and Rayalaseema regions in Andhra Pradesh. Lastly, though the problem of farmers' suicides is quite acute in all the states constituting Group I, it is gravest in the state of Maharashtra. During the twelve years (between 1997 and 2008) the number of farmers' suicides in Maharashtra doubled – from 1,917 to 3,802. Thus, every fifth suicide committed by a farmer in the country during this period was in Maharashtra. So far as other states in this group are concerned, in Andhra Pradesh and Madhya Pradesh, the number of farmers' suicides increased from 1,097 and 2,390 to 2,607 and 2,858 respectively, whereas in Karnataka the number, in fact, decreased from 1,832 to 1,720 (see Table 9.12).

Conclusion

The contemporary agrarian crisis in India, which was caused primarily by the marginalisation of agrarian interests in the national policy agenda, is a direct outcome of the economic reforms since the 1991. The economic reforms led to a gradual withdrawal of state from agriculture, with declining public expenditure and increasing marketisation of agrarian sector. This was an integral part of neo-liberal or free-market policy framework that India adopted to become a partner in the increasingly supra-national regime facilitated by globalisation. Ostensibly, this regime claims to strive for an inclusive, symmetrical, decentralised, and democratically cultivated rules-based world. But, the reality is just the opposite and is full of ironies and paradoxes. For example, we have WTO-backed trade regimes that exert pressure for removal of protection and subsidies vis-à-vis agriculture in the developing countries, while the developed countries are allowed to continue with subsidies in the garb of some artificial technicalities. The supra-national regimes have severely curtailed the policy space that was traditionally available to the developing countries to pursue their development objectives in the best interest of their own citizens.

The process of liberalisation has proved more disastrous for agriculture and peasantry in India because it was adopted without resolving the fundamental agrarian problems such as inegalitarian land structure, depeasantisation, and abysmal condition of agricultural labour, tenants, and small peasants. Although India inherited most of these problems from the British colonial rule, it did too little to resolve them after independence. During the period of economic reforms, state did nothing to transform the depressed traditional institutional framework of agriculture, because it believed that the barriers to lifting up agricultural surplus or growth and, consequently, to rural development, could be surmounted with the Structural Adjustment Programme (SAP). In reality, the opposite happened, and the inherited agrarian problems, in effect, worsened by their associated with the new contradictions generated by the liberalisation process (see Byres 2002; Ramachandran and Swaminathan 2002).

However, despite the crisis generated by economic reforms and liberalisation in the realm of agriculture, it is generally believed that, given the global situation and the economic growth that India has experienced during the period of reforms, the process is irreversible. Therefore, it has been argued that the resolution of the crisis should be explored in the existing economic framework. In this context, a number of state- or region-specific research reports, including the much-discussed research report on agricultural development in Maharashtra by Narendra Jadhav (2008) have proposed various measures. Jadhav's report has advocated that states should develop a district-level body consisting of government officials and experts to carry out data-based studies on agriculture and agriculture related issues, and the body should be assigned the task of implementing the measures in association with other local bodies such as panchayati raj institutions (PRIs) and civil society organisations (CSOs). Among the proposed measures, the following seem pertinent:

Firstly, the state should go for a complete review of the prevailing cropping pattern to find out the possibility of increasing the number of cost-effective and technologically and ecologically sustainable crops, particularly food crops. The review should also be directed towards creating conducive conditions for the cultivation of crops and their marketing and retaining soil fertility. The favourable conditions for the cultivation of crops are linked to proper irrigation facilities along with appropriate technology for rainwater harvesting and retaining soil fertility.

Secondly, the state should restructure the rural financial institutions with the objective of replacing financing by moneylenders with institutional credit to the agricultural sector in a socially sensitive manner. Each village should be adopted by institutional credit agency with an action plan aimed at making the village totally moneylender-loan-free within a short period. Every farming family should be provided a fixed cash credit limit based on its basic needs concerning farming, education, health, and the like. Financial inclusion of all families in the villages should go further by establishing Self-Help Groups (SHGs) with enough cash credit limit in the villages and by making at least one member of each family in the village a member of such a group.

Thirdly, state should make arrangements for a consistent supply of electricity and good quality seeds, pesticides, fertilizers, and other agricultural inputs at appropriate prices in the villages. The farmers, who are in extremely poor and distressed conditions, should be provided free of cost coupons to buy fertilizers, pesticides, and other inputs, and enough food grains to keep them away from debt from traditional moneylenders. This apart, there should be state-funded arrangement to make crops disease-free and state-led initiative to develop an agent-free market to sell agricultural goods at proper prices and to create basic infrastructural facilities such as rural warehouses, cold storage, and agribusiness centres in the villages.

And *lastly*, to maintain the well-being of the farmers and their families, there should be a mechanism in place to facilitate rural non-farm sector so that farmers remain gainfully employed throughout the year. An inclusive Crop Insurance Scheme should be made available at subsidised and reasonable costs to the farmers. To generate self-worth and human capital among the farmers and to keep farmers away from debt, the state should provide good quality free health and educational facilities in the villages.

These measures have been a part of the discourse on agriculture in India for the last few years. The governments, both at the centre and in states, are aware of these measures. In fact, Jadhav, who elaborated on these measures, is now a member of the Planning Commission. However, there has been a lacklustre attitude on the part of successive governments towards these measures. Not surprisingly, therefore, the agrarian crisis has persisted and the incidence of farmers' suicides has remained unabated. What is puzzling is the near absence of farmer/peasant movements, which India was earlier famous for, against the state asking for the implementation of these measures.

Note

1. The 59th Round of the Nation Sample Survey Organisation (NSSO) defines 'marginal farmers' as those possessing 0.01–1 hectare, 'small farmers' as those with 1.01–2 hectares, and 'large farmers' as those with more than 10 hectares.

References

Acharya, S.S. 2000. 'Subsidies in Indian Agriculture and their Beneficiaries', *Agricultural Situation in India*, 47 (5): 251–60.

Acharya, S.S. and R.L. Jogi. 2004. 'Farm Input Subsidies in Indian Agriculture' (*Working Paper 140*). Jaipur: Institute of Development Studies.

Assadi, M. 1998. 'Farmers' Suicides: Signs of Distress in the Rural Economy', *Economic and Political Weekly*, 33 (14): 1562–71.

Balakrishnan, P.; R. Golait and P. Kumar. 2008. 'Agricultural Growth in India since 1991' (*Study No. 27*). Mumbai: Reserve Bank of India.

Bhalla, G.S. 2004. *Globalization and Indian Agriculture: State of the Indian Farmer – A Millennium Study (Vol. 19)*. New Delhi: Academic Foundation.

Bose, A. 2000. 'From Population to Pests in Punjab: American Boll Worm and Suicides in Cotton Belt', *Economic and Political Weekly*, 35 (38): 3375–78.

Byres, T.J. 2002. 'Paths of Capitalist Agrarian Transition in the Past and in the Contemporary World', in V.K. Ramachandran and M. Swaminathan (eds.): *Agrarian Studies: Essays on Agrarian Relations in Less-Developed Countries*. New Delhi: Tulika Books, pp. 54–83.

Chand, R. 2000. 'Emerging Trends and Regional Variations in Agricultural Investments and their Implications for Growth and Equity' (*Policy Paper*). New Delhi: National Centre for Agricultural Economics and Policy Research.

Chandrasekhar, C.P. 2007. *The Progress of 'Reform' and the Retrogression of Agriculture*. New Delhi: Jawaharlal Nehru University.

Chavan, P. 2005. 'How "Inclusive" are Banks under Financial Liberalisation?', *Economic and Political Weekly*, 40 (43): 4647–49.

——. 2007. 'Access to Bank Credit: Implications for Rural Dalit Households', *Economic and Political Weekly*, 42 (31): 3219–23.

Christian Aid. 2005. *The Damage Done: Aid, Death and Dogma*. London: Christian Aid.

Deshpande, R.S. 2002. 'Suicide by Farmers in Karnataka: Agrarian Distress and Possible Alleviatory Steps', *Economic and Political Weekly*, 37 (26): 2601–10.

Dhawan, B.D. 1998. *Studies in Agricultural Investments and Rural Savings*. New Delhi: Commonwealth Publishers.

Government of Andhra Pradesh (GoAP). 2004. *Report of the Commission on Farmers' Welfare*. Hyderabad: GoAP.

——. 2007. *Andhra Pradesh Human Development Report*. Hyderabad: Centre for Economic and Social Studies.

Government of India (GoI). 2005. 'Agriculture and Food Security', *Mid-term Review of the Tenth Five-Year Plan*' (Part II, Chapter 5). New Delhi: The Planning Commission, GoI.

——. 2006. *Report of the Working Group to Suggest Measures to Assist Distressed Farmers*. New Delhi: Reserve Bank of India.

——. 2007. *Report of the Expert Group on Agricultural Indebtedness*. New Delhi: Ministry of Finance.

Grover, D.K., S. Kumar and K. Vatta. 2003. *Market Imperfections and Farmers' Distress in Punjab*. Ludhiana: Agro-Economic Research Centre, Punjab Agricultural University.

Gulati,. A. and S. Bathla. 2001. 'Capital Formation in Indian Agriculture: Revisiting the Debate'. *Economic and Political Weekly*, 36 (20): 1697–1708.

Gulati, A. and K. Mullen. 2003. 'Responding to Policy Reform: Indian Agriculture in the 1990s and After' (*Working Paper No. 189*). Stanford, CA: Stanford Centre for International Development.

Hirashima, S. 2000. 'Issues in Agricultural Reforms: Public Investment and Agricultural Reforms', *Economic and Political Weekly*, 35 (43–44): 3879–84.

Indira Gandhi Institute of Development Research (IGIDR). 2006. *Suicide of Farmers in Maharashtra*. Mumbai: IGIDR.

International Food Policy Research Institute (IFPRI). 2005. 'Indian Agriculture and Rural Development: Strategic Issues and Reform Options' (*Strategy Paper*). Washington DC: IFPRI.

Iyer, K.G. and M.S. Manick. 2000. *Indebtedness, Impoverishment and Suicides in Rural Punjab*. New Delhi: Indian Publishers and Distributors.

Jadhav, N. 2008. *Farmers' Suicide and Debt Waiver: An Action Plan for Agricultural Development of Maharashtra*. Mumbai: Government of Maharashtra.

Menon, Venu S. 2006, 'Globalisation, State and Disempowerment: A Study of Cotton Farmers' Suicides in Warangal', *Munich Personal RePEc Archive Paper No 1633*: http://mpra.ub.uni-muenchen.de/1633/(accessed on 24 August 2011).

Mishra, S. 2006. 'Farmers' Suicides in Maharashtra', *Economic and Political Weekly*, 41 (16): 1538–45.

——. 2007. 'Agrarian Crisis in Post-Reform India: A Story of Distress, Despair and Death', (*Working Paper No. 1*). Mumbai: IGIDR.

Mohanty, B.B. 2001. 'Suicides of Farmers in Maharashtra: A Socio-economic Analysis',

Review of Development and Change, 6 (2): 146–88.

——. 2005. '"We are Like the Living Dead": Farmer Suicides in Maharashtra, Western India', *Journal of Peasant Studies*, 32 (2): 243–76.

Mohanty, B.B. and S. Shroff. 2004. 'Farmers' Suicides in Maharashtra', *Economic and Political Weekly*, 39 (2): 5599–606.

Nagaraj, K. 2008. *Farmers' Suicides in India: Magnitudes, Trends and Spatial Patterns (Research Report)*. Chennai: Madras Institute of Development Studies.

National Crime Records Bureau (NCRB). 1997–2006. *Accidental Deaths and Suicides in India* (Annual Publications). New Delhi: Ministry of Home Affairs, GoI.

Nirmala, A.K. 2003. *Market Imperfections and Farmers' Distress in Andhra Pradesh*. Visakhapatnam: Andhra University.

Parikh, K. 1993. *Economic Reforms and Food and Agriculture Policy*. Mumbai: IGIDR.

——. 1997. 'Overview: Prospects and Retrospect', in K. Parikih (ed.): *India Development Report 1997*. New Delhi: Oxford University Press, pp.1–25.

Parthasarathy, G. and Shameem. 1998. 'Suicides of Cotton Farmers in Andhra Pradesh: An Exploratory Study', *Economic and Political Weekly*, 33 (13): 720–26.

Patnaik, Utsa. 2001. 'Who Benefits When Cheap Rice is Imported?', *Peoples' Democracy*, 25 (18).

——. 2002. 'Deflation and Deja Vu: Indian Agriculture in the World Economy', V. K. Ramachandran and Madhura Swaminathan (eds.): *Agrarian Studies: Essays on Agrarian Relations in Less-Developed Countries*. New Delhi: Tulika Books, 111–43.

Posani, B. 2009. 'Crisis in the Countryside: Farmer Suicides and the Political Economy of Agrarian Distress in India' (*Working Paper Series No. 09–95)*. London: Development Studies Institute, London School of Economics and Political Science.

Prasad, C.S. 1999. 'Suicide Deaths and Quality of Indian Cotton: Perspectives from History of Technology and Khadi Movement', *Economic and Political Weekly*, 34 (5): PE 12–21.

Pursell, G. and A. Gulati. 1993. 'Liberalizing Indian Agriculture: An Agenda for Reform' (*World Bank, Report No. WPS 11721993*). Washington DC: The World Bank.

Ramachandran, V.K. and R. Ramakumar. 2000. 'Agrarian Reforms and Rural Development Policies in India: A Note'. Paper presented at the International Conference on *Agrarian Reform and Rural Development*, Philippines Development Academy and Department of Agrarian Reform, Government of Philippines, Tagaytay, 5–8 December.

Ramachandran, V. K. and M. Swaminathan. 2001. *Does Informal Credit Provide Security? Rural Banking Policy in India*. Geneva: International Labour Office.

——. 2002. 'Introduction', in V.K. Ramachandran and M. Swaminathan (eds.): *Agrarian Studies: Essays on Agrarian Relations in Less-Developed Countries*. New Delhi: Tulika Books, pp. xiii–xxviii.

——. (eds.). 2005. *Financial Liberalisation and Rural Credit in India*. New Delhi: Tulika Books.

Ramakumar, R. 2010. 'Continuity and Change: Notes on Agriculture in "New India"', in Anthony P. D'Costa (ed.): *A New India? Critical Reflections in the Long Twentieth Century*. London: Anthem Press, 43–70.

Ramakumar, R. and P. Chavan. 2007. 'Revival of Agricultural Credit in the 2000s: An Explanation', *Economic and Political Weekly*, 42 (52): 57–64.

Rao, V.M. and D.V. Gopalappa. 2004. 'Agricultural Growth and Farmer Distress: Tentative Perspectives from Karnataka', *Economic and Political Weekly*, 39 (2): 5591–98.

Rao, P. and K. Suri. 2006. 'Dimensions of Agrarian Crisis in Andhra Pradesh', *Economic and Political Weekly*, 41 (16): 1546–52.

Revathi, E. 1998. 'Farmer Suicides: Missing Issues', *Economic and Political Weekly*, 33 (20): 1207.

Sainath, P. 2007. 1.5 lakh farm suicides in 1997–2005, *India Together*. http: //www.indiatogether.org/2007/nov/psa-mids1.htm (accessed on 24 August 2011).

Sarma, E.A.S. 2004. 'Is the Rural Economy Breaking Down? Farmers' Suicides in Andhra Pradesh', *Economic and Political Weekly*, 39 (28): 3087–89.

Sawant, S.D.; V. Daptardar and S. Mhatre. 2002. 'Capital Formation and Growth in Agriculture: Neglected Aspects and Dimensions', *Economic and Political Weekly*, 37 (11): 1068–72.

Sen, A. 1992. 'Economic Liberalisation and Agriculture in India'. *Social Scientist*, 20 (11): 4–19.

——. 2003. 'Changes in Cost Structure and Farm Business Incomes, 1981–82 to 1999–00'. Paper Presented at the All-India Conference on *Agriculture and Rural Society in Contemporary India*, Planning Department, Government of West Bengal, Barddhaman, West Bengal, 17–20 December.

Sen, A. and M.L. Bhatia. 2004. *Cost of Cultivation and Farm Incomes* (*Vol. 14 of State of the Indian Farmer: A Millennium Study*). New Delhi: Academic Foundation.

Shetty, S.L. 1990. 'Investment in Agriculture: A Brief Review of Recent Trends', *Economic and Political Weekly*, 25 (7–8): 389–98.

——. 1997. 'Financial Sector Reforms in India: An Evaluation', *Prajnan*, 25 (3–4): 253–87.

——. 2006. 'Policy Responses to the Failure of Formal Banking Institutions to Expand Credit Delivery for Agriculture and Non-farm Informal Sectors: The Ground Reality and Tasks Ahead', *Monthly Seminar Series on India's Financial Sector*. New Delhi: Indian Council for Research on International Economic Relations.

Shiva, V. 2005. *Earth Democracy: Justice, Sustainability and Peace*. Cambridge, MA: South End Press.

Shiva, V. and A.H. Jafri. 1998. *Seeds of Suicide: The Ecological and Human Costs of Globalisation of Agriculture*. New Delhi: Research Foundation for Science, Technology and Ecology.

Storm, S. 1993. *Macroeconomic Considerations in the Choice of an Agricultural Policy: A Study into Sectoral Interdependence with Reference to India*. Aldershot: Avebury Press.

Suri, K. 2006. 'Political Economy of Agrarian Distress', *Economic and Political Weekly*, 41 (16): 1523–29.

Surjit, V. 2008. *Farm Business Incomes in India: A Study of Two Rice Growing Villages of Thanjavur Region, Tamil Nadu*. PhD thesis. Kolkata: Indian Statistical Institute, University of Calcutta.

Tata Institute of Social Sciences (TISS). 2005. *Causes of Farmers' Suicides in Maharashtra: An Enquiry*. Mumbai: TISS.

Vaidyanathan, A. 2000. 'India's Agricultural Development Policy', *Economic and Political Weekly*, 35 (20): 1735–41.

Vasavi, A. 1999. 'Agrarian Distress in Bidar: Market, State and Suicides', *Economic and Political Weekly*, 34 (2): 2263–68.

World Bank, The. 1986. *World Development Report – 1986*. New York: Oxford University Press.

——. 1991. *1991 Country Memorandum for India*. New York: The World Bank.

10

Social Security for Unorganised Workers in India

D. RAJASEKHAR

The proportion of workers in the unorganised sector in India has been growing since the independence. These workers now form over 93 per cent of the total workforce in the country. While this growth need not necessarily be linked to globalisation, there is no gainsaying that the unorganised workers have become more vulnerable under the influence of globalisation. This chapter, therefore, focuses on the provision of social security for the unorganised workers as one of the important ways of managing their vulnerability. Social security (protective measures to assist households and people facing severe shortages in income and basic survival needs due to different work, health, or family related risks) is an important instrument for the well-being of workers (especially for those in the unorganised sector) and their family members, as well as those too young, old, or unable to earn an income for a variety of reasons. Ironically, although unorganised workers make a significant contribution to the national wealth, they do not have sufficient and reliable access to social security.

This chapter is presented in six sections. In the first section, the demographic, labour market, economic, and fiscal situation of the country is examined to bring out the importance of provision of social security to her workforce. In the second section, we examine the policies of the Government of India with reference to the provision of social security to the unorganised workers. After examining the status of the contributory and non-contributory social security schemes in the country in the next two sections, we will draw the implications of availability and accessibility of social security schemes for the poverty among workers in the fifth section. Social security needs of the unorganised workers are examined in the last section, following which conclusions are provided.

Unorganised Workers in India

In recent years, India's economic growth has been impressive. On an average, the growth rate has been about 8.8 per cent during the four years ending with 2007–08. The targeted growth rate during the Eleventh Five-Year Plan is 9 per cent. The total GDP is projected to be 51.46 trillion in the fiscal year 2007–08.[1]

It must be noted that much of this growth was on account of the growth in services and manufacturing sectors. The process of liberalisation of the economy has thrown up newer opportunities for employment in emerging and dynamic economic activities, and at locations that provide an environment conducive for the growth of such activities. The growth in employment in the private sector, in cities like Bangalore and Hyderabad, has been high in recent years. But, the rate of growth in agriculture, where the bulk of the workforce has been engaged, has been low. As a result, the work participation rates, both for males and females, have hardly increased in India in the last one-and-half decades (Rao 2007). The work participation rate for women has continued to be low. Age-specific labour-force participation rates show that, while higher rates have been the norm for all age groups among men, those for women sharply decline after 30 years of age, especially in rural areas (ibid.).

It has been estimated that the total employment (principal plus subsidiary) in the Indian economy in 2004–05 was 458 million, of which the unorganised sector accounted for 395 million (86.24%) (see Table 10.1). Of the 395 million unorganised sector workers, agriculture accounted for 253 million (64.05%) and the rest 142 million (35.95%) are employed in the non-agriculture sector. Between 1999–2000 and 2004–05, the percentage of non-agricultural workers in the unorganised sector rose from 32 to 36. The agriculture sector almost entirely consists of the unorganised workers who are mainly self-employed (65%) or casual workers (35%). Even in the non-agriculture sector, nearly 72 per cent of the workers are in the unorganised sector – an increase of 4 percentage points from 68 per cent in 1999–2000. These workers are mainly self-employed (63%). The rest of the workers in the non-agriculture unorganised sector are more or less equally distributed between the regular (17%) and casual (20%) categories (NCEUS 2007).

Table 10.1

Distribution of total Indian workforce by formal and informal sectors in 1999–2000 and 2004–05

Sector/Worker	*Total employment (in millions)*		
	Informal/un-organised workers	*Formal/organised workers*	*Total*
		1999–2000	
Informal/unorganised sector	341.3 (99.6)	1.4 (0.4)	342.6 (100.0)
Formal/organised sector	20.5 (37.8)	33.7 (62.2)	54.1 (100.0)
Total	361.7 (91.2)	35.0 (8.8)	396.8 (100.0)
		2004–05	
Informal/unorganised sector	393.5 (99.6)	1.4 (0.4)	394.9 (100.0)
Formal/organised sector	29.1 (46.6)	33.4 (53.4)	62.6 (100.0)
Total	422.6 (92.4)	34.9 (7.6)	457.5 (100.0)

Note: Figures in brackets are row-wise percentages.

Source: Computed by NCEUS (2007) from National Sample Survey 55th Round (1999–2000) and 61st Round (2004–05), Employment-Unemployment Survey.

Between 1999–2000 and 2004–05, the total employment in the economy has increased from 397 million to 457 million (see Table 10.1). The change in the organised or formal employment is nil or even marginally negative. The increase in employment (for about 61 million workers) has been only of the informal type. If one looks at the changes in employment across organised and unorganised sectors, employment increased by 8.5 million in the organised sector. According to NCEUS,

> What this means in simple terms is that the entire increase in the employment in the organised sector over this period has been informal in nature, that is, without any job and social security. This constitutes what can be termed as informalisation of the formal sector, where any employment increase consists of regular workers without social security benefits and casual or contract workers again without the benefits that should accrue to formal workers. (ibid.: 4)

Poverty and Vulnerability among the Unorganised Workers

When 93 per cent of the country's workforce is employed in the informal or unorganised economy, it is but natural that there is a high congruence between the poor and the vulnerable segments of the society. In order to highlight this congruence, NCEUS (2007) has attempted, as a first approximation, to measure this category by dividing the total population of the country into six groups based on their consumption expenditure: (i) 'Extremely Poor': those who have a monthly per capita consumer expenditure of up to three-fourths of the official poverty line (that is, an average of ₹ 8.9 per capita per day [pcpd] in 2004–05); (ii) 'Poor': those between the extremely poor and up to the official poverty line (average expenditure of ₹ 11.6 pcpd); (iii) 'Marginally Poor': those with per capita consumer expenditure of only 1.25 times the poverty line (that is, ₹ 14.6 pcpd); (iv) 'Vulnerable': those who have per capita consumer expenditure of only two times the poverty line (that is, ₹ 20.3 pcpd); (v) 'Middle Income': those with per capita consumer expenditure of two to four times the poverty line (that is, between ₹ 20.3 and 40.6 pcpd); and (vi) 'High Income': those with the per capita per day consumption expenditure of more than four times of the poverty line (that is, more than ₹ 40.6 pcpd).

Table 10.2

Population in different expenditure classes

Expenditure class	*Number of persons*	*Percentage*
Extremely poor (up to 0.75PL)	70	6.4
Poor (0.75PL to PL)	167	15.4
Marginally poor (PL to 1.25PL)	207	19.0
Vulnerable (1.25PL to 2PL)	392	36.0
Middle income (2PL to 4PL)	210	19.3
High income (>4PL)	44	4.0
Extremely poor and poor (1+2)	237	21.8
Marginal and vulnerable (3+4)	599	55.0
Poor and vulnerable (7+8)	836	76.7
Middle and high income (5+6)	253	23.3
Total	1090	100.0

Note: PL refers to the official poverty line.

Source: Computed by NCEUS (2007) from unit level data of National Sample Survey 50th Round (1993–94), 55th Round (1999–2000), and 61st Round (2004–05), Employment-Unemployment Survey.

The poor and the vulnerable groups would together constitute 77 per cent of the population (see Table 10.2). This group, totalling 836 million people with an income roughly below ₹ 88.73 in PPP (purchasing power parity) terms, can be called as the poor and vulnerable segment of the Indian population.

Table 10.3

Percentage distribution of expenditure classes by social identity, informal work status, and education, 2004–05

Economic status	*Social category (percentage share in own total)*				*Percent age of unorganised workers*	*Education**	
	STs/ SCs	*All OBCs, except Muslims*	*All Muslims, except STs/SCs*	*Others (without STs/SCs, OBCs and Muslims)*		*Illiterates*	*Primary and below primary*
Extremely poor	10.9	5.1	8.2	2.1	5.8	8.1	5.0
Poor	21.5	15.1	19.2	6.4	15.0	19.0	14.2
Marginally poor	22.4	20.4	22.3	11.1	19.6	22.2	19.4
Vulnerable	33.0	39.2	34.8	35.2	38.4	36.9	40.0
Middle income	11.1	17.8	13.3	34.2	18.7	12.8	18.9
High income	1.0	2.4	2.2	11.0	2.7	1.0	2.5
Extremely poor and poor (1+2)	32.4	20.3	27.4	8.5	20.8	27.1	19.2
Marginal and vulnerable (3+4)	55.4	59.6	57.1	46.3	57.9	59.1	59.4
Poor and vulnerable (7+8)	87.8	79.9	84.5	54.8	78.7	86.2	78.6
Middle and high income (5+6)	12.2	20.1	15.5	45.2	21.3	13.8	21.4
All	100.0	100.0	100.0	100.0	100.0	100.0	100.0
All (million)	302	391	138	258	423	270	164

* Refers to persons aged 15 years and above.

Source: Computed by NCEUS (2007) from NSS 61st Round (2004–05), Employment-Unemployment Survey.

As seen in Table 10.3, 79 per cent of the informal or unorganised workers, 88 per cent of the Scheduled Castes (SCs) and Scheduled Tribes (STs), 80 per cent of the OBC (Other Backward Classes) population, and 84 per cent of Muslims belong to the poor and vulnerable group.

> They have remained poor at a bare subsistence level without any job or social security, working in the most miserable, unhygienic and unliveable conditions, throughout this period of high economic growth since the early nineties... The illiterates have a very high probability of being poor or vulnerable, almost nine out of ten, and they are predominantly unorganised workers. Even with education up to only primary level 83 per cent are in the poor and vulnerable group. (ibid.: 8)

The relationship between poverty and vulnerability, on the one hand, and the type of employment that the unorganised workers engage in, on the other, is shown in Table 10.4. Among these workers, 21 per cent belonging to the middle and high income groups are mostly self-employed or regular workers. The category of self-employed here consists of those with sufficient capital and skills, such as urban traders, independent skilled workers, or professionals. Regular employees could be those whose services are critical to the running of small informal enterprises or establishments such as accountants or master craftsmen or such similar critical skilled workers.

Table 10.4

Percentage distribution of unorganised workers across expenditure classes

Status	*Total*	*Self-employed*	*Regular wage workers*	*Casual workers*
Poor and vulnerable	78.7	74.7	66.7	90.0
Higher income	21.3	25.3	33.3	10.0
Total	100.0	100.0	100.0	100.0

Source: Computed by NCEUS (2007) from NSS 61st Round (2004–05), Employment-Unemployment Survey.

The high congruence between informal work status and poverty/vulnerability becomes almost complete in the case of casual workers, with 90 per cent of them belonging to the poor and vulnerable group. As noted earlier, overwhelmingly, this group includes the SCs, STs, OBCs, and Muslims.

National Policies and Programmes for the Unorganised Workers

In all countries including India, typically, there are two sectors – organised and unorganised.[2] In India, the organised sector is defined as consisting of all government institutions, and of enterprises using electricity and employing ten or more persons, and those not using electricity but employing twenty or more persons (ILO 2000: 2). This sector is characterised by skilled labour, regular employment and remuneration, and the use of sophisticated technology; it mostly includes registered factories and service establishments. Workers in this sector have a high level of bargaining power.

The unorganised sector comprises those workers who do not have formal and direct relationships with their employers. Therefore, they do not have access to social security. They are also unable to organise themselves in pursuit of a common objective. This is because of constraints such as the casual nature of employment, ignorance and illiteracy, small size of establishment and low capital investment per person employed, scattered nature of establishments, superior strength of the employer operating singly, or in combination (Government of India 2002).[3]

An important criterion that separates the organised sector from the unorganised sector is the availability of and access to different types of social security benefits for the workers in these sectors. The social security measures planned and implemented in India since independence have been limited to the organised sector workers, despite a majority of the workforce being dependent on the unorganised labour market for its sustenance. Recognising this, the Tenth Five-Year Plan (2002–07) noted that

> a policy framework at the national level, on social security provisions for different groups of workers and employees, will be formulated. A legislative and administrative framework has to be created for significant coverage of the unorganised sector by social security cover. The strategy would be to motivate and encourage the State Governments to formulate and implement

> schemes and programmes targeted at certain occupational groups in the unorganised sector without putting any additional pressure on the budget. (Planning Commission n.d.: 396)

Towards this, in 2004, an attempt was made to introduce universal contributory health insurance scheme for the unorganised workers. There were also a number of health insurance schemes which have been initiated by different state governments. A study commissioned by the International Labour Organisation (ILO) shows that eleven health insurance schemes were started by different state governments during 2002–07 (Rajasekhar, Suchitra and Manjula 2008a). Two or more schemes have been implemented each year between 2002 and 2007, except 2004. Three schemes were introduced in 2006. Thus, there has been a spurt in the initiation of state government-run health insurance schemes in the last five years.

In his speech delivered on 8 July 2004, the Union Finance Minister P. Chidamabaram stated that the Government of India is

> firmly committed to ensure the welfare and well-being of all workers, particularly those in the unorganised sector who constitute 93 per cent of our workforce. Social security, health insurance and other schemes for such workers like weavers, handloom workers, fishermen and fisherwomen, toddy tappers, leather workers, plantation labour, beedi workers, etc. will be expanded. (NCEUS 2006: 1)

In keeping with this commitment, in 2004, the Government of India constituted the National Commission for Enterprises in the Unorganised Sector (NCEUS) to look into the conditions of unorganised sector workers and prepare a bill on appropriate social security benefits for them (NCEUS 2006). The Commission has prepared the Unorganised Sector Workers' Social Security Bill, 2007, which has since been approved by parliament. The Commission proposed a minimum social security cover consisting of life insurance, old age pensions, and health insurance for unorganised sector workers belonging to the BPL (below poverty line) households.

To provide social security in a phased manner to workers living in BPL households in the unorganised sector, the central government has introduced the following three schemes during

2008-09: (i) the Aam Admi Bima Yojana to provide insurance cover to poor households, (ii) the National Health Insurance Scheme is planned to be launched in a phased manner so as to reach 300 million people from BPL households over the next five years, and (iii) the Indira Gandhi National Old Age Pension scheme was enlarged to include all persons falling under BPL category and is being implemented.

The Government of India has yet again recognised the need to provide social security in its Eleventh Five-Year Plan (2007–12), whose central vision is 'faster but socially inclusive growth'. The plan aims at the creation of productive and gainful employment and improved quality of work for the workforce, both in the formal and the informal sectors, through sound macro-economic policies. Importantly, the need to ensure social security for all, especially those in the unorganised sector, is recognised as an overarching concern. The plan prioritises the improvement and expansion of social security schemes as a mechanism of inclusive growth and seeks to introduce measures to achieve this.

Social Security Policies and Programmes for the Organised Sector Workers

The Constitution of India provides strength and spirit to the social security legislation for organised workers through its Directive Principles of the State Policy. These workers are provided with budget-financed medical and old age benefits. These mandatory benefits are provided either solely at the cost of employers or on the basis of joint contribution of the employers and the employees. The social security benefits are entitlements that accrue to the employees, while the responsibility for compliance largely rests with the employers. The enactments for major social security benefits for the organised sector workers are the Employee's Provident Funds and Miscellaneous Provisions Act, 1952; the Employees State Insurance (ESI) Act, 1948; the Payment of Gratuity Act, 1972; the Maternity Benefit Act, 1961; and the Workmen's Compensation Act, 1923.

These legally provided and budget-based social security benefits are available only to the organised sector workers. As a result, a larger proportion of the organised sector workers have been receiving statutory benefits. The Planning Commission has observed that

> the social security schemes in India cover only a very small segment of the workers... Out of an estimated workforce of about 397 million, only 28 million workers are having the benefits of formal social security protection. About 24 million workers were covered under various employees provident funds schemes and 8 million workers were covered under the ESI schemes, in addition to about 4.5 million under the Workmen Compensation Act and about 0.5 million under the Maternity Benefit Act in the year 2000. (2006: 18)

But, the critical point is that the organised sector in India is shrinking due to the growth of contractor system in several industries, labour laws, globalisation, etc. The use of contract labour in the organised manufacturing sector has grown from 7 per cent of total persondays in 1984 to 21 per cent in 1998 (ILO 2007: 34). Those in the organised sector have been opting out of this sector. D. Rajasekhar and G. Sreedhar (2002) have shown that workers in the *beedi* (country cigarette) industry in Karnataka, who were initially benefiting from statutory provisions such as minimum wages, provident fund, etc., have chosen to become 'unorganised' by withdrawing from their accumulated provident funds to meet the life-cycle needs. The *agarbathi*-rolling and garment-manufacturing industries have experienced changes in the mix of workers: the proportion of unorganised workers has increased at the expense of organised workers (Rajasekhar, Suchitra and Manjula 2007). As a result, the growth proceeds on account of globalisation have disproportionately gone for the organised workers. In contrast, the unorganised workers in these industries, majority of whom were women, were obtaining wages lower than those prescribed by the government, outside the formal social security system and suffering from a range of health problems for which there was no protection.

Social Security Schemes for the Unorganised Sector Workers

Unlike social security benefits for the organised sector workers that take the form of entitlements and which are budget-financed, those for the unorganised sector workers only take the form of schemes.

The benefits for the unorganised workers can be divided into three types: social assistance, social insurance, and health insurance. In addition, there are state-specific schemes meant for specific categories of unorganised workers.

National Social Assistance Schemes

Many social assistance schemes have been implemented for the unorganised worker households living below the poverty line. These are old age pensions, maternity benefits, family benefits, disability pensions, and widow pensions. While the first three are central government sponsored schemes, the last two are the state schemes. There are two important problems with regard to these schemes: first, the amount of benefit is paltry, and second, the performance of social assistance schemes in the country, in terms of number of persons assisted, has varied over time (see Rajasekhar 2008). This suggests that access to these schemes is poor.

What factors influence access to social assistance schemes? First, financial constraints compelling the state governments to tighten the eligibility criteria resulted in restricting old age pensions to only the destitute among BPL households and excluding a large number of unorganised workers living under vulnerable conditions. Second, the poor access to old age pensions was due to low levels of awareness about the schemes – eligibility conditions, whom to approach, and how to approach – and difficulties of documentation. These, together with poor responses from the officials concerned and high opportunity cost of wage-labour income foregone in going around the government offices, force the unorganised workers to depend on middlemen and spend considerable amount of money in the process. Third, the access to maternity benefits has been adversely affected by the mandatory rule of institutional delivery. However, institutional delivery to access meagre amounts of maternity benefits is costly for the poor, as this would involve costs on account of travel to the place where the facility is available and staying at a distant place away from home for a few days. Finally, the poor bargaining power on account of limited membership in trade unions and peoples' organisations such as self-help groups (SHGs) has adversely affected the access to social assistance schemes.

Social Insurance

In 2000, a group-based social insurance scheme, called the Janashree Bima Yojana,[5] was introduced for persons in the age group of 18 to 60 years belonging to BPL households. The insurance cover provided under this scheme is up to ₹ 30,000, in case of natural death; ₹ 75,000, in case of accidental death or permanent disability; and ₹ 37,500, in case of partial disability. An innovative feature of this scheme has been that two school-going children of insurers are provided with financial assistance of ₹ 100 per month to complete school education.[6] Fifty per cent of the annual premium of ₹ 200 is subsidised by the central government.

Two striking positive features of the Janashree Bima Yojana scheme are: (i) improvement in the coverage of unorganised workers, and (ii) a high rate (over 60%) of renewal (see Rajasekhar 2008). The scheme would have better coverage if the following issues are addressed: First, the awareness of the programme is found to be low. Rajasekhar, Suchitra, Madeshwaran and Karanth (2006) found that only less than 5 per cent of the sample of unorganised workers in Karnataka was aware of the scheme. Second, by restricting its benefits only to the BPL households, the scheme ignored heterogeneity among the unorganised workers. While all the BPL households are likely to be in the unorganised sector, the reverse is not necessarily true. The BPL criterion is a minimalist and inappropriate approach to extend social security to the unorganised workers (Rao, Rajasekhar and Suchitra 2006). Finally, the poor are sceptical of contributing to a scheme wherein they realise that they will not get any returns unless and until the eventuality that they have taken the insurance for occurs. Since the Janashree Bima Yojana is not designed as a moneyback scheme, people prefer saving elsewhere.

Review

While a larger proportion of the organised workers have been benefiting from legally mandated and budget-provided social security benefits since independence, those in the unorganised sector have been left out. It is often stated that all the social security schemes (initiated by the government and non-government agencies) cover even less than 10 per cent of the total unorganised workers. What ails the social security policies and programmes for the unorganised workers?

First, despite the multiplicity of schemes and programmes of the central and the state governments aiming at social protection of the underprivileged, there is no consistent policy on social security in the country (Prabhu and Iyer 2001). The schemes and programmes have been framed at random at various points in time in response to the expedience of the day without conforming to any overall design. These schemes do not represent a uniform policy or plan.

Second, the multiplicity of social security schemes initiated by the Government of India, lacking in an overall cohesion in design and management, have often proved to be counterproductive to the economy (ibid.). This is because of the administrative costs of implementing them are too high in relation to the paltry benefits accruing from them and the negligible impact they have on the target population (Dreze and Sen 1991). The state welfare boards, which have been administering the social security schemes, incur disproportionately high administrative costs. Given the bureaucratic administrative machinery, there are several demands and compulsions of administrative procedures that have to be met, all of which cause delays and add to the mounting cost of administering the schemes.

Third, the expenditure on social security across the states has been meagre. According to the World Labour Report (2000), the public sector expenditure on social security in India was 1.8 per cent of the GDP, whereas it was 4.7 per cent in Sri Lanka and 3.6 per cent in China. This is the case across the states as well: Karnataka spends only 1.52 per cent of its total expenditure (amounting to ₹ 3,570 million) on social security measures for the unorganised sector; Tamil Nadu, which has efficient social security programmes, spends 2.64 per cent of its total expenditure on social security (CMIE 2002).

Fourth, the financial constraints in the past have often compelled the governments to tighten the eligibility criteria. For instance, old age pensions have been, until recently, restricted to only the destitute and the BPL households. As a result, a large number of elderly living under vulnerable conditions were excluded.

Fifth, fragmented, as against universal, approach has been followed in formulating social security schemes. For instance, the benefits under most of the schemes have been confined to the unorganised workers belonging to the BPL households. While the poor unorganised workers are the neediest, those workers not falling under the BPL category of households yet vulnerable have been left out. V.M. Rao, D. Rajasekhar and J.Y. Suchitra (2006) show that unorganised workers above the poverty line suffer from a number of deprivations and hence argue that the BPL criterion is a minimalist and inappropriate approach to extend social security to the unorganised workers. As NCEUS (2007) has shown, 55 per cent of the population in India are not poor but vulnerable; about 58 per cent of them are unorganised workers.

Finally, the unorganised workers do not have bargaining power on account of limited membership in trade unions and SHGs. Consequently, they suffer from lack of awareness on social security schemes. In any case, since social security in India is delivered through schemes, the workers cannot demand it as a matter of right.

Vulnerability among Unorganised Workers

An overwhelming majority of the unorganised sector workers do not, thus, have access to sufficient and reliable social security. Faced with such a situation, what risks do they face and what coping mechanisms do they adopt? An analysis of evidence to answer these two questions is important given the debilitating impact that risks can have on the poorer unorganised worker households. The research by Anirudh Krishna (2004) shows that crises on account of limited or non-access to social security have been the single most important factor pushing households deeper into poverty. It is in this context that we look at the evidence on risks faced by the unorganised workers in the absence of access to sufficient and reliable social security and coping mechanism adopted by them. This is done with the help of studies that we have undertaken.[7]

We consider that risks are emergencies, which include health emergencies, accidents and deaths, crop failures, drought situations, social functions like wedding and religious/ritualistic ceremonies, social obligations such as village festivals, etc. The social functions and obligations are not 'risks' in the true sense of the term, but we treat them as emergencies because the poor perceive even such predictable events as risks.[8] The term 'emergencies' has thus been used to include both predictable and unpredictable events; for households typically lacking risk-management tools, predictable events would also have negative welfare effects (Rajasekhar, Suchitra, Madeshwaran and Karanth 2006; Rajasekhar, Reddy and Suchitra 2006).

In all these studies, we asked the sample households on crises or emergencies faced during the three years prior to the survey date. In Table 10.5, the data on the proportion of households facing at least one crisis have been presented. It can be seen that across the states and different groups, more than 30 per cent of the households had faced at least one crisis in the reference period. The incidence was the highest among the unorganised agricultural workers belonging to the two most disadvantaged groups, namely, SCs and STs. The incidence was also high among the agarbathi workers (65%), while it was low among domestic workers (35.58%).

Table 10.5

Incidence of emergency needs in unorganised sector households

State and category of workers	*Households (%) facing at least one crisis*
Karnataka (n = 1,213)	
Agricultural labourers	41.39
Construction workers	41.86
Domestic workers	35.58
Agarbathi workers	65.00
Garments workers	43.00
Andhra Pradesh (n = 149)	
Agricultural labourers	64.43
Tamil Nadu (n = 131)	
Dalit agricultural labourers	90.00
Adivasi agricultural labourers	83.10

Source: Field survey.

In Table 10.6, we have presented all the emergencies faced by households in different groups by the types. Health emergencies were the most significant crises faced across all categories of workers, followed by death of household members and marriages and other social obligations. Health emergencies have been largely due to the workers' inability to access the public health delivery system due to distance, irregular attendance of doctors, lack of facilities, etc. Hence, the unorganised workers have to depend on private health providers. In addition, early marriages lead to childbirth at a young age leading to gynaecological problems. This is further corroborated by the macro data. About 82 per cent of total health care expenditure in India is accounted for by the private sector, and almost all of this is out-of-pocket expenses (on consultation, diagnostics, in-patient care, etc.) (PriceWaterHouseCoopers 2007).

Table 10.6

Distribution of all emergencies faced by households by type

Categories of workers	*Death of household member*	*Health crises*	*Marriages and social obligations*	*Accidents*	*Other*	*Total (No.)*
Karnataka						
Agricultural labourers	23.77	47.08	16.59	11.66	0.90	223
Construction workers	14.60	48.90	19.71	16.06	0.73	137
Domestic workers	15.79	52.64	23.68	7.89	0.00	38
Agarbathi workers	14.53	58.91	18.75	7.69	0.12	117
Garment workers	7.25	77.46	13.04	1.45	0.80	69
Andhra Pradesh						
Agricultural labourers	12.50	50.00	20.83	7.29	9.38	96
Tamil Nadu						
Dalits	7.25	59.41	17.39	8.70	7.25	69
Adivasis	11.27	47.88	21.13	11.27	8.45	71

Source: Field survey.

In sum, a large proportion of the crises confronted by the unorganised worker households were on account of their inability to access social security benefits relating to life cover, accident benefit, and health insurance. Such crises impose a heavy cost burden on these households. Table 10.7 presents the total expenditure on all crises faced by the different categories of workers and the distribution of this expenditure across the sources from which they were financed. It can be seen that the extent of expenditure on all the household crises has been very high. Significantly, it is

Table 10.7

Distribution of total expenditure on crises by sources from which financed

States and categories of workers	*Sources of financing for the household crises faced by unorganised workers*							
	Own sources	*Money-lenders*	*Relatives*	*SHGs*	*Employer*	*Sale of assets*	*Other source*	*Total expenditure (in Rs)*
Karnataka								
Agricultural labourers	18.06	54.92	12.21	0.00	8.49	2.79	3.53	26,84,600
Construction workers	25.32	48.29	12.17	0.00	4.26	3.04	6.92	27,95,100
Domestic workers	18.65	50.79	17.28	0.00	2.60	3.62	7.06	5,52,650
Agarbathi workers	21.86	37.01	24.27	0.00	2.19	8.90	5.77	21,50,500
Garments workers	30.86	59.26	4.94	0.00	0.00	2.47	2.47	8,45,000
Andhra Pradesh								
Agricultural labourers	3.03	54.13	22.84	5.10	2.49	11.05	1.36	14,03,100 (9,417)
Tamil Nadu								
Dalits	30.74	32.79	6.53	11.59	0.00	4.02	14.33	544,300 (7,888)
Adivasis	16.56	58.66	4.29	10.20	0.00	3.05	7.24	524,700 (7,249)

Note: Figures in parentheses are average amounts in Rs.

Source: Field survey.

informal coping strategies that households mostly fell back on to meet these expenditures. Borrowing from moneylenders was the dominant coping mechanism, with anywhere between 37 and 60 per cent of the total expenditure being through this source. A somewhat large share of the expenditure was incurred through borrowing from relatives, another example of informal mechanisms of risk management, that is, drawing upon family and other social capital. A significant proportion of the expenditure was from own sources, that is, money that the households had saved either in banks or micro-finance groups or simply kept aside at home. Important to note here is the limited role played by the employers of the unorganised workers and the significant role played by SHGs, wherever unorganised workers have had membership in these microfinance groups.

Table 10.8

Distribution of workers by proportion of expenditure to average monthly per capita income

Categories of workers	*<100 per cent*	*100–250 per cent*	*>250 per cent*
Agricultural	22.92	29.17	47.91
Construction	41.82	25.45	32.73
Domestic	72.27	22.73	5.00

Source: Field survey.

In order to understand the devastating impact that such high dependence on informal sources had on the workers and their households, we have worked out the proportion of the expenditure incurred by agricultural labourers, construction workers, and domestic workers in Karnataka to the average monthly per capita income (PCI) of the households (see Table 10.8). We have taken the expenditure on these risks as 'at one point in time' expenses, and therefore, when the expenditure is incurred, it is likely to have an adverse impact on the household during that particular period. This period was taken to be a month.

The agricultural workers were the worst off, as nearly 48 per cent of them spent more than two-and-a-half times their monthly per capita income on crises, and almost 30 per cent spent 100–200 per cent of the same. The construction workers were relatively better off in terms of the extent of impact the expenditure had during that particular period. The domestic workers' expenditure was not as hard-hitting to their households as the agricultural and construction workers' expenditures were. The implication of this is that when the unorganised workers encountered the kind of crises that involved expenditure to this degree, they were forced to draw upon other sources, such as their household consumption (including food and education), to meet these needs.

A large contributor to the debilitating impact of such borrowings is the high rates of interest levied by informal lenders. On many occasions, these workers paid interest amounts for years together without having returned any part of the principal amount borrowed. Table 10.9 shows the proportion of interest amount paid on the principal amount borrowed. It is clear that costs incurred by the workers in the form of interest payments were substantial. Payment of more than 100 per cent of the principal amount borrowed merely by way of interest indicates a situation of absolute vulnerability.

Table 10.9

Distribution of households by worker categories and proportion of interest amount paid to principal amount

Categories of workers	*<50 per cent*	*50–100 per cent*	*>100 per cent*
Agricultural	76.43	15.71	7.86
Construction	84.95	10.75	4.30
Domestic	75.00	10.71	14.29

Source: Field survey.

Thus, there has been extreme dependence by the unorganised workers on informal sources of risk management, primarily through borrowing from moneylenders at high rates of interest. This perpetuates vulnerability among these households. These households are unable to send their children to school, access health facilities, etc. This will deepen their poverty.

Social Security Needs of the Unorganised Workers

The unorganised sector includes a vast spectrum of occupations and activities from agricultural labour, construction work, and domestic help to employment in informal industries and services such as garments, *agarbathi*-rolling, *beedi*-rolling, transport, etc., to self-employed workers like railway porters, auto-rickshaw drivers, vegetable vendors, and others. Examining the employment security faced by three categories of workers, i.e., agricultural, construction and domestic, Suchitra and Rajasekhar (2006) found that the degree and kind of employment security faced by each of these groups was different from the others, and depended on both general factors and factors specific to the sectors. This is important because employment security is the most basic component of work-based social security, and it forms a crucial platform for the workers to demand other components.

In order to capture the workers' preferences on these other components of social security, we use the data collected for the studies by Rajasekhar, Suchitra, Madeshwaran and Karanth (2006), Rajasekhar and Suchitra (2006), and Rajasekhar and Manjula (2006). While the first study collected data from 910 unorganised workers undertaking agricultural labour (505), construction work (301), and domestic help (104), the latter two collected the data from 148 *agarbathi* rollers and 150 garment workers respectively.[9]

Table 10.10

Preference mapping of social security needs by unorganised sector workers

Social security needs	*Agri-cultural workers*	*Con-struction workers*	*Domestic workers*	*Agarbathi workers*	*Garment workers*
Unemployment	164 (32.48)	90 (29.90)	26 (25.00)	37 (25.00)	50 (33.33)
Sickness	48 (9.50)	37 (12.29)	12 (11.54)	26 (17.57)	74 (49.33)
Employment injury	39 (7.72)	69 (22.92)	6 (5.77)	4 (2.71)	7 (4.67)
Old age pensions	180 (35.64)	75 (24.92)	38 (36.54)	59 (39.86)	9 (12.67)
Death	26 (5.15)	20 (6.64)	11 (10.58)	22 (14.86)	0 (0.00)
Did not rank	48 (9.51)	10 (3.33)	11 (10.57)	0 (0.00)	0 (0.00)
Total	505	301	104	148	150

Note: The figures within the parentheses are percentages and represent the proportion of workers in each category who indicated the first preferences for the five needs, and also those who did not express their preferences at all.

The data collected enabled a detailed analysis of the preference-mapping of the different social security needs by the different categories of unorganised workers. Using PRA techniques,[10] the workers were asked to prioritise the needs. The figures in Table 10.10 are the numbers and proportion of workers assigning first priority to different needs. As evident from the figures, unemployment benefits, old age pensions and medical benefits (sickness) were the three key needs, but the incidence of these felt needs differed across the sectors. Old age pensions were the most highly preferred by agricultural labourers, *agarbathi* workers, and domestic workers, while construction workers gave the highest preference to unemployment benefits,[11] and garment workers to health insurance (sickness).

Not only were there differences across the sectors, the studies found heterogeneity within each sub-sector as well – across age, sex, education, regions, etc. Old age pension, for instance, was found to be highly preferred by workers above 40 years of age, while unemployment benefits were more highly preferred by the younger workers. In the relatively backward areas, a greater proportion of workers preferred unemployment benefits, while better developed areas found more takers for old age pension. Similarly, those households which had attained relatively higher levels of education showed higher preference for old age pension, while the lesser educated households indicated higher preference for unemployment benefits. The need for unemployment benefits was starker for women workers as compared to their male counterparts. Benefits for employment injury were highly preferred across age groups among the construction workers – a highly risk-prone group.

The second important area of heterogeneity was the willingness of the workers to participate in contributory social security schemes. Table 10.11 brings this out clearly: across the sectors, more than 60 per cent of the workers are willing to contribute towards their social security. The proportion of workers willing to contribute varies across the different sectors depending on a range of reasons such as economic conditions of households, existing coverage under other schemes, etc. In Table 10.12, we have shown the minimum, maximum, and average amounts that workers in each of the sectors are willing to contribute towards their first two priority social security needs. We find considerable differences across the sectors in this aspect as well.

Table 10.11

Willingness of unorganised sector workers to participate in contributory social security schemes

Categories of unorganised workers	*Proportion of workers willing to contribute*
Agricultural labourers (n = 505)	67.30
Construction workers (n = 301)	82.00
Domestic workers (n = 104)	73.00
Agarbathi workers (n = 148)	68.42
Garment workers (n = 152)	78.15

Source: Field survey.

Table 10.12

Amounts different categories of workers are willing to contribute towards priority social security needs

Categories of unorganised workers	*Amounts workers are willing to contribute (Rs. per annum)*					
	*1st priority social security need**			*2nd priority social security need***		
	Minimum	*Maximum*	*Average*	*Minimum*	*Maximum*	*Average*
Agricultural labourers (n = 505)	25	3,000	624	60	3,600	758
Construction workers (n = 301)	100	9,600	1,092	200	6,012	1,397
Domestic workers (n = 104)	100	2,400	906	200	2,400	842
Agarbathi workers (n = 148)	240	6,000	1,106	120	3,600	1,014
Garment workers (n = 152)	240	12,000	1,246	120	7,200	1,101

* First priority for agricultural labourers, domestic workers, and agarbathi workers was old age pensions; for construction workers, was unemployment benefits; and for garments workers, was health benefits.

** Second priority for agricultural labourers, domestic workers, agarbathi and garment workers was unemployment benefits, while for construction workers, it was old age pensions.

As seen from Table 10.12, the amounts that workers were willing to contribute were positively associated with the extent of organisation in the sectors in which they worked. For instance, construction workers are relatively more unionised than all the other sectors, and *agarbathi* and garment workers are employed by factories either directly or through layers of sub-contracting, ultimately implying that at some level above, there is a certain degree of organisation that they can take recourse to. These groups were willing to contribute higher amounts as compared to the domestic workers and agricultural labourers. This was, to a large extent, because the latter's inability to organise themselves effectively.

Another important aspect is that there are a good number of workers in each of the sectors who are not willing to contribute for a variety of reasons. Dominant among these reasons is that these workers belong to households whose basic entitlements or promotional social security needs have not been adequately met. For these workers, therefore, there is a need to facilitate reliable access to the social assistance programmes of the state, as well as ensure satisfactory fulfilment of the basic entitlements, both of which have been lagging currently, in part due to the poor institutional mechanisms of implementing the schemes.

Conclusion

In India, 93 per cent of the 458 million workers are in the unorganised sector. These workers suffer from indecent work conditions and the consequent deficits ranging from social exclusion to unemployment, health hazards, lack of social security, deep poverty, and the denial of basic human and labour rights. Among these deficits, lack of social security is prominent.

Statutory, budget-financed, and contributory social security benefits are provided to organised workers, who constitute only 8 per cent of the total workforce. In terms of coverage, the contributory social security schemes become somewhat important only in the case of organised workers. If one looks at the coverage of these schemes for the total workforce in India, it is miniscule.

Unlike social security benefits for the organised sector workers that take the form of entitlements, those for the unorganised sector workers take the form of only schemes. In terms of coverage, all the non-contributory schemes put together do not even cover 10 per cent of the unorganised workers. The formal social security benefits, provided to unorganised workers, have also been inadequate. Several studies have revealed that these amounts have been paltry and very inadequate in relation to the cost of living. The amounts become even smaller if one takes transaction costs into consideration. Thus, unorganised workers in India do not have access to sufficient and reliable formal social security benefits.

Faced with such a situation, unorganised workers routinely face risks on account of ill-health, accidents to and death of an earning member, and incur considerable expenditure to meet these emergencies. It is informal coping strategies that the unorganised workers mostly adopt to meet the expenditure on account of crises. An important coping mechanism has been to borrow from informal lending agencies such as moneylenders at very high rates of interest. This perpetuates vulnerability among the unorganised worker households and deepens poverty among them. Most of the unorganised workers are willing to contribute to social security provided that effective and efficient social security systems are established and functioning.

There is, therefore, a need to provide adequate and reliable social security to the unorganised workers as an entitlement. Furthermore, the social security benefits need to be universal rather than scheme-based. This is important for poverty reduction and human resource development. In the current context of globalisation, effective and efficient social security system is a key instrument to reduce income gaps, to redistribute incomes, and to ensure the vast majority of the unorganised workforce do not face social harshness.

Notes

1. However, with the per capita income of ₹ 45,292, India still belongs to the category of 'low-income countries'.
2. These two sectors are alternatively referred to as the formal and the informal sectors, respectively. While the distinction between the formal sector and the informal sector is based on the coverage

under statutory government regulations and provisions, this is not true of the distinction between the organised and the unorganised sector. Strictly speaking, these are different sets of definitions. The dividing line, however, is thin and hazy, and these classifications are seldom mutually exclusive. To avoid getting bogged down by taxonomic details, we will continue to treat the 'formal' and the 'organised' sectors and the 'informal' and the 'unorganised' sectors synonymously, and henceforth, we use only the latter terms.

3. In the records of the National Commission on Labour (NCL), the unorganised sector is simply defined as the residual of the organised sector (GoI 2002). However, due to the problems of underestimation and insufficient coverage, it is difficult to arrive at this residual estimate.
4. Broadly, this includes the following interlinked points: rapid growth that reduces poverty; creates employment opportunities, access to essential services in health and education especially for the poor; equality of opportunity; empowerment through skills development and education; environmental sustainability; recognition of women as agents of sustained socio-economic development; and good governance.
5. This is implemented through Life Insurance Corporation of India. In the Annual Budget of 2008–09, ₹ 500 crores of additional allocation has been earmarked for this scheme.
6. Initially, this facility was available to all the insurers. Since 2007–08, it has been restricted to 15 per cent of the poorest households.
7. These studies are Rajasekhar, Suchitra, Madeshwaran and Karanth (2006), Rajasekhar, Reddy and Suchitra (2006), Rajasekhar, Manjula and Suchitra (2006), Rajasekhar, Suchitra and Manjula (2006), and Rajasekhar, Suchitra and Manjula (2008b).
8. For instance, a less vulnerable household may not perceive a routine wedding as a crisis. But, the same may be seen as a crisis by a 'highly vulnerable' household, because such an event is likely to render them even more vulnerable.
9. Though these studies were conducted in Karnataka, their results would be applicable to workers in the respective sectors elsewhere in the country.
10. Picture cards on each of the contingencies were shown and described to the workers. They were then asked which of these contingencies they felt the greatest need to acquire protection

against. Although we have presented only the first priority indicated by the workers, they were asked to preference map all the five needs.

11. Although by unemployment benefits, we normally mean benefits such as doles given to workers during times of unemployment, in the context of the unorganised workers, we found that the workers interpreted this benefit to mean employment guarantee. And rightly so, since, for these workers, unemployment was not really a contingency but rather a way of life – more the norm than an exception. Not surprisingly, even if not as the most highly ranked need across the categories of workers, at least 25 per cent of all categories of workers gave the highest preference for this need.

References

CMIE [Centre for Monitoring Indian Economy]. 2002. *Public Finance, Economic Intelligence Service.* Mumbai: Centre for Monitoring Indian Economy.

Dreze, Jean and Amartya Sen. 1991. 'Public Action for Social Security: Foundations and Strategy', in E. Ahmad et al. (eds.): *Social Security in Developing Countries.* New Delhi: Oxford University Press, pp. 1–40.

Government of India [GoI]. 2002. *Report of the National Commission on Labour.* New Delhi: Government of India.

——. 2004. Budget Speech of the finance minister, P Chidambaram, delivered on 8 July 2004. New Delhi: Ministry of Finance, Government of India.

International Labour Office [ILO]. 2000. *India: Social Protection for the Unorganised Sector.* Geneva: ILO.

——. 2007. *Towards Globalisation for the People: The Role of Social Protection in Shaping a Fair Globalisation.* Geneva: ILO.

Krishna, Anirudh. 2004. 'Escaping Poverty and Becoming Poor: Who Gains, Who Loses, and Why?', *World Development,* 32 (1): 121–36.

National Commission for Enterprises in the Unorganised Sector [NCEUS]. 2006. *Report on the Unorganised Sector.* New Delhi: NCEUS.

——. 2007. *Report on Conditions of Work and Promotion of Livelihoods in the Unorganised Sector.* New Delhi: Academic Foundation.

Planning Commission, GoI. 2006. *Report of the Working Group on Social Security.* New Delhi: Planning Commission, GoI.

——. n.d. *Tenth Five Year Plan (2002–2007), Volume II: Sectoral Policies and Programmes*. New Delhi: Planning Commission, GoI.

Prabhu, K.S. and S.V. Iyer. 2001. 'Public Provision of Social Security: The Challenge in South Asia', *South Asia Economic Journal*, 2 (1): 31–66.

PriceWaterHouseCoopers. 2007. *Healthcare in India: Emerging Market Report* – 2007.

Rajasekhar, D. 2008. 'Social Security for Unorganised Workers in India: Status and Issues', *The India Economy Review*, 5 (1): 124–31.

Rajasekhar, D. and R. Manjula. 2006. 'Voices of the Women Garment Workers', in B.C. Prabhakar (ed.): *Gender Sensitivity at Workplace*. Bangalore: KEA and ILO, pp. 148–62.

Rajasekhar, D. and G. Sreedhar. 2002. 'Changing Face of Beedi Industry in Karnataka', *Economic and Political Weekly*, 37 (39): 4023–28.

Rajasekhar, D. and J.Y. Suchitra. 2006. 'Women Agarbathi Workers: Contributing a Lot, but Obtaining Very Little', in B.C. Prabhakar (ed.): *Gender Sensitivity at Workplace*. Bangalore: KEA and ILO, pp. 138–47.

Rajasekhar, D.; J.Y. Suchitra and R. Manjula. 2006. *Social Security Needs and Willingness to Contribute to Social Security: Agarbathi Workers in Karnataka* (mimeo). New Delhi: GTZ (German Technical Cooperation).

——. 2007. 'Women Workers in Urban Informal Employment: The Status of Agarbathi and Garment Workers in Karnataka', *Indian Journal of Labour Economics*, 50 (4): 835–46.

——. 2008a. *Government Sponsored Health Insurance Schemes in India: An Overview*. New Delhi: ILO.

——. 2008b. *Assessing the Micro-Finance Needs of Vulnerable Groups* (mimeo). Bangalore: Institute for Social and Economic Change.

Rajasekhar, D.; J.Y. Suchitra, S. Madheswaran and G.K. Karanth. 2006. *Design and Management of Social Security Benefits for the Unorganised Sector Workers in Karnataka*. New Delhi: GTZ (German Technical Cooperation).

Rajasekhar, D; N.L. Narasimha Reddy and J.Y. Suchitra. 2006. *Effectiveness of Micro-Finance Programmes in Reducing Vulnerability to Debt Bondage* (ISEC Research Report (www.bondedlabour.org). Bangalore: Institute for Social and Economic Change.

Rajasekhar, D.; R. Manjula and J.Y. Suchitra. 2006. *Social Security Needs and Willingness to Contribute to Social Security: Garment*

Workers in Karnataka (mimeo). New Delhi: GTZ (German Technical Cooperation).

Rao, Hanumantha K. 2007. *Rural Development Statistics 2005–2006.* Hyderabad: National Institute of Rural Development.

Rao, V.M.; D. Rajasekhar and J.Y. Suchitra. 2006. 'The Unorganised Worker: Deprivations, Social Security and Policy Implications', *Economic and Political Weekly*. 41 (19): 1913–30.

Suchitra, J.Y. and D. Rajasekhar. 2006. 'One-Size-Does-Not-Fit-All: Employment Insecurity of Unorganised Workers in Karnataka', *The Indian Journal of Labour Economics,* 49 (3): 455–73.

World Labour Report. 2000. *Income Security and Social Protection in a Changing World*. Geneva: ILO.

11

Globalisation, Social Justice, and the Vulnerable Sections

Some Bygone and Burning Impressions

MANOHAR YADAV

Globalisation, as understood in terms of its developments since the 1990s, does not portray its full-length picture in India. Like in the other erstwhile colonised countries of the world, globalisation has a trajectory, record, and consequences of its own in India. It has passed through different historical phases and each phase has produced unique contextual results. On many counts, India benefited as well as was let down and deceived itself in each phase because of the ill initiatives pushed by the vested interest both from within and outside the country. In accordance with the nature of the native social structure and cultural milieu, incorporating bewildering variety of unequal human segments, placed in ascending–descending, vertical–horizontal orders, each segment of the population received the quantum of benefits or losses it 'deserved'. This historically etched and enduring environment determined the functioning of globalisation in India. The high and the privileged castes and the various competing religious groups got the best out of each phase of globalisation. For the vulnerable sections too, to some extent, globalisation heralded the boon; but, in course of time, it turned out to be a bane, as it went on pushing them towards the fringes. Naturally, as an already suffering lot, these sections lost hopes of revival though they kept on driven by the glimmers of globalisation. They became apathetic to the agonies experienced either in the persisting old order or in the emerging new context. Qualitatively, the experience of life appeared to them to be the same in both the situations.

The old and the new frameworks systematically got integrated into one whole system to further worsen the deteriorating local state of affairs. In this, India shows itself to be specific and distinctive. Nothing, that is apathetic to just and humane condition is new to India: inequality, exclusion, deprivation, etc. have been characteristic of her social fabric. But, that is not the issue; the issue is why are these unjust forms not disappearing or, at least, mitigating. It seems, and very strangely so, the social system in India has only such inherent tendencies, which produce and reproduce those structures that generate still harsher and stronger forms of inequalities and corresponding consequences. That is why democracy has failed in India. There is no reciprocity of interests, no concern for fellow human beings, and no sense of brotherhood – these render democracy in India to be no more than a mere form of government. As a consequence, freedom, justice, and fair treatment, which ought to place one on par with the other in all spheres of life, have no meaning for the masses. The lower and the lowest castes have been worst hit. Every time in history, when new consignment of benefits occurred, being equipped with historically endowed advantageous structural positions, the forward communities have garnered them the most. The benefits arising out of the process of globalisation have been, not surprisingly, reinforcing the persisting inequities and inequalities.

Thus, two issues need to be kept in mind while analysing the situation of dalits in the globalisation era. One is historical and structural condition, carrying over the inbuilt tendency to reinforce inequalities and related consequences, and the other is the tendency to absorb new and emerging inequalities, due to the compelling and inevitable circumstances created by the prevailing world order. The contextual variations of sufferings based on the location of dalits are located is an additional factor: the binaries like rural–urban, public–private, agricultural–non-agricultural, and lucrative–non-lucrative are important here.

Impact of the British Rule: Reinforced Vulnerability

For India, globalisation, in the modern sense of the term, began with the dawn of British rule. It ushered in a revolution of an unprecedented scale in many domains of life. The new modes of transport, communication, education, and law were themselves enough to change the face of India. Indeed, it was positive in many respects and proved to be a profound experience for a society characterised by feudalistic, parochial, and inert propensities. For the British, however, there were certain immediate and complex challenges to encounter with in India. First of all, the integration of highly parcelled bits of regions spread across the vast territory of the subcontinent and assimilation of its large mass of heterogeneous population into one unified whole proved to be a Herculean task. Determined as they were to bring the whole of India under their sole suzerainty, the British usurped and consolidated every portion of the land, irrespective of whether it was under the sway of a small or big native ruler. During the process, as if to bless India in disguise, they gave it a shape of an exclusive common nation; so far, it was not one as such. Simultaneously, they gave birth to the consciousness of Indianness and the spirit of nationalism, too, although it remained upper-caste/upper-class nationalism for a long time. The sense of nationalism among Indians mainly grew because of the influence of English education introduced by the British in India. It was through English education that few of the top classes of the Indians were exposed to western philosophy and the value of liberalism and humanism. That, in turn, urged them to realise their flaws back at home and forced them to think and act to rectify the same. As a result, there sprang up some reform movements. But those who organised such movements did not incorporate in their agenda the most plaguing historical and structural issues like caste and untouchability. Instead, they focused on derivative issues like bar on widow remarriage, etc.

So far as the British were concerned, they maintained distance from the native affairs and allowed everything to go on as they had been before. Their main concern was to loot India of its rich resources. For this, they aligned with the native exploitative forces and negotiated with the prevailing structures of Brahmanism. Karl Marx thought the British rule would destroy the old Indian society; on the contrary, it revitalised every element of Hindu social order: the distinction between high and low, and pure and impure, and the corresponding social, cultural, and economic distinctions. Thus, in reality, the western ideals of liberty, equality, and justice did not transform the age-old arrangements of unfair relations in India. The British rule consolidated the privileges of the upper castes and communities. These castes and communities, in so far as they saw the benefits for themselves, accepted the changes brought about by the British rule. The British introduced English education in India with the intention of training Indian substitutes for their company services. But, it was only the traditional elite, especially the Brahmins and the Kayasthas, among the Hindus who benefited from it. As B.P. Lamb puts it, 'When British first came to India, their main contacts were with Brahmins, who with a few other upper castes, were the first to profit by the British education and to enter government service under the East India Company' (1963: 143).

At the higher level, caste, no doubt, changed its character; it became an adaptive element of the structure. However, the ingenious upper castes utilised western philosophy, thoughts, ideas, skills, expertise, and ability to perform new jobs only to consolidate their own advantageous positions. They never let those opportunities trickle down to the lower castes. As a result, whatever the good things that the British initiated remained within the confines of these castes. This aggravated the traditional caste inequalities. As Satish Saberwal writes,

> The caste order served, on one side, to *facilitate* the absorption of western ideas, skills, styles of working and the like by groups within few *jatis*; and, on the other, to *impede* their flow across *jatis*. That is to say, groups, which absorbed the western ideas, tended often to act like cysts, with strong ties of kinship and friendship internally, and continuing privileged access to the sources of the west. Part of their insulation from the larger milieu comes from their using English language in myriad settings. (1996: 17)

It was, indeed, a double benefit for the higher castes: inheriting caste reverence and attaining gentlemen's honour. The combined power of traditional superiority and westernised supremacy helped them to secure a greater grip on the subjugated masses. Hence, the British were of no use, especially, for the downtrodden and the stigmatised castes like the 'untouchables'.

Their rule helped only old elites, those who were rooted in high caste and landlord backgrounds like the zamindars, deshmukhs, and other dominant groups. It is not from education alone, but also from the new systems of land revenue that the upper castes benefited. By introducing new revenue systems, the British promoted the landowning dominant castes who exploited the lower castes. As Francine Frankel says,

> In the *Zamindars* of north Bihar, Oudh, inland Orissa, and parts of Madras, the dominance of established status-oriented upper caste land holding families over the cultivating peasantry was greatly enhanced by the acquisition of individual property rights upheld under British law and enforced by state power. By contrast, in the western Doab of the United Provinces, many traditional Muslim and some Rajput Zamindars were replaced by Brahmins, Khatris and Banias. These helped to create a new class of owner – cultivators who took an interest in commercial agriculture. The situation was still different in most parts of Bengal, coastal Orissa and tribal Middle India, where a large share of landed property was on Brahmin, Bania and other local urban upper castes, most of whom constituted a new rich class of absentee landlords lacking any personal involvement in cultivation. (1990: 483)

Similarly, whatever economic modernisation that took place during the British rule benefited the upper castes. For example, Brahmins, Parsis, Vaniyas, and Kunbis got the lion's share of the emergent industrialisation in cities like Ahmedabad and Bombay (now Mumbai), while lower castes, like Dheds and Mahars, worked as low-paid labourers in the new industries.

Thus, whether it is new agriculture, industry, commerce, administration, art, literature, or whatever that sprouted as a part of the process of British colonisation in India facilitated the elites to advance their interests. Their positions were restructured to retain their old power while simultaneously reinforcing the historical positions of the subordinate caste groups. The British did intervene in Indian affairs, but it was only to add up the economic and other interests of the powerful classes and not to mould the age-old structural arrangements of the Indian society, including untouchability, the most heinous of social institutions. Therefore, this devious neutral stance of the British rule in India came under attack of revolutionaries like B.R. Ambedkar. Participating in the deliberations of the First Round Table Conference held in London, Ambedkar he had charged that 'the British Government has accepted the social arrangements as it found them and has preserved them faithfully... Our wrongs have remained as open sores and they have not been righted, although 150 years of the British rule have rolled away...' (cited in Moon 1982: 504).

Thus, as highlighted by Ambedkar, even under the British rule, the condition of the vulnerable sections, particularly those of the lower castes remained the same. Being helpless, and left to themselves, these castes were forced to carry over their historically entrenched problems on to the next phase of globalisation, which emerged with many new ventures in independent India.

Vulnerability: The Post-Independence Scenario

During the middle and the later phases of the British rule in India, there had evolved non-Brahmin movements in some parts of South India seeking social justice and emancipation from the age-old shackles of caste discrimination. But, during the later phase of the freedom movement, what got built up as depressed classes movement under the leadership of Ambedkar created such an atmosphere that it became inevitable for both the British and the Hindus to accept certain constitutional arrangements that could lead to the eventual overall advancement of the historically fallen and depressed communities in the country. This culminated in creating elaborate legal provisions intended to take care of the woes of these unfortunate groups of people.

After independence, with the new constitution in place, positive beginnings were made. As Manohar Yadav writes,

> Adoption of a universal franchise, a system of planned economic growth, equality of opportunity for education and employment and, of treatment, created a new socio-economic and political environment in India. Also ... dalit upliftment received a special political fillip. A vast array of untouchable and adivasi communities came to be identified as the Scheduled Groups [under] the new constitution entitled for a positive discriminatory treatment in the course of their over all advancement. No doubt, the entire state apparatus, in its aims and objectives, stood to promote the ensuing good of the dalit masses in India. To these trends of

> development, several other processes like urbanisation, westernisation, etc., were added ... to catapult India into a modern, secular, democratic society. (Yadav 1998: 25)

However, in a very short time, it lost its force and direction as well. To the suppressed communities, there arose, no doubt, some opportunities to rise above their ranks due to the policies like reservation in government jobs. But they were not equipped with literacy and education to qualify themselves to utilise the new opportunities, particularly those in the higher echelons of the new power structure. Among the 'untouchable' and the adivasi communities, there were hardly any graduates during the 1950s. Structural handicaps too operated with fierce force to keep them at bay. So, nothing more happened in terms of improving their status, except that they got nominal representation in parliament and the state legislative assemblies as representatives of the Scheduled Castes/Scheduled Tribes (SCs/STs) through reserved constituencies. Those who migrated to cities ended up becoming Class IV, municipality workers, or manual labourers.

The new system started operating as per the dictates of the upper castes. It was they who had dominated the freedom movement and, on that count, they had the hold over every controlling point. Some of the upper castes enjoyed positions too disproportionate to their percentage in population. Lamb submits: 'Of twenty-three Hindus in the Cabinet or Council of Ministers of the Indian Government in 1956, thirteen were Brahmins' (1963: 144). The same fact was applicable also to the other vibrant and gainful areas of the new jobs the independence generated. But here it is not the Brahmins alone but other upper castes also who shared the benefits. To all intents and purposes, the upper castes, with their English education background, virtually monopolised the opportunities in the power structure. Describing the social background of the new bureaucracy, Prayag Mehta says,

> Like their fore runners, (ICS [Indian Civil Service] cadres during the British regime), most of the IAS [Indian Administrative Service] officers, (after independence), also come from dominant social groups having access to English medium education, with stress on respect for authority and discipline, character building, leadership quality and good manners. (1998: 77)

Quoting S.N. Singh, Mehta further says,

> that during 1980–81, 71 per cent of IAS officers were recruited from this class, 19 per cent from agriculture and the rest from the other categories. They were, therefore, not representatives of the wider society as, at that time, the middle class was not even 10 per cent of the India's work force .... No wonder, their social background contributes to promoting a thought pattern in support of the social status quo and the privileged sections of the society. (ibid.)

Further, what had begun as development through five-year plans did not address the immediate pressing problems of the masses. Of course, the state began building basic industrial units that were more capital intensive than labour intensive. Agriculture, on whose support the poor and the marginalised were struggling to survive, did not flourish. It was a distorted approach to development without space for popular urges and aspirations. So, it did not help people experience real freedom and justice.

Not until the Fourth Five-Year Plan period could dalits receive any real relief in crucial matters like poverty, hunger, and unemployment, although it was mandatory for the state to guarantee sufficient means of livelihood to each of its citizens as per the Directive Principles of State Policy. Thus, dalits had to wait for almost twenty years after independence for the state to tackle their burning problems. Whether the various ventures introduced in this respect were successful or not, the catchphrases like 'Food for Work' and '*Garibi Hatao*' (banish poverty) earned much acclamation all over the country. In the subsequent plan periods, many intervention programmes were designed and implemented – Integrated Rural Development Programmes, National Rural Employment Programme, Rural Landless Employment Guarantee Programme, Jawahar Rozgar Yojana, Nehru Rozgar Yojana, and in recent years, National Rural Employment Guarantee Act, to mention but a few. It is claimed that dalits have gained from these general pool of programmes broadly meant for all sections of the society. In addition, some exclusive programmes like Special Component Plan and Integrated Tribal Development Plan have also been introduced for the amelioration of the conditions of SCs and STs respectively.

How far have dalits and other vulnerable sections of the society been able to gain by these various interventions of the state, however, is a controversial matter. There is one view that these programmes have not yielded any meaningful benefits to dalits. Rather than empowering them, it has been argued, these programmes have resulted in fostering a sort of dependency syndrome in them. It is because these programmes have not generated in them the strength needed to take care of themselves. Hence, these programmes appear as if they are provisions meant to keep dalits ever needy and dependent human beings. One thing is very clear: while espousing such policy measures, the complexities that underlie the situation of dalits have not been taken into consideration. Hence, the nude fact that dalits are too weak on all the frontiers of life.

As has been already said, even after the constitution of independent India came into force, for about two-and-half decades, the entry of dalits into government jobs was hampered by many factors: non-availability of qualified candidates, lack of awareness, and manipulation by vested interests prevented dalits from accessing available opportunities. Political reservation is a different story, as it did not require any qualification. However, whatever political reservation dalits got did not matter much to them, as except the elected representatives no one benefited from it. Since the later half of the 1970s and though the 1980s, dalits started securing entry into government and public sector jobs. Yet it is a bare fact that they are still due to secure full measure of opportunities in this respect. Hence, inferring from the figures presented in Twenty-Eighth Report of the Commissioner for SCs and STs, Government of India, S.C. Behar says, 'It is clear that in the case of both Central and State Governments, a large percentage of the reserved posts remain vacant. The situation in respect of tribals would even be worse if one was to exclude from the consideration the predominantly tribal states of the North-East' (2002: 316).

Globalisation and Persisting Vulnerabilities

What has emerged as globalisation since the 1990s is distinctive disposition as compared to the earlier phases of globalisation. It has been variously termed and interpreted, as it happens to have critical implications for the economy and society in India. With this phase of globalisation in motion, it is said, a free flow of money and capital across the globe has extensively raised the network of the rich from all over the world, which, by its united power, has been subduing the poor around the world. Naturally, the masses in India, too, have tasted it more as a bitter process. Particularly, dalits, tribal people, and women have experienced an unparalleled measure of marginalisation due to this process.

However, the immediate anxiety of these masses has been the shattering base of the framework called the 'democratic state' in which they had dreamt to settle down with their taken-for-granted notions of 'equity' and 'justice'. This state has been struggling to retain its authentic base even as its new managers have begun to eat into its very vitals. Sixty-four years ago, as it freshly emerged from the historical mint of independence, the state held many high promises. All those promises have gone astray or have totally withered away in the hostile wind of globalisation. Currently, the Indian state is at the mercy of external agencies. It is directly or indirectly controlled by the World Bank, International Monetary Fund, World Trade Organisation, the trans-national corporations, and so on working in tandem with each other. All these agencies, being in favour of for-profit enterprise, have no regard for equity or distributive justice. Of course, half-heartedly, they claim to owe some social responsibility towards the affected sections of the society, but in reality they are antagonistic to the very idea of welfare. The masses have been made to feel content with fringe benefits doled out to them in the form of programmes to raise their literacy level or such other development indicators. Apparently, there is some improvement in this regard, but, overall, there has hardly been any significant development.

It is with self-interest that the Indian elites have joined hands with global capitalist classes and global financial institutions and have laid excessive emphasis on economic growth, which has been destroying the livelihoods of the majority. Also, these elites have managed to acquire fertile agricultural lands to grow cash crops and earn quick profits. In addition, the rapid growth of cities and associated industrial hubs and other developmental activities have also led to the loss of common land.

Persisting Bleak Realities

In his analysis of the status of SCs, Duncan Forrester reveals that 'whatever index one may use – poverty, social status, health, life expectancy, literacy, education – [they] come under the bottom of the scale' (quoted in Gaikwad 1999: 2). Although the concentration of vulnerability counted in terms of these indicators is more among SCs, the situation among tribal communities and other most-backward castes may not too different. So, what is true of SCs is more or less true of other lowest castes and the tribal communities as well. Below, we will examine the condition of SCs in relation to few main indicators of development.

Land and Employment Situation

When the loss of land is occurring on in such a massive scale, the landless can hardly dream of owning land. Yet, there are researches that claim, that obtaining property rights would create a positive impact on the lives of dalits and women. A research conducted by Washington-based Rural Development Institute asserts that 'landlessness is the best predicator of poverty in India – a much better predicator than either illiteracy or membership of a traditionally "untouchable" caste'. It further argues that 'important livelihood benefits such as improved nutrition, income, place for residence, enhanced social status and access to credit, and bargaining leverage in labour markets can be easily derived by a family in case it owns a required plot of land' (quoted in Yadav and Ramaswamy 2010: 3). But, sadly, the vulnerable sections like dalits in Karnataka own only 7 per cent of the total agricultural land in the state. Also, their land is highly fragmented: some of the dalits in northern Karnataka own a piece of land worth sowing only two rows of crops. But such households are also counted as 'marginal farmers'. The fragmentation process is so rapid among the SCs in Karnataka that, between 1991 and 2001, their operational holdings in marginal size class have increased from 45 per cent to 52 per cent. Despite land reforms and land purchase measures of the Government of Karnataka, during this period, the total area of operational holdings among dalits has increased from 9.95 lakh hectares to 10.71 lakh hectares – a mere addition of 0.76 lakh hectares of land. And, according to some micro studies, 'there is also a doubt about the quality of land that the SCs got as result of land reforms efforts in Karnataka' (Aziz and Krishna 1997: 55). Left with such precarious land base, dalits have no option but to live with floating opportunities in the filed of dying agriculture. Alternatively, they migrate to the cities and end up in slums there.

According to 2001 census, about 20.54 per cent and 43.41 per cent of the total SC workers are reported to be the cultivators and landless agricultural labourers respectively. Only 2.53 per cent of them are accounted for as household workers, while 33.12 per cent of them are enumerated as other workers. Thus, though, in comparison with 1991 census figures, their dependency on agricultural labour has decreased by 6 percentage points, their situation as cultivators has not improved. In fact, their number as cultivators has decreased by 3 percentage points. Since the enumeration as 'other workers' in the 2001 census includes whole lot of sub-occupations, including those jobs falling under the service sector, it is possible that, due to pull and push factors, the other SCs may have been absorbed by the infrastructure building process, which is endlessly going on in urban centres, mostly as construction workers, etc. The infrastructure-building sector appears to be very enigmatic since it does not make available any data with respect to the kind of work the various caste people handle there. According to the President of the Karnataka State Construction Workers Federation (affiliated to the All India Trade Union Congress), 'in Bangalore alone there are about 8.5 lakh construction workers without any social security and work place security' (cited in Yadav and Ramaswamy 2010: 5)). And, the entire construction industry consists of about sixty categories of workers. Almost all of them are out of the framework of Workers Welfare Fund. Dalits, being unskilled labourers, get very low wages besides not having any such security. There are certain works that happen to be too dangerous and hazardous, and, in such occupations, majority are found to be dalits. All this means that employment scenario among dalits is grim despite such programmes as National Rural Employment Guarantee Act. Dalits form a large segment of the new urban toilers or, what Sandeep Pendse non-specifically terms them, 'workers, labouring masses, the poor, the underprivileged, urban subaltern, and slum dwellers' (1995: 6).

Worthless Education

The so-called educated youth among dalits in Karnataka have not benefited much from the lucrative jobs generated by globalisation.

This is because most of them do not have the type of skills or quality of education that these new jobs demand. The excellent zones of education in science, medicine, mathematics, information technology, bio-technology, etc. are either beyond their reach or attraction. This has also inadvertently created the false notion that dalits or the other backward classes (OBCs) are generally without merit or incompetent. Obviously, the private schooling of the children belonging to the upper strata of society is far superior to that of the public schooling of the poor and dalit children. This makes the latter too weak to vie with the former. Generally, the children of the upper strata go to the English-medium schools, whereas those of dalits and the poor sections have no option but to attend the vernacular medium schools.

In education system today, enrolment has become the most important indicator of development. Once enrolled, whether a child attends the school or not, he/she is promoted to the next higher class. Many of the students passing School Leaving Certification Examination do not even know how they cleared their examination! Even after matriculation, many of them do not know how to read, let alone to write. Thus, the quality of education that the students get from the vernacular medium government schools lacks the essence to make them competent enough to compete with their counterparts from English-medium private schools. The present education system is also worthless on the count that it hardly generates creative, innovative, and self-making abilities.

Assetlessness

The asset position of dalits is also woeful; any casual observation of their households would reveal that they hardly own anything other than a hut or a dilapidated structure of a small house constructed as part of a governmental housing scheme. In Karnataka, a house is built at a cost of about ₹ 20,000 under the Ashraya or Ambedkar Housing Scheme. But, given the kind of material and labour used in building these houses, it is hardly surprising that they collapse within few months of their construction. The 2001 census informs us that, in Karnataka, more than half (55%) of the SC families in rural areas live in semi-permanent or temporary houses. About 31.13 per cent of their urban counterparts also live in semi-permanent or temporary houses. These data, however, do not reveal the true picture: in rural areas, every SC holder of a hopeless land is counted as a marginal farmer; in urban areas, anyone owning a 10 square feet tenement is counted as owning a house.

Thus, mainstreaming of dalits is long way to go; it is a dream to find pathways for them to gain from, what Owen Lynch once termed, 'power, prestige, wealth and education' (1969: 3). Unless some strong policy measures are worked out in the cause of creating an enduring and naturally thriving base of life for dalits, the so-called freedom and justice will remain as a mirage in their case. Some policy measures, which would help dalits share the fine goods of life are discussed below.

Policy Measures

Land Policy

Dalits form the largest proportion of the landless agricultural labourers. Hence, their real well-being lies in getting some fixed amount of land, which can ensure them over all security – social, economic, and physical. It is said, owning a piece of land enhances one's pride as well as the status in the society. It also enables one to have access to credit and bargaining power in the labour market. The state government may also think of making provisions in the budget to build up 'Dalit Agricultural Colonies and Industrial Units'. In Kalaghatagi taluk of Dharwad district in Karnataka, on an experimental basis, a Dalit Agricultural Colony has been established and named after a ruined village called Kalasanakoppa. This has been a wonderful success story. Emulation of such a model of dalit empowerment would yield appreciable results. This can make dalits' life more stable and sustainable.

Improvement in Asset Position

To restate, the persistence of thick concentration of dalits in the primary sector underlines their excessive vulnerability. Such being their situation, the government should ensure that the asset position of dalits is sufficient enough to enhance their capital accumulation capability so that they are slowly merged into the mainstream economy. At present, except land records, nothing else exists in the form of the plain data that indicates the degree of their presence in commerce, industry, business, and technology.

Education Policy

The existence of extreme disparities in the quality of education is against the principle of equity and justice. Thus, the government needs to think beyond formal enrolments in schools to check the rapidly growing discrepancies in education. Unless the prevailing system of education is fully channelised to create proper and matching excellence among dalits or the BCs, it will have no real value for them. The strategic intervention of the government with liberal budget provisions can fill up the educational deficiencies that dalits experience. It can happen only when public education is elevated to the same standard as that of private education, or when dalits get equal access to private schools with full aid from the government. The deprivation that the dalit children suffer from not being fully educated in English warrants urgent attention of the government. It is not enough to introduce English as one of the subjects to be taught from first standard onwards, as the government of Karnataka has done. What needs to be attained is actual correction of accumulated disparities in terms of sharing the relevant and advanced knowledge that English education has been incessantly producing. To begin with, the government may launch a few 'Centres of Excellence for Dalit Education' to ensure that dalits get proficiency in functionally valuable education.

Poverty and Hunger

Dalits have been the victims of historically rooted cumulative inequalities. Ameliorating their situation necessarily calls for extra efforts. Presently, though hunger is not a persistent phenomenon among dalits in all states, the government has not properly addressed their food and nutritional needs. The quality of food grains they get from fair price shops is too low to meet their nutritional needs. Moreover, because of their poor income position, they cannot afford additional intake of other food items like eggs, milk, fish, or fruits. According to National Family Health Survey (1998–99) report, not even half of the SC women and children consume milk or curd, as compared to 80 per cent of other women and children, in Karnataka. Naturally, the body mass index of SCs has been counted to be much below the national/state average. In terms of all health indicators – life expectancy at birth, infant mortality, maternal mortality, etc. –

the SCs' situation still remains to be matched with the general population. Thus, there is a dire necessity of state intervention to improve the health conditions of dalits.

It is said that India's food policy is going to be conditioned by global level circumstances. Already, the prices of wheat and other staple crops have sharply gone up in the global markets. Food has also a tendency to deplete from the stock. Under such conditions, the state has to come to the rescue of dalits and other vulnerable groups with suitable policy measures. Indeed, the state needs to shed its present capitalist complex and go back to its original role as the welfare state.

Conclusion

One needs to take cognisance of the caution that Ambedkar sounded in the Constituent Assembly while presenting the draft constitution of which he was an architect. His main concern was that things should not go wrong after independence and after the adoption of the new, secular constitution. Apart from protecting civil rights and implementing measures for reducing poverty and unemployment, the state needs to ensure endogenous development of dalits through building up their natural strengths by imparting functionally relevant and useful education and by mainstreaming them in the entire domain of economy, polity, and culture so that they no more feel left out or alienated in the process nation-building.

It is common for dalits to speak about state intervention, which is no doubt imperative in absolute terms. But it is also desirable that dalits take stock of their own situation and see whether they have a role to play in their own betterment. The dalit intellectuals and the elite of the community have a significant function in this respect. The dalit intellectuals need to peel off every layer of the complex situation of the dalit world filled with dilemmas and paradoxes and find out some valuable means to bring them dalit brethern into their own. One way is to reconstruct the organic link between the dalit elites, intellectuals, and ordinary masses by devising such strategies, which bring their cultural and material resources together for their self-empowerment. The top bureaucrats and politicians ably assisted by intellectuals can help create an alternative identity for dalits in terms of building their own economy, polity, and culture in such a way that simultaneously, and in terms of equality, every thing gets integrated into the mainstream society concomitantly keeping its distinctiveness intact.

Independent of constitutional remedies, Ambedkar could have envisaged a 'Self-Reliant Parallel Economy of Dalits', where dalits have their own organised banking system, cooperative societies, agricultural colonies, and industrial units. The dalit elites, by investing in some viable and profitable areas of industry, trade, or commerce, can give rise to self-reliant economy of their own with channels leading to its integration into the larger economy. There are castes that have come out with their own economy exclusively using their community power at the same time drawing sufficient aid from the government to protect their economy. The government should take initiatives to facilitate and promote the wealth-generating activities among dalits. So far, either through the political representation or jobs in the government sector, some dalits have secured some wealth, but rarely through industrial or business enterprises. The emergence of a visible section of dalits with industrial and wealth backgrounds can earn the community the respect it deserves from the larger society. And, that will give an alternative identity for dalits.

Furthermore, when the government is facilitating so many huge ventures, like promoting Special Economic Zones (SEZs), it can also think of acquiring land to promote some SEZs for dalits and the tribal communities. The government can also help restore and rejuvenate subsistence economy in cases where it already exists among dalits and the tribal communities. Of late, the idea of development of 'green economy' is gaining ground in the country. Dalits can be encouraged to develop their own green economies. But there should be more stress on making possible an endogenous economy to emerge from amongst dalits themselves through the method of mustering and mobilising their own strength and resources along with the support from the government.

Dalits have not made much headway in the development of institutional and cultural resources in the cause of their upliftment. Of course, they have established a few higher education institutions, but that is too scanty to meet the needs of the community. Moreover, there is utter lack of initiative on the part of dalits in starting primary or middle schools. The elite among dalits can take lead in initiating action on this matter of urgent importance on their own besides seeking strategic intervention of the government to bridge the educational gulf that dalits continue to experience with the privileged.

References

Aziz, Abdul and Sudhir Krishna. 1997. *Land Reforms in India: Karnataka: Promises Kept and Missed.* New Delhi: Sage Publications.

Behar, S.C. 2002. 'Reservation: An Insufficient Condition for Social Transformation', in Ghanshyam Shah (ed.): *Dalits and the State.* New Delhi: Concept Publishing Company, pp. 310–24.

Frankel, Francine R. 1990. 'Decline of a Social Order', in Francine R. Frankel and M.S.A. Rao (eds.): *Dominance and State Power in Modern India – Vol II.* New Delhi: Oxford University Press, pp. 482–517.

Gaikwad, S.L. 1999. *Protective Discrimination Policy and Social Change.* New Delhi: Rawat Publications.

Lamb, B.P. 1963. *A World in Transition.* New York: Frederick A. Praeger.

Lynch, Owen. 1969. *The Politics of Untouchability.* New York: Columbia University Press.

Mehta, Prayag. 1998. *A Psychological Strategy for Alternative Human Development: India's Performance since Independence.* New Delhi: Sage Publications.

Moon, Vasant. 1982. *Dr Babasaheb Ambedkar: Writings and Speeches – Vol. 2.* Mumbai: Department of Education, Government of Maharashtra.

Pendse, Sandeep. 1995. 'Toil, Sweat and the City', in Sujata Patel and Alice Thorner (eds.): *Bombay: Metaphor for Modern India.* New Delhi: Oxford University Press, pp. 3–25.

Saberwal, Satish. 1996. *Roots of Crisis: Interpreting Contemporary Indian Society.* New Delhi: Sage Publications.

Yadav, Manohar. 1998. 'Development: A Dalit Perspective', *Journal of Bangalore Theological Forum,* 30 (3 & 4): 24–32.

Yadav, Manohar and V. Ramaswamy. 2010. 'The Land Situation of Dalits in Karnataka'. Paper presented at the national workshop on 'The Dalits and Land Rights', jointly organised by the Institute for Social and Economic Change and DRISTI at Bangalore, 29–31 March 2011.

12

Does Micro-Finance Reduce Vulnerability?

A Study of Dalit Households in Karnataka and Tamil Nadu

D. RAJASEKHAR, MANJULA R. AND SUCHITRA J.Y.

Micro-finance implies the provision of financial services such as savings, credit, and insurance for the poor in rural and urban areas to meet consumption credit needs, or to start new economic activities, or to strengthen the existing ones. Governments, donors and NGOs all over the world have been advised to take up micro-finance programmes for the poor and vulnerable sections of society as these programmes have the potential to reduce poverty and empower the poor (Rajasekhar 2002), especially in the context of globalisation and privatisation.

The knowledge on achievements of micro-finance is partial and contested. While one group of scholars (Hashemi, Schuler and Riley 1996; Puhazhendi and Badatya 2002) argues that micro-finance has very beneficial social and economic impact, others caution against such optimism (see Goetz and Sen Gupta 1996, Rogaly 1996; Buckley 1997; Mayoux 1998; Kropp and Suran 2002; Banerjee et al., 2010). Other studies (see Hulme and Mosley 1996; Rajasekhar 2002; Coleman 2006) suggest beneficial impact of micro-finance programmes, but argue that the programme does not assist the poorest. This suggests considerable gap between theory and evidence (Morduch 1999) and calls for a discussion on why 'micro-finance promise' has not been fulfilled. In particular, there is need to discuss the relationship between micro-finance and the reduction of vulnerability.

This chapter discusses the extent to which micro-finance has reduced poverty and vulnerability. The data presented here were collected from dalit households having membership in micro-finance groups formed by NGOs supported by New Entity for Social Action (NESA)[1] in Karnataka and Tamil Nadu states. After obtaining a list of all NGOs with their respective target groups from NESA, those predominantly working with dalits were identified. From this list, six NGOs (three each from Karnataka and Tamil Nadu) were selected randomly. After reaching the project area of the selected NGOs, three self-help groups (SHGs) (existing for at least three years prior to the survey date) from each project area were selected randomly with the help of a list obtained from the sample NGOs. Thus, in all, eighteen SHGs were studied in-depth. After reaching the village where the sample SHG was located, a focus group discussion was conducted and ranking/mapping techniques were adopted to map the micro-finance needs. In order to explore the issues in a detailed manner, 40 per cent of the members from each of the selected SHGs were selected randomly in the presence of SHG members for canvassing the household questionnaire. In all, we have interviewed 120 dalit households having membership in eighteen SHGs in the project area of six NGOs located in six different districts in Karnataka and Tamil Nadu during 2006–07. Regional consultations were held with representatives of dalit SHGs and leaders of NGOs working with dalits in each state to share key findings, validate the same, and obtain suggestions. After incorporating the comments and suggestions coming from these workshops, the findings were revised and presented in a national seminar.

The chapter is presented in five sections. The first section outlines the situation of dalit households in Karnataka and Tamil Nadu, and also at the all-India level. The second section discusses the background of the sample households and the micro-finance benefits received by them. The third section examines the relation between micro-finance and access to basic amenities, health, and education among the households. The fourth section analyses the relationship between membership in micro-finance groups and vulnerability. Concluding remarks are provided in the last section.

Dalits in Karnataka and Tamil Nadu

In 2004–05, there were 301.2 million poor in India. Over 77 per cent of them lived in rural areas (GoI 2007). The programmes and policies followed by the Government of India since independence seem to have had a positive impact on poverty. The figures compiled by the Planning Commission show that the incidence of poverty has declined from 51.3 per cent in 1977–78 to 27.5 per cent in 2004–05.

In the selected states of Karnataka and Tamil Nadu also, there has been a decline in the incidence of poverty at the aggregate level as well as among the Scheduled Castes (SCs) (see Table 12.1). In Karnataka, the incidence of rural poverty declined from 36.3 per cent in 1983 to 17.4 per cent in 1999–2000, while that among SCs it declined from 52.7 per cent to 26.2 per cent during the same period. Similarly, the incidence of rural poverty in Tamil Nadu declined from 54 per cent to 20.6 per cent, while poverty among SCs in rural areas it declined from 67.5 per cent to 32.6 per cent during this period. Two points need to be noted here. First, the decline in the incidence of poverty among SCs has been faster as compared to the overall population. This is a positive aspect. Second, despite this decline, the incidence of poverty was high among SCs even in 1999–2000. Why it is so? In what follows, we shall examine this question.

Table 12.1

Prevalence of poverty in rural India and among the scheduled castes

	Years		
	1983	*1993–94*	*1999–2000*
Karnataka			
All	36.3	29.9	17.4
SCs	52.7	46.6	26.2
Tamil Nadu			
All	54.0	32.4	20.5
SCs	67.5	44.1	32.6
India			
All	45.6	37.1	27.1
SCs	58.1	48.1	36.2

Note: SCs = Scheduled Castes

Source: Biradar (2011).

Differences in Landownership

Access to land, an important productive asset in rural India, not only influences income, but also vulnerability. Table 12.2 shows that the proportion of medium and large farmers has been lower among the SC households as compared to the other households. On the other hand, the proportion of landless among SCs was 2.7 per cent in 2004–05 as compared to 1.8 per cent among others. This suggests that the incidence of landlessness among the SC households has not been very high. However, the incidence of marginal farmers was considerably high among SCs as compared to others. The low incidence of landlessness and high proportion of marginal farmers among the SC households can be attributed to the distribution of land under Land Reforms Programme (Rajasekhar 1988: 48, 1992: 216; Bakshi 2008). As has been reported by many studies, these lands have often been marginal (Rajasekhar 1992: 215; Planning Commission 2009). This suggests that most of the SC households are marginal farmers owning inferior and unproductive land. Although the ownership of productive assets such as land is inversely related to the level of vulnerability, the ownership of inferior and dry land exposes farmers to weather-related uncertainty and higher level of vulnerability, especially in the context of dependency on informal credit market for the purchase of agricultural inputs.

Table 12.2

Distribution of households (%) by landholding size and social groups (2004–05)

Size classes (in hectares)	*Scheduled Castes*	*Scheduled Tribes*	*Others*
Landless households	2.7	3.6	1.8
>1.0 (Marginal)	86.9	66.7	71.5
1.1 –2.0 (Small)	6.7	16.3	13.1
2.1-4.0 (Medium)	2.7	10.6	8.8
>4.1 (Large)	1.0	2.9	4.9
All	100	100	100

Source: Biradar (2011).

Deprivation in Capabilities

Human capital influences the 'life-span' income-earning levels of individuals. SCs seem to be particularly worse off in terms of educational attainment. In 2001, the rate of literacy among the rural population was 68.8 per cent, while it was only 54.7 per cent among SCs. It is important to look at educational levels of the workforce belonging to different social groups, as education influences the quality of employment and income levels. The NSSO (National Sample Survey Organisation) data for 2004–05 show that the proportion of workforce with illiteracy or being literate at lower levels was higher among SCs as compared to those belonging to other castes. R.R. Biradar (2011) found a negative relationship between literacy (proxy for human capital) and poverty among social groups. An obvious implication of this is that low literacy rate among the SC workers has resulted in poor access to quality employment, lower earnings, and higher incidence of poverty. This is further corroborated by the NSSO data on quality of employment and earnings.

Quality of Employment and Earnings

The NSSO data for 2004–05 show that 41.3 per cent of the SC workers in rural India were in self-employment, 6.6 per cent in regular employment, and 52.1 per cent in casual employment. In contrast, as many as 66.9 per cent of the workers belonging to other castes were in self-employment, 7.8 per cent in regular employment, and only 25.3 per cent in casual employment. Thus, a higher proportion of the SC workers were in casual employment, which implies that a larger proportion of the SC workers were facing uncertainty of employment and were obtaining lower wages. Underemployment was also high among the SC workers: in rural India, 30 per cent of the workforce among the SC households was underemployed, whereas the percentage of underemployed was only 24.1 among other castes.

The foregoing reveals that the incidence of poverty has been higher among the SC households as compared to others. The high incidence of poverty has been largely on account of tiny and unproductive landholdings and low rates of human-capital formation leading to poor skills, low quality of employment, and poor earnings. This suggests high level of vulnerability among the SC households due to lack of access to productive assets, poor access to education, labour market discrimination, and caste-based discrimination.

Micro-finance and the Sample Households

Micro-finance has the potential to reduce poverty and empower the poor. The savings facilities offered by SHGs enable the poor dalit households to save. The accumulated amounts of savings give confidence to the poor and contribute towards the reduction of vulnerability. The credit facility enables the member households to borrow for social consumption (such as payment of school fees, purchase of medicines, etc.), carrying on the productive activities (such as buying fertilisers for crop production, and meeting working capital needs in small manufacturing, trades, and services), and initiate new income-generating activities. Against this background, let us now look at the evidence gathered from the field.

Background Information on the SHG Members

All except one SHG from Tamil Nadu were formed for women. Thus, while all the sample SHG members in Karnataka were women, 85 per cent in Tamil Nadu were women. Most of the members belonged to the age group 25–40 years. About 15 per cent of the members in Karnataka, however, belonged to the age group of less than 20 years (Table 12.3). Most of them were unmarried. It was found out that even college-going/school-going girls were enrolled in the group, especially in Karnataka, as they were perceived to be useful for mobilising small savings. We were told that two or more persons from the same household joined the same group. In such cases, the other members would be unmarried girls. This suggests errors in the targeting of micro-finance programmes, which have been popularised as savings schemes rather than those bringing socio-economic empowerment among women members.

It may be noted that a small proportion of the members were either widows or deserted or separated. It is also possible that a few of the married women were heading the households. In the case of female-headed households, as the NGO leaders have maintained during the interviews, the vulnerability levels would be quite high.

The distribution of members by number of years of membership, as presented in Table 12.4, shows that 55 per cent and 60 per cent of the members in Karnataka and Tamil Nadu, respectively, had SHG membership for three or more years. This period is adequate to see the impact of micro-finance benefits on vulnerability levels.

Table 12.3
Basic information of sample SHG members

Particulars	*Karnataka (n = 60)*	*Tamil Nadu (n = 60)*
Sex of the members (%)		
Male	0.00	15.0
Female	100.00	85.0
Age (in years) of members (%)		
< 20	15.00	0.00
20-25	8.33	21.67
25-30	28.33	20.00
30-40	28.33	38.33
More than 40	20.00	20.00
Education of members (%)		
Illiterate	61.67	51.67
Primary	21.67	25.00
Secondary	5.00	8.33
High school and above	11.66	15.00
Marital status of members (%)		
Unmarried	11.67	1.67
Married	83.33	91.67
Widowed	3.33	3.33
Separated/deserted	1.67	3.33

Source: Field survey.

Table 12.4
Distribution of members (%) by duration of SHG membership

Duration of membership	*Karnataka (n = 60)*	*Tamil Nadu (n = 60)*
< 2 years	45	40
3 years	23	25
> 4 years	32	35
Total	100	100

Source: Field survey.

The major motivation for the sample members to join SHGs was either to avail savings facility or access credit. Importantly, only a few sample SHG members mentioned that social and economic empowerment was the major motivation for them to join the group. Thus, the expectations of members appear to be simple.

One would, therefore, expect NGOs to provide training to members to broaden their horizons on the importance of SHG membership and the long-term benefits that would accrue to the members through such membership.

Did the sample members hold leadership positions either in the past or do so currently? The response was positive from 25 per cent of the sample members in Karnataka and 18 per cent in Tamil Nadu. A larger proportion of older members in Karnataka held leadership positions as compared to Tamil Nadu. This also suggests that leadership rotation has not been as frequent as one often expects (that is, once in a year). If the frequent rotation of leadership has been practised, the proportion of members holding leadership positions would have been higher.

An important feature of SHGs is that they hold regular meetings to enable the members to discuss their problems and take corrective collective actions. While some SHGs fixed fortnightly meetings, others fixed weekly meetings. The evidence collected from the representatives of sample SHGs shows that most of them held the meetings as scheduled. Did the sample members attend all the meetings regularly? While all the sample SHG members in Tamil Nadu stated that they attended the meetings regularly, only 85 per cent of the sample members in Karnataka stated so. The remaining members attended the meetings either once in a while or never attended. The problem of irregular attendance in Karnataka has been confined to the project area of one NGO. In this case, the problems such as inappropriate rules relating to savings and credit, elite capture, and poor processes relating to the formation of the groups have contributed to the reluctance towards group affairs and irregular attendance. In this project area, the dependence of members on the NGO staff was very high. Unless the NGO staff visits the village, the meeting would not be held.

Savings Benefits

Contribution of savings by each member to the group is a mandatory requirement in SHGs. Regular savings contributions are a not only proof of the participation by members but it also enhances the members' stakes in the programme. Growing amounts of savings go a long way in instilling confidence among members and enable them to avail loans either from the group itself or banks to undertake income-generating activities.

As per the norms, each SHG is expected to fix savings amounts to be contributed by a member and also frequency of contributions through a process of consultation and collective decision-making. The usual practice is that the amount of savings to be contributed by each member is fixed and uniformly applied to all the members in the group. But, the groups do provide flexibility in so far as the frequency of contributions is concerned. In other words, if a member cannot contribute savings in a week, she can pay savings amount of two weeks in one go in the following week. Since savings amount is linked to credit amounts requested by each member, any new member joining the group is not allowed to contribute the savings amount in one go at the beginning. The usual practice followed by the groups is to collect savings amounts in the meetings held once in a week or fortnight.

The distribution of sample members by monthly amounts of savings (see Table 12.5) shows that the micro-finance programmes in Tamil Nadu have fixed larger amounts. While about 73 per cent of the sample members contributed ₹ 40 per month in Karnataka, over 63 per cent of the sample members in Tamil Nadu have contributed ₹ 80 or more per month. Interestingly, about 20 per cent of the members in Tamil Nadu were contributing1 ₹ 20 per month or ₹ 30 per week.

Table 12.5
Distribution of members (%) by monthly amount of savings (Rs) contributed to SHGs

Savings (Rs per month)	*Karnataka (n = 60)*	*Tamil Nadu (n = 60)*
40	73.3	16.7
50	0.0	20.0
80	16.7	43.3
100	0.0	0.0
120	0.0	20.0
Total	100	100

Source: Field survey.

Thus, it can be anticipated that the cumulative amount of savings would be high in Tamil Nadu, as compared with Karnataka (see Table 12.6). While over 63 per cent of the SHG members in Tamil Nadu have cumulative savings of more than ₹ 2,000, more than 58 per cent of SHG members in Karnataka have savings of less than ₹ 1,000. As will be shown in the next section, this was not primarily due to differences in monthly savings amounts or the period of membership.

Table 12.6

Distribution of sample SHG members (%) by cumulative amount of savings

Cumulative amount of savings (Rs)	*Karnataka (n = 60)*	*Tamil Nadu (n = 60)*
< 500	36.67	0.00
500–1,000	21.67	11.67
1,000–1,500	23.32	10.00
1,500–2,000	11.67	15.00
2,000–3,000	6.67	23.33
> 3000	0.00	40.00
Total	100	100

Source: Field survey.

Low level of savings among micro-finance groups in Karnataka can be attributed to many reasons. First, best practices required for the mobilisation of savings were not followed by the Karnataka SHGs. For instance, SHGs adopt such rules as 'regular savings is taken into consideration while taking a decision on disbursal of income generating loan', 'savings amounts are linked to the size of loan disbursed', and 'fine is imposed on those who do not contribute savings regularly' as incentives to motivate or influence the members to contribute savings regularly. This was, however, not done in the case of several sample SHGs from Karnataka. Second, micro-finance groups did not fix the amount of savings after having discussions in the group and ascertaining the capacity of the members to save. As a result, although members in some of the groups were in a position to contribute higher amounts of savings, this potential was not tapped. Third, the principle of reciprocity was not followed. As will be discussed further, groups have taken a decision that, until the accumulated amount of savings reaches a 'certain' level, loans will not be sanctioned to members. In the absence of facility to avail small loan amounts for consumption and other purposes, group members tended not to put their savings in the group.

Credit Operations

An important function of SHGs is to provide credit facility to members, not only for consumption, but also for productive activities. In the first year of SHG existence, the savings of members would be built into a revolving credit fund from which members' credit needs relating to consumption will be met. Typically, these purposes include paying school fees, purchase of medicines, buying of food grains from the public distribution system, etc. Since the loan amounts required for these purposes would be small, they can easily be met through the revolving credit fund built with the help of members' savings, and can be repaid in small instalments in two or three months. Thus, in the initial phases of an SHG, there will be frequent borrowing from members for consumption. Such a frequent borrowing would help in the inculcation of credit discipline among members.

Only when the revolving credit fund becomes substantial would SHGs entertain applications for short-term production credit. Typically, short-term production credit would involve loans for the purchase of fertilizers, working capital for trade or business, purchase of inputs for dairying, etc. These loans are usually availed at the end of the first year or in the second year.

However, members cannot initiate income-generating activities through revolving credit fund built with the help of members' savings, as these activities would involve larger sums of money. Hence, SHGs have to obtain funds from outside sources such as banks. Under the Bank–SHG linkage programme of the National Bank for Agriculture and Rural Development, SHGs are eligible to receive additional bulk loans in the ratio of 1: 1 to 1: 5 of the group's savings. However, the banks will not provide additional resources unless they are satisfied with the group's performance with regard to regularity of meetings, rotation of leadership, mobilisation of savings, and repayment of loans. Banks have developed a protocol to rate SHGs on a scale of 1 to 10, and only those SHGs obtaining a higher rating are eligible to receive bulk loans.

The sample members in Karnataka obtained 94 loans from their SHGs since inception. This implies that, on an average, each member obtained one-and-half loans. In contrast, the sample members in Tamil Nadu obtained as many as 300 loans since inception. The average number of loans works out to be five.

Source-wise distribution of loans also informs us of the status of micro-finance programmes across the states. While nearly 93 per cent of the loans were obtained through SHGs (that is, revolving credit fund built with the help of members' savings) in Karnataka, the corresponding proportion in Tamil Nadu was only 58 per cent. More importantly, over 42 per cent of the loans in the latter state were obtained from banks through SHGs.

Table 12.7 shows that one-third of the sample SHG members in Karnataka did not obtain any loans. (This, however, does not mean that they did not need credit.) There are three reasons for this. First, NGOs from Karnataka did not provide small loans in the initial stages of group formation for consumption purposes. Several members noted that they were, in fact, in need of loans for consumption, education, and health. For instance, Sakamma from Jabgare village in Hunsur taluk of Mysore district was educating two of her children. She was in need of money to pay school fees. When she approached the group for a loan, she was denied on the grounds that SHG would start providing loan only when the accumulated amount in the group reaches a certain level. This is in contrast to SHGs in Tamil Nadu; they started lending right from their inception. Second, a few of the groups have become defunct due to poor governance. The leadership of these groups was vested with those related to the NGO staff. There was a suspicion among members that loans were issued to relatives of leaders, and this had blessing of the NGO staff. This resulted in widespread discontent among members, non-attendance in group meetings, and non-payment of savings contributions. Third, elite capture was also a reason why the number of loans availed by members tended to be low. One group took the decision that only representatives should take the loan in the initial rounds. This led to widespread discontent, elite capture, and ultimately the group becoming defunct.

Table 12.7
Distribution of sample members (%) by number of loans received since inception

Number of loans	*Karnataka (n = 60)*	*Tamil Nadu (n = 60)*
0	33.3	3.30
1	28.3	6.67
2–3	25.0	43.33
4–6	13.4	25.00
7>	0.0	21.70
Total	100	100

Source: Field survey.

In addition, the number of loans obtained by the SHG members in Karnataka was fewer as compared with their counterparts in Tamil Nadu. The proportion of SHG members obtaining four or more loans was nearly 47 per cent in Tamil Nadu, but it was only about 13 per cent in Karnataka. The proportion of SHG members obtaining two or three loans was only 25 per cent in Karnataka, whereas it was as high as 43.33 per cent in Tamil Nadu. While over 28 per cent of the SHG members in Karnataka obtained only one loan, the corresponding proportion was only 6.67 in Tamil Nadu. This implies that the SHG members in Tamil Nadu went through several credit cycles. This would have, as noted earlier, met their consumption and production credit needs, and inculcated credit discipline among them. This would have also led to greater satisfaction among them.

The distribution of loans and loan amount across the states as shown in Table 12.8 brings out the some important points. First, the emphasis on household consumption appears to be high in Tamil Nadu, but not so when one looks at the distribution of total credit. The proportion of loans for household consumption was very high in Tamil Nadu, because the programmes encouraged members to borrow for consumption in the initial phases. Second, it appears that, in Karnataka, a significant proportion of loans and the highest proportion of loan amount were given for income generation. But, the proportion of the loan amount lent for income generation was the second highest in Tamil Nadu, thus, making average amounts for income generation significant in that state. On the whole, the sample groups in both the states emphasised the consumption credit needs. However, the average loan amount for consumption has been consistently higher in Tamil Nadu.

Table 12.8
Purpose-wise distribution (%) of loans

Purpose	*Number of loans*	*%*	*Total loan (in Rs)*	*%*	*Average loan (in Rs)*
Karnataka (n = 60)					
Household consumption	28	29.5	18,500	6.7	661
Health	20	21.1	20,700	7.5	1,035
Social functions	9	9.5	26,500	9.6	2,944
Income-generating activities	23	24.2	143,580	52.0	6,243
House construction/repair	7	7.4	51,200	18.5	7,314
Repayment of old debts	7	7.4	14,700	5.3	2,100
Others	1	1.1	1,000	0.4	1,000
Total	95	100.0	276,180	100.0	2,907
Tamil Nadu (n = 60)					
Household consumption	197	65.7	449,877	46.6	2,284
Health	25	8.3	58,990	6.1	2,360
Social functions	12	4.0	37,000	3.8	3,083
Income-generating activities	35	11.7	275,300	28.5	7,866
House construction/ repair	14	4.7	79,738	8.3	5,696
Repay old debts	4	1.3	17,076	1.8	4,269
Other	13	4.3	47,301	4.9	3,639
Total	300	100.0	965,282	100.0	3,218

Source: Field survey.

Micro-Finance and Access to Basic Amenities, Health, and Education

The SHG membership has the potential to enable the poor to organise themselves and approach the government collectively for accessing basic amenities, for obtaining ration cards to avail subsidised food from the public distribution system, for seeking educational and health facilities, and for accessing social assistance benefits such as old age, widow, and disability pensions. It also provides an opportunity to voice protest whenever the human rights and dignity of dalits is violated. It will, thus, help them have economic and social empowerment. Despite this, it is difficult to explore the links between the SHG membership and access to basic amenities, health, and education with these data for the following reasons. First, membership in SHGs has not been very long. Second, we do not have information on the situation among the sample households before they obtained membership in these groups. We also do not have information on the control group. Nevertheless, an attempt is made to look at the access to basic amenities, health and education as this may provide some insights on micro-finance and vulnerability.

Access to Basic Amenities

Access to basic amenities has been fairly good for the sample households in both Karnataka and Tamil Nadu (see Table 12.9). A majority of these households were living in their own house. The proportion of houses constructed or obtained through housing programmes of the government is relatively higher in Karnataka. The proportion of households owning pucca or semi-pucca houses has been substantially higher in Tamil Nadu. Some of the sample households were residing in katcha houses. It should be noted that micro-finance groups provided loans for the purpose of house repairs. Even then, several respondents have noted that vulnerability level has not come down after becoming an SHG member because they continue to reside in non-durable houses. They were of the opinion that NGOs did not either initiate activities to enable members to obtain housing assistance from the government or provided assistance to construct better houses. The proportion of households not having electricity facility was higher in Karnataka, notwithstanding the fact that nearly 47 per cent of them have obtained electricity connection through the state government's 'Bhagyajyothi' programme. In both the states, the proportion of households without sanitation facility is very high.

A large proportion of the sample households in both states depend on public stand-posts. A number aspects are noteworthy in this regard. First, only 8 to 10 per cent of the households in these states depended on private water supply sources. Second, a few households in Karnataka depended on mini-water supply source, while none in Tamil Nadu depended on this source. Third, adequacy levels varied depending on the source.

Table 12.9

Access of sample households to basic amenities, health, and education

Particulars	*Karnataka (n = 60)*	*Tamil Nadu (n = 60)*
Distribution of sample households (%) by ownership of house		
Own house	75.0	81.7
Government provided	20.0	10.00
Others	5.0	8.3
Total	100.0	100.0
Distribution of sample households (%) by type of house		
Katcha	10.0	26.7
Semi-pucca	80.0	56.7
Pucca	10.0	16.6
Total	100.0	100.0
Electrification (%)		
Electrified (own)	28.3	73.3
Electrified (government)	46.7	10.0
No electrification	25.0	16.7
Total	100.0	100.0
Adequacy of water (%)		
More than adequate	10.0	11.7
Adequate	55.0	78.3
Inadequate	35.0	10.0
Sanitation (%)		
Own or community	23.3	26.67
No facility	76.7	73.33
Total	100.0	100.00
Type of Ration Card (%)		
BPL Card	78.3	56.7
APL Card	10.0	36.7
No ration card	11.7	6.6
Proportion of literate to total household members (%)		
Zero	3.3	5.0
Less than or equal to 50	50.0	33.3
50 to 75	35.0	33.3
75 to 100	11.7	28.4
Use of health facility (%)		
Public Health Centre/Government hospital	63.3	66.7
Private clinic	35.0	20.00
Nursing home	1.7	13.3

Source: Field survey.

An important point is that a relatively larger proportion of the sample households in Tamil Nadu termed the water supply through public stand-posts as more than adequate or adequate. This suggests that the supply of water through public sources has been fairly good in Tamil Nadu. The same can be corroborated by the data on adequacy of water supply through private water supply sources. While a significant proportion of the households depending on private households connections in Karnataka stated that water supply through this source has been more than adequate, none of the households depending on private household connection in Tamil Nadu stated that the water supply was more than adequate. Some households reporting inadequate water supply manage the situation either by taking water from neighbours or relatives, while most of them (especially in Karnataka) manage with whatever water is available.

Most of the sample households in the two states have either Below Poverty Level card or Above Poverty Level card – the proportion having the former card being relatively higher in Karnataka (Table 12.9). The proportion of households not having any type of card was relatively higher in Karnataka. This was mainly in the case of households that have been recently formed. A majority of the households having ration cards in Karnataka reported that they obtain all the food grains and other provisions that they are entitled to from the public distribution system. In contrast, a majority of the sample households in Tamil Nadu reported that they obtained only a few items – not out of compulsion, but out of choice.[2] At the same time, a few households have noted that SHGs neither provided credit to obtain provisions from the ration shop nor allowed withdrawal of their savings for purchasing of provisions from the ration shop.

The educational attainment (literacy level) of the sample households is comparatively better in Tamil Nadu (see Table 12.9). One of the reasons for this is that micro-finance groups supported their members in their efforts to educate their children by way of providing loans to pay school fees, buy bus pass, etc. In contrast, as noted earlier, this was not done in Karnataka. Although the proportion of households not having any literate member is marginally higher in Tamil Nadu, the proportion of households having more than 50 per cent literate members was about 62 per cent in Tamil Nadu as compared to about 46 per cent in Karnataka. The evidence, thus, suggests that micro-finance has been used to finance the education of children, especially in Tamil Nadu.

A larger proportion of the households from both the states regularly depend on public health centres for obtaining health care facilities (see Table 12.9). At the same time, the proportion of households depending on private health providers (private practitioners or hospitals) (about 35%) is significant in Karnataka. As the purpose-wise distribution of loans shows, SHGs in both the states have supported their members in accessing health facilities by way of providing loans for the purpose.

In brief, it can be stated that the access of sample households to basic amenities such as house, electricity, food grains through the public distribution system, and drinking water supply has been fairly good. However, members have noted that NGOs and SHGs have not undertaken sufficient and regular work for improving the access to basic amenities. For instance, one SHG member from Hunsur taluk in Karnataka stated that she wants her group to take up issues such as lack of access to ration cards, electricity, etc. In contrast, dalit micro-finance groups in Bidar in Karnataka and those in Tamil Nadu have taken up the issue of inadequate access to basic amenities, and initiated actions towards the same.

Before we proceed further, it is important to keep some points in mind. First, the proportion of households having katcha (non-durable) houses has been significant in Tamil Nadu. Second, the proportion of the sample households not having access to electricity has been significant in both the states. Third, a majority of the sample households in both the states did not have access to sanitation. This may have had implications for the health status of the sample households. Fourth, although a majority of the households regularly depended on public health facilities, the quality of health care services through this source has been perceived to be poor. As a result, a significant proportion of them stated that they depended on private health providers. This has implications for expenditure on health among the sample households.

Micro-Finance and Vulnerability

As has been observed in the previous sections, the sample households have benefited from both savings and credit facility. Although the extent of benefits varied across the two states and project areas within each state, the fact remains that these households have been having a mechanism through which they can come together, discuss their problems, and solve them collectively. The solving of problems can be either through collective action to put pressure on the government to access basic necessities or accessing credit for income generation. Thus, the SHG membership has the potential to reduce vulnerability among dalits. However, it must be clarified that the sample households have had membership in SHGs for only a short duration; it is not long enough period to examine the impact of micro-finance on the vulnerability levels. Hence, we will only explore the links between SHG group membership and levels of vulnerability.

SHG Membership and Levels of Savings

Increasing and larger amounts of savings in the groups would imply that the financial assets owned by the poor are growing and this would give confidence to the members. We have, therefore, worked out the distribution of sample members by the duration of their membership and the cumulative amounts of their savings (see Table 12.10). It is observed that members with a longer duration of membership have larger amounts of savings. This is only to be expected since the duration and the amount of savings contributed in a month influence the total amount of savings in the group. However, in Karnataka, a significant proportion of members with four or more years of membership have saved less than ₹ 500 or ₹ 1,000 since inception. This could be either because of the failure of the programme to mobilise members' savings by adopting the principle of reciprocity, or because of the poverty of members leading to their inability to contribute. Whatever the reason, this does not suggest that the members have savings large enough to gain confidence or have a sense of security.

Table 12.10

Distribution of sample members (%) by duration of membership and cumulative amount of savings

Duration of membership (in years)	*Size classes of cumulative saving amount (Rs)*						
	< 500	*500–1,000*	*1,000–1,500*	*1,500–2,000*	*2,000–3,000*	*> 3000*	*Total*
Karnataka (n = 60)							
< Two	37.04	37.04	22.22	3.70	0.00	0.00	100 (27)
Three	57.14	0.00	7.14	35.71	0.00	0.00	100 (14)
> Four	21.05	15.79	36.84	5.26	21.05	0.00	100 (19)
Total	36.67	21.67	23.33	11.67	6.67	0.00	100 (60)
Tamil Nadu (n = 60)							
< Two	0.00	0.00	4.17	4.17	58.33	33.33	100 (24)
Three	0.00	46.67	0.00	33.33	0.00	20.00	100 (15)
> Four	0.00	0.00	23.81	14.29	0.00	61.90	100 (21)
Total	0.00	11.67	10.00	15.00	23.33	40.00	100 (60)

Source: Field survey.

Micro-Finance and Number of Loans

Table 12.11 shows no clear-cut association between the duration of membership and the number of loans availed. One cannot conclude that the new members have availed lesser number of loans as compared to older members. This could be for many reasons. First, the NGO programmes have not built the capacity of members to borrow. Had the programmes done so, the new members with capacity to borrow may have benefited significantly. Second, the capacity of NGOs may itself be the problem. Some NGO programmes were more successful in providing training, encouraging members to save or borrow repeatedly for meeting consumption and production credit, and linking groups with banks. These have contributed to repeated credit cycles and larger number of loans.

Disbursal of most of the loans for consumption has also some implications. First, these loans may have helped the member households to resort to greater social consumption and achieve better educational and health outcomes. For this, we need to look at the health crises that the households faced. Second, income generation has not been significant among the sample member households. This further implies that micro-finance programmes could not reduce vulnerability.

Table 12.11

Distribution of members by duration of membership and number of loans availed from SHG

Duration of membership (in years)	Number of loans availed					
	0	1–3	4–6	7–10	> 10	Total
Karnataka (n = 60)						
<2	70.37	25.93	3.70	0.00	0.00	27
3	7.14	71.43	21.43	0.00	0.00	14
> 4	0.00	78.95	21.05	0.00	0.00	19
Total	33.33	53.33	13.33	0.00	0.00	60
Tamil Nadu (n = 60)						
<2	0.00	37.50	29.17	4.17	29.17	24
3	13.33	66.67	20.00	0.00	0.00	15
> 4	0.00	52.38	23.81	0.00	23.81	21
Total	3.33	50.00	25.00	1.67	20.00	60

Source: Field survey.

Micro-Finance and Income

The link between the duration of SHG membership and income of the sample households is weak. Not all the member households with longer duration of SHG membership fall into higher income brackets (see Table 12.12). Similarly, the proportion of wage income to total income was not low in the case of older SHG members (see Table 12.13). This essentially implies that there are other factors contributing to vulnerability.

Table 12.12

Distribution of sample households by duration of membership and total annual household income

Duration of membership (in years)	Total annual household income (in Rs)					Total
	< 10,000	10,000– 25,000	25,000– 50,000	50,000– 100,000	>100,000	
Karnataka (n = 60)						
<2 years	7.41	44.44	40.74	7.41	0.00	100 (27)
3 years	3.45	20.69	55.17	17.24	3.45	100 (29)
> 4 years	25.00	25.00	25.00	25.00	0.00	100 (04)
Total	6.67	31.67	46.67	13.33	1.67	100 (60)
Tamil Nadu (n = 60)						
<2 years	0.00	20.83	62.50	16.67	0.00	100 (24)
3 years	0.00	20.00	37.14	40.00	2.86	100 (35)
> 4 years	0.00	0.00	100.00	0.00	0.00	100 (01)
Total	0.00	20.00	48.33	30.00	1.67	100 (60)

Source: Field survey

Table 12.13

Distribution of sample households by duration of membership and proportion of wage income to total income

Duration of membership (in years)	Proportion of wage income to total income					Total
	0	<1–25%	25–50%	50–75%	>75%	
Karnataka (n = 60)						
<2 years	23.08	75.00	44.44	44.44	52.00	45.00
3 years	30.77	25.00	11.11	22.22	24.00	23.33
> 4	46.15	0.00	44.44	33.33	24.00	31.67
Total (Nos.)	13	4	9	9	25	60
Tamil Nadu (n = 60)						
<2 years	72.73	60.00	50.00	25.00	26.67	40.00
3 years	0.00	40.00	16.67	62.50	23.33	25.00
> 4	27.27	0.00	33.33	12.50	50.00	35.00
Total (Nos.)	11	5	6	8	30	60

Source: Field survey.

Micro-Finance and Emergencies

R. Holzmann and S. Jorgensen (2003) discuss risks caused by four sets of factors, namely, individual, household, community, and national. *Individual-level risk factors* (disease and old age) determine the risk exposure of a person regardless of the household or community to which the person belongs. *Household-level risk factors* (high dependency ratios, low social standing, limited access to means of production and low or uncertain returns to labour) relate to the household structure and composition, and to its socio-economic characteristics. These two factors are, however, the result of socio-cultural norms that assign different values to ascribed characteristics such as age, gender, ethnic group, etc. *Community risk factors* are primarily determined by ecological and infrastructural conditions, such as soil degradation, difficult access to basic social services, etc. And, *national risk factors* relate to laws, policies, and geographical and political conditions. They affect the whole population, but tend to be more burdensome on the poor.

In this paper, we have used a broader term, 'emergencies', to include the above mentioned sets of risks and many more. The emergency needs of a household are those that occur suddenly and for which the households have seldom any prior preparation to meet. Holzmann and Jorgensen categorise such prior preparation into two types of risk management strategies: *prevention* and *mitigation*, as against a complete lack of preparation in which case the households are forced to cope ('coping strategy') with the risk as best as they can. Emergencies include health emergencies, accidents and deaths, crop failures, drought situations, social functions like wedding and religious/ritualistic ceremonies, social obligations such as village festivals, etc. The social functions and obligations are not 'risks' in the true sense of the term, but we treat them as emergencies because the poor perceive even such predictable events as risks.

We asked the sample households about the crises or emergencies they faced during the three years prior to the survey date. Table 12.14 shows the distribution of the sample households by the number of crises faced. A majority of the sample households have faced at least one crisis. The weak association between the duration of SHG membership and the number of crises should not be seen as an indicator of the failure of micro-finance programmes in reducing vulnerability. It should be seen as indicating certain gaps in the way micro-finance programmes are designed and/or lack of link between micro-finance and others having more capacity to reduce the vulnerability among poor households. This is further explained with the help of information on the exact nature of the crises.

Table 12.14

Distribution of sample households (%) by duration of membership and number of emergencies faced

Duration of membership (in years)	*Number of emergencies faced*				*Total*
	0	*1*	*2*	*3*	
Karnataka (n = 60)					
<2 years	37.04	51.85	11.11	0.00	100 (27)
3 years	21.43	64.29	14.29	0.00	100 (14)
>4 years	15.79	57.89	21.05	5.26	100 (19)
Total	26.67	56.67	15.00	1.67	100 (60)
Tamil Nadu (n = 60)					
<2 years	12.50	62.50	16.67	8.33	100 (24)
3 years	6.67	66.67	20.00	6.67	100 (15)
>4 years	9.52	71.43	19.05	0.00	100 (21)
Total	10.00	66.67	18.33	5.00	100 (60)

Source: Field survey.

About 67 per cent of the emergencies faced by the sample households in Karnataka were related to health, death, accident, and child birth. The corresponding proportion in Tamil Nadu was 76 per cent. As can be inferred, the sample households faced these crises because they do not have sufficient and reliable access to formal social security. In other words, the poor are not provided health and life insurance, and adequate maternity and accident benefits. The poor households facing these emergencies are, therefore, compelled to spend money from their own pockets. However, since the money required to cope with crises on account of limited access to social security is usually large, they are forced to borrow at very high rates of interest from informal credit agencies such as moneylenders. By borrowing large sums at very high interest rates, the sample households have further slipped into poverty and vulnerability. This suggests that SHGs have to enable the member households to access social security schemes implemented by the government, or they have to introduce appropriate social security products.

The member households are also exposed to vulnerability as they do not have access to appropriate savings products. Micro-finance programmes often do not adequately meet the savings needs of micro-finance group members. In general, micro-credit is the most important component of micro-finance programmes. The savings component is introduced more as collateral for the credit provided to the members rather than in its own right. Credit is usually provided for a range of income-generating activities, as also some household consumption needs. Although the sample SHGs collected savings, these were only a means to join the groups and access credit. The NGO programmes do not tap all the savings potential that exists among the member households and link with banks to meet life-cycle needs such as education, construction of house, marriage, etc. This led to a situation where members of the sample SHGs had to borrow from moneylenders and other informal agencies at exorbitant interest rates to meet these needs. Unable to repay these loans, the member households often slip into poverty or are unable to come out of the poverty trap. This, to be sure, also perpetuates vulnerability.

Conclusion

We have shown in this paper that the micro-finance programmes in Tamil Nadu have been more successful in enabling member dalit households to attend group meetings, to contribute larger amounts of savings, and in providing loans to meet consumption and production credit needs. This has had some positive impact on the member households to cope with vulnerability. It should be noted, however, that such a positive impact is both region-specific and NGO-specific. In other words, NGOs adopting good governance principles in the formation and functioning of micro-finance programmes were more successful in having positive impact.

It should also be noted that dalit households faced vulnerability on account of a number of factors, and not all of them were within the purview of micro-finance programme. The vulnerability among dalit households was on account of limited access to formal social security. Although micro-insurance is, by definition, part of micro-finance, many groups do not provide insurance services to the member households. In this context, there is need for micro-finance programmes to enable the member households to access the social security schemes provided by the government. Vulnerability among dalit households was also due to their inability to meet the expenditure on life-cycle events such as education of children, construction of house, marriage, etc., on their own. Consequently, the member households typically borrow from moneylenders at high interest rates to meet all this expenditure. Hence, there is need for the dalit households to have good access to appropriate savings products. Thus, micro-finance programme will be in a better position to reduce vulnerability among poor in general, and dalit households in particular, if they provide access to appropriate insurance (social security) and savings products either on their own or in collaboration with other actors such as government or banks.

Notes

1. New Entity for Social Action (NESA) is Bangalore-based NGO which supported a diverse group of NGOs in undertaking a number of activities including micro-finance. The study on Micro-Finance Needs of Vulnerable Groups, from which this paper is culled out, was supported by NESA.

2. Some of the households in Tamil Nadu have chosen not to buy wheat, though the same was available from the public distribution system. Similarly, some of the households chose not to buy kerosene.

References

Bakshi, Aparajita. 2008. 'Social Inequality in Land Ownership in India: A Study with Particular Reference to West Bengal', *Social Scientist*, 39 (9–10): 95–116.

Banerjee, Abhijit; Esther Duflo, Rachel Glennerster and Cynthia Kinnan. 2010. 'The Miracle of Micro-Finance? Evidence from a Randomized Evaluation' (Mimeo).

Biradar, R.R. 2011. *Incidence of Poverty among Social Groups in Rural India: Who are the Poorest and Why?* (ISEC Monograph No. 24). Bangalore: Institute for Social and Economic Change.

Buckley, Graeme. 1997. 'Micro-finance in Africa: Is it Either the Problem or the Solution?', *World Development*, 25 (7): 1081–93.

Coleman, Brett E. 2006. 'Micro-Finance in Northeast Thailand: Who Benefits and How Much', *World Development*, 34 (9): 1612–38.

Goetz, Anne Marie and Rina Sen Gupta. 1996. 'Who Takes the Credit? Gender, Power and Control over Loan Use in Rural Credit Programs in Bangladesh', *World Development*, 24 (1): 45–63.

Government of India [GoI]. 2007. 'Poverty Estimates for 2004–05'. New Delhi: Press Information Bureau. Planning Commission: Government of India (21 March).

Hashemi, Syed M.; Sidney Ruth Schuler and Ann P Riley. 1996. 'Rural Credit Programs and Women's Empowerment in Bangladesh', *World Development*, 24 (4): 635–53.

Holzmann, R. and S. Jorgensen. 2003. 'Social Risk Management: A New Conceptual Framework for Social Protection and Beyond' (*Social Protection Discussion Paper – No. 6*). Washington, D.C.: World Bank.

Hulme, David and Paul Mosley. 1996. *Finance against Poverty*. London: Routledge.

Kropp, Erhard W. and B.S. Suran. 2002. *Linking Banks and Self Help Groups in India: An Assessment.* Mumbai: National Bank for Agriculture and Rural Development.

Mayoux, Linda. 1998. 'Women's Empowerment and Micro-Finance Programs: Approaches, Evidence and Ways Forward' (*Discussion Paper*). Milton Keynes: The Open University.

Morduch, Jonathan. 1999. 'The Micro-finance Promise'. *Journal of Economic Literature*, 37 (4): 1569–1614.

Planning Commission, The. 2009. *Study of Present Status and Utilisation of Land Allotted to the SC Families and its Impact in Andhra Pradesh, Gujarat, Madhya Pradesh, Uttar Pradesh and West Bengal* (Report prepared by Haryali Centre for Rural Development, New Delhi). New Delhi: The Planning Commission, Government of India.

Puhazhendi, V. and K.C. Badatya. 2002. *Self-Help Group–Bank Linkage Program for Rural Poor in India: An Impact Assessment*. Mumbai: National Bank for Agriculture and Rural Development.

Rajasekhar, D. 1988. *Land Transfers and Family Partitioning: A Historical Study of an Andhra Village*. New Delhi: Oxford & IBH and Trivandrum: Centre for Development Studies.

——. 1992. *Economic Mobility of Rural Households: A Study of Kurnool District in Andhra Pradesh (c. 1860–1989)* (unpublished PhD thesis). New Delhi: Jawaharlal Nehru University.

——. 2002. 'Impact of Micro-Finance Programs on Poverty and Gender Equality: Some Evidence from Indian NGOs', in Shahra Razavi (ed.): *Shifting Burdens: Gender and Agrarian Change under Neoliberalism*. Bloomfield: Kumarian Press, pp. 151–96.

Rogaly, Ben. 1996. 'Micro-finance Evangelism, Destitute Women and the Hard Selling of New Anti-Poverty Formula', *Development in Practice*, 6 (2): 100–12.

Contributors

D.N. Dhanagare was Professor of Sociology at the University of Pune, Vice-Chancellor of Shivaji University, Kolhapur, and President of the Indian Sociological Society (2002–03). Email: dhanagare.dn@gmail.com

N. Jayaram is Professor at the Centre for Research Methodology, Tata Institute of Social Sciences, Mumbai. Email: njayaram2@rediffmail.com

Manjula R. is Research Officer at the Centre for Decentralisation and Development, Institute for Social and Economic Change, Bangalore. Email: manjula@isec.ac.in

M.V. Nadkarni is Honorary Visiting Professor at the Institute for Social and Economic Change, Bangalore. Email: mv_nadkarni@rediffmail.com

P.K.B. Nayar was Professor of Sociology at the University of Kerala, Thiruvananthapuram and President of the Indian Sociological Society (2006–07). E-mail: pkbnayar@rediffmail.com

Narendar Pani is Professor at the National Institute of Advanced Studies, Bangalore. Email: narendar.pani@gmail.com

D. Rajasekhar is Professor at the Centre for Decentralisation and Development, Institute for Social and Economic Change, Bangalore. Email: raja@isec.ac.in

V.M. Rao is Honorary Professor at the Institute for Social and Economic Change, Bangalore. Email: vimora29@yahoo.com.

Gaurang R. Sahay is Associate Professor at the Centre for Development Studies, Tata Institute of Social Sciences, Mumbai. Email: gaurangsahay@gmail.com

Suchitra J.Y. works with the Centre for Public Policy, Indian Institute of Management, Bangalore as Project Director of the Gender Asset Gap Project. Email: suchitra.jy@iimp.ernet.in.

Manish Thakur is Associate Professor with the Public Policy and Management Group, Indian Institute of Management (Calcutta), Kolkata and Fellow, Indian Institute of Advanced Study, Shimla. Email: mt@iimcal.ac.in

Michael Walton is at the Centre for Policy Research, New Delhi and the Harvard Kennedy School. He was V.K.R.V. Rao Chair Professor (2007–09) at the Institute for Social and Economic Change, Bangalore. Email: michael_walton@harvard.edu.

Manohar Yadav is Associate Professor at the Centre for Study of Social Change and Development, Institute for Social and Economic Change, Bangalore. Email: yadav@isec.ac.in

Index